UNDERSTANDING
RELIGIOUS CONVICTIONS

Understanding Religious Convictions

James Wm. McClendon, Jr.

and

James M. Smith

UNIVERSITY OF NOTRE DAME PRESS

NOTRE DAME   LONDON

A section of chapter 2 was previously published as "Ian Ramsey's Model of Religious Language," *Journal of the American Academy of Religion* 41, no. 3 (September, 1973). Reprinted with permission. Parts of chapter 2 appeared in "Saturday's Child: A New Approach to the Philosophy of Religion," *Theology Today*, October, 1970. A section of chapter 3 is based on the author's article "Religious Language after J. L. Austin," *Religious Studies* 8, March, 1972.

200.1
M126u

Library of Congress Cataloging in Publication Data

McClendon, James William.
  Understanding religious convictions.

  Includes bibliographical references and index.
    1. Religion—Philosophy. 2. Religion and language.
I. Smith, James Marvin, 1933-   joint author.
II. Title.
BL51.M17   200'.1   74-34519
ISBN 0-268-01903-7
ISBN 0-268-01904-5 pbk.

216044

Contents

Preface

There is a dark
Inscrutable workmanship that reconciles
Discordant elements, makes them cling together
In one society . . .

Wordsworth, The Prelude

OUR GOAL IN THIS BOOK IS TO DISCUSS THE DISCORDANT elements which divide our own society into fragments and to discover what Wordsworth calls the "dark inscrutable workmanship" that can make even discordant elements one. Since this is our goal, it may be helpful to point out that we two authors are representative of the discord we examine, one of us being a social philosopher who long ago gave up the foolishness of Christian faith and would appear on census as a secular atheist, while the other is a theologian who believes and (unevenly) practices that very Christian foolishness. So we are, in apparent disregard of the Apostle's warning, "unequally yoked together" (2 Cor. 6:14) as writing partners and hence are in better position than some to know the conflicts and paradoxes of a pluralistic world.

Nevertheless, the book that has grown from our discussion and trial drafting is not a debate or a dialog; we have composed it together and are alike responsible for every paragraph, every word. No unequality in *this* sense. That we could do this (and that the course of our friendship has resulted in no small shiftings in our respective conviction sets) is itself a reason for hope regarding wider convictional conflicts. For we believe that here we are indeed engaged with that inscrutable workmanship which the worlds of religion, of race, of politics need even more desperately than does the academic world in which we both live.

Our success here, such as it is, has not come without others' prior work or others' correction and encouragement. Knowledge-able readers will see that the notes within are a very inadequate guide to the help we have received from the literature. The list which follows may likewise (but in this case unintentionally) omit some who have read parts of the successive versions of our type-script and written comments and criticism: Peter Winch, Robert Cunningham, Michael Novak, Hugh Fleetwood, Claude Welch, Daniel O'Hanlon, Paul van Buren, Durwood Foster, John Cobb, Van Harvey, Terrence Tilley, Ismail al Faruqi, John Hutchison, Stanley Hauerwas, David Burrell, David Armstrong, Axel Steuer, John Boler, LeRoy Moore, Nelson Pike. We are indebted to each one for help generously given. We also thank the American Philosophical Asso-ciation and the American Academy of Religion, where portions of the work were tried before lively audiences, and especially the members of the Pacific Coast Theological Society, who heard most of our ideas in their earliest form and gave us generous critical encouragement.

Portions of our work, noted within, have been published in *Religious Studies, Theology Today,* and *Journal of the American Academy of Religion,* and we thank their editors, H. D. Lewis, Diogenes Allen, Ray Hart, again here.

Many have helped with typing, correcting, and editing: we think especially of Thomas Caruso, Sonja Ridenour, Esther Davis, Char-lotte Utting, Yvonne Burke, Aurora Avakian, Joan Creighton, Ralph Frey, and the excellent staff of the University of Notre Dame Press, especially our editor, Ann Rice.

For encouragement and for practical aid with money, facilities, typists, and materials we are grateful to institutions where we have worked: for McClendon these include the Universities of San Francisco, Stanford, and Temple, Goucher College, St. Mary's in Baltimore, and the Church Divinity School of the Pacific in Berkeley; for Smith they include the University of Washington and California State University, Fresno. Our students will see, too, how much or how little they have changed our minds by their good questions and comments on our work.

Our dedication page cannot adequately represent our debt to our two families, whose members have helped in many ways as we did the work. We think especially of their willingness to adjust vacation times and work schedules over eight years (and on two continents) to the demands of this work, while those who were old enough have taken share in reading and correcting as well.

And not least, we thank each other, here in print, for sharing a happy task happily ended for us though only begun for our readers—whom we now cordially greet.

McClendon & Smith

To Peg and to Marie

NOTE

In the following pages double quotation marks (" ") are used for all direct quotations and for the mention (as opposed to the use) of words or terms, except in the special case of quotations within quotations (" ' ' "). Single quotation marks (' ') are used (with that exception) only as 'scare-quotes.'

UNDERSTANDING
RELIGIOUS CONVICTIONS

1

The statement "There is someone who feeds the cattle upon a thousand hills, who can match the powers of evil and lift up the everlasting doors" is not one to which what is still hidden from us in Space and Time is all irrelevant. But it seems to me it is not only this that makes the question, "Is that statement true?" a hard one. It is also the fact that this question calls upon us to consider all that is already before us, in case it should happen that having eyes we see not, and having ears we hear not.

John Wisdom[1]

The philosophers have interpreted the world in various ways; the point, however, is to change it.

Karl Marx[2]

Understanding Religion

UNDERSTANDING RELIGIOUS CONVICTIONS IS A WAY OF UNDER-
standing religion; we shall claim it is the best way. There is now no
generally agreed way to understand religion, and proposals for
understanding it must take that lack of agreement as a main
feature to be explained. To some, the scholarly understanding of
religion is founded upon a principle of stainless neutrality and
detachment: the truth about religion is never to be confused with
the 'truth' *of* religion, and the understanding seeks the former
alone. To others, the knowledge of religion involves an intense
subjectivity, whether this be the subjectivity of the research
scholar confronting his chosen Asian cultures or that of involved
underclassmen evoking religious experience from classroom encounter sessions. Others find the true understanding of religion in
a sociological approach, or historical, or economic, or anthropo-
logical, or through 'history of religions' or in philosophy, while
even theology survives in isolated centers. Perhaps most common
is a random bundle of several approaches, providing everything—
except unity of inquiry.

Varied as are these approaches to religion, they confront a body
of material or subject matter more varied still. For besides the
endless assortment of methods of observation (sociologists noting
communities; anthropologists, ritual and folklore, and so on),
there is the actual diversity of religious outlooks and practices.
Middle-aged Americans, having learned to identify religion with
their own Protestant-Catholic-Jewish religious culture, are now
obliged to see that this is only a narrow band in a vast spectrum,
particularly when their children come home cooly announcing
that they have embraced Yoga or Zen. Meanwhile, beneath the old
familiar Western labels, scholars have been noting an unsuspected
diversity of local creeds and homegrown pieties: plurality turns

3

out to have been the flavor of our native religion and our native irreligion, too.[3]

Certainly this variety in the world is not limited to religion: national loyalties, economic ideologies, artistic preferences, and moral styles also exist in large and apparently increasing number. Such variety is in many ways a cause for celebration. After all, as Mill pointed out, it is precisely this variety in ideas and styles which provides the experiments in living which enable us to expand our horizons. But there is a darker side as well. Differences frequently become passionate and violent conflicts: Arab against Israeli, communist against capitalist, monarchist against democrat, Catholic against Protestant. One might expect that with an increase in scientific knowledge and the spread of educational advantages and advancing communication technology, the variety of views and perhaps the passion with which they are held would diminish. Should not a view founded on ignorance yield to knowledge, one based on misunderstanding give way to explanation, one based on bad arguments be corrected by more adequate or valid counterarguments? No such expectations can survive an examination of the history of the twentieth century. While some views have disappeared and some differences have been resolved, the general trend seems to be in quite the opposite direction.

The conflicting variety of religious and other human commitments presents us with two slippery tangles of difficulties. First, arising from our convictional differences is a tangle of practical difficulties which are at best inconvenient or annoying or wasteful, at worst destructive or horrible or tragic in their consequences. To grasp this tangle and alleviate its dangers is, at least for the short run, the work of diplomats and other conciliators. The other tangle is more theoretical: the Buddhist and Christian, the Marxist revolutionary and democratic reformist, the materialist and idealist are not mere opponents in a power struggle. Rather each claims to have a fundamental truth which the others lack. Each, therefore, would persuade his rivals and others more neutral of the correctness of his view and the rightness of his cause and (at least indirectly) of the incorrectness of his opponent's view and the wrongness of his cause. Indeed, it is one indication that we hold our views seriously and strongly that we seek the assent of others to them. As Jonathan Edwards put it, "it is the necessary consequence of true esteem and love [of an object] that we value others' esteem of the same object, and dislike the contrary."[4] From what standpoint, then, and by what means shall we assess these apparently rival truth claims? Why have the abiding differences been so impervious to practical attempts at settlement? Such tangled theoretical problems are the concern of this book.

Significantly, problems in the outer world of creeds and party cries often correspond to conflicts within thoughtful persons who seek to make sense of their own deep prehensions and tenacious practices, religious or other. It may be that the strongest tension with which we must struggle here is between recognition of the full range of human wants, fears, hopes, faith, doubts, and commitments on the one hand, and the drive to purely rational understanding of these very phenomena on the other. And we must confront this tension in a world convictionally divided, so that there is no easy division between our own inner conflicts and our conflicts with outsiders.

It will be seen that we have freely shifted from religious to other sorts of difference and back again. This is not inadvertent. We will argue soon that there is no easy and satisfactory way to isolate religious concerns or concepts from other concerns and concepts, and we will treat the variety and conflict of religious convictions as paradigmatic of (if not central to) other sorts of conflicting human variety. This treatment of religion seems to overlook the undoubted role which more than one great religion has played as a reconciler of men and as a proponent of theoretical solutions to the problems of pluralism; however, it was the intractability of religious conflicts, whether intercultural or intrasubjective, which first called forth our interest in the problems of pluralism.

What are these problems? An appropriate answer to this question depends on how one defines or characterizes pluralism. Rather than offer what must seem a tendentious definition, we will indicate several descriptions of life today, each of which is sometimes appealed to as evidence that pluralism prevails or that the world is pluralistic.

First, of course, there is the variety of viewpoints of all sorts. This is "pluralism" in its broadest sense, and those who deny it usually claim that the variety is merely in style or surface expression rather than profound or fundamental. But the narrower senses of the term presuppose this broader meaning.

Second, some of the differences among viewpoints are intractable to argument or persuasion. Those who deny pluralism in this sense urge on us the potential of education and communication as ways of resolving conflict. Those who affirm it, as we do, generally regard recent history as grounds for skepticism about any straight-forward resolution by these means.

Third, many political writers mean by "pluralism" the relative equality of power or prestige possessed by the variety of interest groups, racial and religious subcultures, or ideological positions. In this sense, the United States is more pluralistic than South Africa or the Soviet Union, and the rise of the Third World, the Arab States, and the dissident socialist nations makes the world more pluralist than it was fifty years ago. This sense of "pluralism" is outside our concern, except insofar as it is simply a special instance of pluralism in the broad sense.

Several questions arise if one concedes that our world today is pluralistic in one or more of these senses. Two in particular will concern us throughout the remainder of the book:

(1) Are there any common elements linking the world's communities so that rational discourse, persuasion, justification, about their differing convictions can occur?

(2) What is the nature of the justification of convictions, or, as we shall put it later, how are convictions justifiable?

To the first and more fundamental of these questions there are three possible answers. One, which we shall call "hard perspectivism"[5] maintains that differences on fundamental questions—convictional differences—are an inevitable, ineradicable, and ultimate fact of human existence, and that no common element, relevant to mutual understanding, exists. According to this view, human communities and their convictions are so constituted that interconvictional persuasion is impossible; indeed, even communication along these lines is impossible on any significant level. Though the hard perspectivist would not put it this way, in his view the communities we live in and our perspectives on the world are perceptual and conceptual prisons, so much so that those with different perspectives see, think about, and speak about different worlds. This view, often called relativism as well, holds that conflict among those of different perspectives cannot be resolved by any means which presuppose serious communication among the opponents. If there should be a conversion from one perspective to another, it must be the result of some non- or extra-rational cause or process, and the shift would put the convert as completely outside his former view as he had been completely inside it before.

Hard perspectivism has acquired a contemporary following partly in response to what seemed the excessive optimism or imperialism of non-perspectivism. According to non-perspectivism the conflicts among persons or communities are wholly contingent and, since they are also trivial or illusory, given time and effort they are completely eradicable. Of course the non-perspectivist recognizes real differences among human communities, but he is more likely to attribute these to ignorance, or perversity, or both than to serious differences about what it means to be rational or humane or reverent or scientific. So if a Marxist and a Christian democrat (or a Buddhist mystic and a scientific humanist) do not now understand one another or if they now disagree on any fundamental question, such as the meaning of reasonableness, it is only because one or both are ignorant of some facts or incapable of thinking straight.

There is, finally, a third view of these convictional conflicts, which can be called "soft perspectivism." It regards convictional differences, and the conflicts flowing out of them, as expected but not inevitable, fundamental but not ultimate, and enduring but not inherently ineradicable. One or more common elements exist, but to discover and use these elements requires measures which cannot be limited along perspectival lines.

The question of which of these perspectivisms is correct is partly answerable by empirical methods, by careful and patient observation of human affairs. But there are non-empirical issues here as well. One of these is what we take the differences and conflicts to be about. Conflict, even violent conflict, can arise momentarily out of almost anything: a disputed comma, an unexpected jostling, an insolent look. But we are concerned with those conflicts which the participants themselves regard as crucial and which have endured, as our examples illustrate, over long stretches of human history: conflicts about *convictions*. A "conviction," as we shall use the term, is a persistent belief such that if X (a person or a community) has a conviction, it will not easily be relinquished and it cannot be relinquished without making X a significantly different person (or community) than before. Later we shall be saying a good deal about convictions. For now we are content to make a few remarks to warn the unwary and to soothe the suspicious. We note, first, that we have not defined convictions topically. So far as our definition is concerned, a person or a community may have convictions about ice cream flavors or hair styles and not have convictions about God, the nature of truth, or the good life. If that situation is unlikely (as we think it is), it is not impossible by definition. What a person cares most about—

what makes him the person he is—is something that must be found out from the person, not settled *a priori.*

Of course, what one cares about is not just a matter of argument and evidence. But (we shall argue) these are part of the story. Thus we hold that convictions are a species of belief, intending by "belief" to indicate that they are cognitive as well as conative and affective. In our usage, beliefs not only include what one thinks or suspects is true, but also what one regards as highly probable, certain, or even knows to be the case.[6] Convictions are often the subject of controversy, but they need not be, and perhaps some never are.

Convictions are the beliefs which make people what they are. They must therefore be taken very seriously by those who have them. This means that to take any person seriously we must take that person's convictions seriously, even if we do not ourselves share them. If we regard integrity and a certain degree of consistency as important elements in being a person, we should neither expect nor want others' convictions to be easily changed or lightly given up. On the other hand, if we have a true esteem for our own convictions, we will want them to be shared in appropriate ways by anyone whom we regard. A certain tension appears here. If persons who hold opposed convictions are to come to share common ones, then some sort of exchange must take place in which the disparate partners communicate with, persuade, change one another in significant ways, so that one or both become significantly different persons than they were. Soft perspectivism believes that such changes are both rational and possible, and we intend to defend a version of soft perspectivism. At the outset, however, we recognize that soft perspectivism's view is only partly empirical. For there is a self-fulfilling element in all the 'perspectivisms': the success of attempts to persuade across convictional lines depends to some extent on what one takes to be the nature of those convictions, and the nature of the persons who have convictions, to begin with. We acknowledge that a view of human nature is implicit in our work here; its defense is the business of what is to follow.

Nevertheless, we cannot assume the truth of soft perspectivism at this stage. To do so would constitute an egregious begging of the question. We must be careful, therefore, to adopt a method of investigating convictions (and, particularly, religious convictions) which does not prejudge the issue from the start. The investigator cannot, for example, simply make up questionnaires asking people about their convictions, or observe their behavior and infer their convictions from that. Both of these methods have the look of being scientific. They start from observations that any investigator can make (public availability) and they yield quantifiable data. The problem is that for such methods to be meaningful, hard perspectivism must be false and non-perspectivism, or a very soft soft perspectivism, must be true. For such 'objective' methods to be successful in revealing convictions, it must be possible for the investigator's questions to be understood properly and for the investigator genuinely to understand the answers or the other behavior of the 'subjects.' No doubt the investigator could attach some significance to whatever answers he gathered; no doubt he could *assign* significance to whatever behavior he observed. But a proper understanding of such evidence is possible only if communication among those with differing convictions is straightforward and unproblematic. By what right, though, could the investigator make that assumption? On the other hand, neither is there warrant for giving up the investigative task *ab initio,* as hard perspectivism would seem to dictate.

What we propose is examining in its context the language in which people express, appeal to, and reveal their convictions, particularly their religious convictions. The precise details of this method will be set out in the next two chapters, but we can state here the basic principles from which we will work.

(1) The starting point of our inquiry, the data, is what the members of the religious communities say (including what they write), especially to each other.

(2) In determining what is meant by what they say, the crucial evidence will be the testimony of the community as it is embodied in its linguistic and other practices.

(3) The categories of assessment (true or false, appropriate or inappropriate) to be employed for the utterances of the community will be, insofar as possible, those dictated by the sorts of utterances they are within that community.

(4) It is *not* assumed (though it may be true) that the standards of adequacy appropriate in one community are appropriate in others, or in general.

No mere method, of course, can guarantee a complete, precise, and undistorted account of religious (or any other) activity. What these procedures will amount to in the present work can become clear only as we do the work itself. But it is already evident that our method presupposes that the language of convinced persons does reveal their convictions. This is a special case of the more general principle that our beliefs are revealed in our actions. Lipchitz' telling us that he believes it will rain is as much his act as putting on his raincoat or opening his umbrella. Which kind of act gives us a better idea of Lipchitz' belief will depend on the surrounding circumstances, including his other beliefs, intentions, and desires (which we come to know in the same ways). Lipchitz' putting on a raincoat may be unnecessary, precipitous, or dissembling; while his statement, "It is going to rain" or his avowal, "I believe it is going to rain," may be false, unsupported, or insincere. Still, there is a point in emphasizing the especially close connection between our beliefs (including convictional beliefs) and our acts of speaking. For while in many contexts and for many purposes all sorts of actions may evince our beliefs, there is a set of speech-acts whose point is to do just this. If we say with Austin[7] that utterances may be classed as "happy" or "unhappy" depending on the extent to which they fulfill certain conditions based upon the circumstances in which they are made, then we can also class beliefs in an analogous way as happy or unhappy. One spectrum of such conditions for both beliefs and speech-acts is associated with truth or falsity. Beliefs are happily true, accurate, or correct, or they are unhappily false, distorted, or vague. (Of course, these sample assessments do not exhaust the possibilities.) Yet the same could be said for speech-acts such as statements, assertions, and some judgments.

These parallels tend to show that it is indeed our speech, among all our acts, which is especially suited to the expression of many of our beliefs. Moreover, there is another spectrum of assessments of beliefs, attitudes, and responses which is even more closely matched by a spectrum of assessments of speech-acts, namely, being well-founded or ill-founded. Thus guesses are said to be more or less accurate, more or less informed. We speak also of "wild" guesses—so not all guesses are wild. Not only beliefs, but assumptions, agreements (with), suspicions, and surmises are among the mental states or acts which are unhappy unless there is evidence in their favor. In strictly parallel fashion statements, assertions, reports, confessions, and warnings commit their utterers to responding to requests for argument or evidence. If I *rank* a man first, *find* the accused guilty, *classify* this bone as neolithic, or *evaluate* a performance of Hamlet, my act will prove to be unhappy in some degree if when challenged I can offer no considerations in its defense. Finally, beliefs (as well as some other mental states) may also be absurd, outrageous, banal, eccentric, etc.—just as various speech-acts may be.

In general, then, wherever one finds a belief or belieflike state, one should be able to specify a speech-act having conditions for happy utterance which include the conditions for happily holding or having that belief.[8] In setting out the conditions for happy utterance, we would also be setting out the conditions for happily believing. We can reckon also with the fact that people do not always say what they think or think what they say—that is, with the facts of secrecy and hypocrisy, as well as self-deception and self-ignorance.[9] Beliefs, attitudes, and the like are secret when we keep them secret: we pretend, dissemble, keep a straight face, lie, or just keep silent. Note however that such secrecy is the result of something the secret-keeper does, even if what he does in the circumstances is to refrain from acting. To pretend, even to lie, is a fairly sophisticated activity, which we must learn to do and which we perform with some difficulty. To be an accomplished liar is indeed an accomplishment, requiring skill and effort. This suggests that there is some point in saying, as many philosophers have, that it is normal or natural for beliefs to be communicated or expressed and that secrecy or privacy of this kind is the exception not the rule. Of course, beliefs may be unclear or unknown to the believer until he is called on to act. In the action, whether it is speaking or some other doing, his beliefs are revealed to the believer and to his fellows alike—and also to the investigator of religious language.

Thus we have grounds for believing that an analysis of what religious people say—religious talk—will, when we understand it, enable us to know what they mean, what they believe, what their convictions are, provided only that religious talk and religious convictions are in appropriate respects like the talk and beliefs we have examined so far. Is that a valid proviso?

Our full defense of the proviso will emerge in the rest of the book, especially in chapters 3 and 4. We wish now only to forestall a dogmatic or *a priori* claim that religious convictions *must* be different, *could not* be studied and analyzed like other convictions. Such a claim might come from two very different sources. On the one hand, there is the person who holds that religious convictions are not to be considered along with political or scientific or aesthetic convictions, but must instead be exposed, along with any other superstitious hangovers from the past or prescientific era. He contends there is nothing to understand *in* religious convictions, and the only thing to understand *about* them is that they are irrational, nonsensical hocus pocus. On the other hand is the person who denies that true religion is open to investigation as a human phenomenon. Religion, properly regarded, is a response to the transcendent, the ineffable, to that which is precisely not human or earthly. From this point of view, it is irreverent even to attempt a merely human understanding of true religion.

Now either of these claims might turn out to be right. One might decide, after full investigation, that religious convictions are all irrational nonsense, or instead that they (or some of them) have a grasp of some ultimate and transcendent reality which disqualifies our human attempts to talk about it. Our method does not commit us either to the defense or to the denial of religious or irreligious claims, but only to the understanding of them. Moreover, we are bound as far as we are able to understand them as the members of religious communities understand them, not as we would like them to be for whatever reason. We don't quarrel directly with either of the claims made against our proviso that religious convictions can be studied and examined for their meaning and justification just as other sorts of convictions can be. We only want to ask how either objector can be so sure in advance that he is right. There seems to be only one way to be so sure so soon, and that is by having some grasp of the 'essence of religion,' thereby knowing what religion and religious convictions must be. We do not believe that anyone has such a grasp because we do not believe there is such an 'essence.'

"When I mention religion," said Parson Thwackum to Mr. Square, "I mean the Christian religion; and not only the Christian religion, but the Protestant religion; and not only the Protestant religion, but the Church of England."[10] His announcement may serve to remind us that this word has a thousand meanings, that we are obliged to specify our own intended sense, and also that even after such specification is made, the 999 other senses remain. Historians of ideas have familiarized us with the fact that many of the concepts we apply to the world, present and past, are relatively new-coined ones. Such is the case with "religion" in its use in the expression "the religions of the world," and in its use to represent the sum or the essence of those 'religions.' These uses arose in the nineteenth century; before that time, though the noun "religion" and the adjective "religious" were used (as well as their correspondents in other European languages), their meaning was different in a variety of ways.[11] For example, these terms once referred to conscientiousness and scrupulosity (cf. "He practices the piano religiously every day"); then to conscientious ritual observance or devotion to gods or to human persons. Later, the 'religious' were those in monastic orders (as opposed to 'secular' clergy). Still later, during the Enlightenment, the *philosophes* used "religion" to refer to systems of doctrine or ideas (cf. "the religion of reason"), and it was in reaction to that that Schleiermacher used the term to refer to a feeling or grasp of reality available in many such systems. It remained for the later nineteenth century, with its interest in the many peoples and varied cultures of the world, to designate as religion "not only in the Enlightenment sense the various systems of what people believed, and not only in the Catholic sense what they ritually practised, and not only in Schleiermacher's sense what they inwardly felt, but increasingly the historical development of all this over the long sweep of the centuries."[12] Thus came the distinctively modern senses of the term "religion," as referring to what we nowadays call 'the religions of the world,' or, in the singular, 'world religion,' meaning the sum of these, or (again with a difference) "religion," meaning the supposed 'essence' of the latter.

Now we shall have no quarrel with those who want to use the words "religion" and "religious" in any or almost all of these ways evolved in the history of these terms, particularly if they do so with the knowledge that there are also other uses. We shall however be somewhat chary of those who speak as if "religion" denoted, or "religious" ascribed, some *one* quality or character or essence. What is that quality to be? Scrupulous conscientiousness? But other human concerns have that quality—for example, the playing of delicate musical instruments. Adherence to a god or gods? But some of the religions turn out to be atheistic. Concern with the sacred or holy? Again, the same objection—not all that is called "religion" turns out to have this concern. Whatever property is proposed, ritual, myth, ethical concern, social adhesion, sacrifice, numinous awareness, some 'religion' turns out not to have it. Some writers have proposed that it is exactly their *importance to the holder* that makes certain beliefs and practices religious.[13] The difficulty here is that not everyone does treat his religious beliefs as being very important, or act as if they were. This may tempt someone to say, "Well, then, those are not *really* religious beliefs." That seems, however, to define religion by stipulation, and in that event we are back to Parson Thwackum.

If the lack of an acceptable common definition of "religion" makes the essentialist's position arbitrary, it admittedly makes our own investigation more difficult as well. What language shall fairly be designated religious? What shall we investigate? Perhaps here we can take our clue from Ferré's definition of religion. For while it may be true, as we have argued, that not all participants in religion regard religion as important, it is necessarily the case that all convinced persons and convinced communities treat their own convictions as important. Thus what Ferré has actually done, we believe, is to point to the (necessary) centrality of convictions in human life. So our own approach will be to attend to the analysis and understanding of convictions, leaving the qualifier 'religious' to be determined by each according to his own usage and need. As far as we can in this book, we will choose as examples for analysis language used in ways most readers will take to be (in some sense) religious. In this loose sense we will attend to religious convictions, however conceptually elusive religion itself may be. In doing so, we intend to provide ways of understanding which will be useful to those of the most diverse schools of thought about 'religion,' without adopting the view of any one school.[14]

We are sensitive, even now, to the charge that there is a certain incongruity between the task we have set ourselves and the problem we described at the beginning of this chapter. There we described a situation, the plurality of convictions in conflict, which has had and continues to have tragic consequences. (We are not forgetting the happier aspects of this plurality, but they do not make the tragic aspects less urgent.) Indeed, given mankind's technological sophistication, we cannot ignore the potential for ultimate catastrophe in the conflict of convictions. Yet what we propose is *another* investigation: more study—and of words! Marx's criticism of philosophers fairly rings in our ears.

And yet. . . . If the world is to be changed, where should we begin? In what direction should we go? What is the most effective means of change? Any attempt to change the world which slights or ignores the answers to these questions is unworthy of the support of reasonable men, however passionate and impatient they are. Even to try to answer such questions requires just the understanding of the pluralistic human condition (and therefore of human convictions in their plurality) that is our aim. We are sensitive, therefore, but not apologetic. For we recognize that understanding of convictions is a necessary part of changing them and even of knowing which ones need to be changed.

In fact, we make an even more ambitious claim than that. In the present essay, we shall not only point the way to the understanding of convictions, but also to their justification or rejection. Indeed, we will show that *the former is the latter;* that fully to understand what a conviction means or is, is the only way, and a sufficient way, to know whether that conviction deserves to be believed; to put it compactly, that the full analysis of some convictions is tantamount to their justification. There are catches in that claim as it stands, but none, we hope, which will be fatal to our work. As, however, we show how, if at all, convictions can be justified, we admit that we do not here try to show which convictions pass the test. To admit that is to recognize that our work is more like a *code duello* than like the fighting of a duel. Our only excuse for making it so is that without rules, no one can win a duel (though he might, of course, injure his 'opponent' in some way); our hope is that we will set down the 'rules' by which the best convictions must prevail. That does not mean, however, that we conceive atheism triumphing over Christianity, or Buddhism over Western secularism (or vice versa, in either case) as the appropriate consequence of our work; it might be that the triumph of the best would involve a plurality in practice, or the emergence of new convictional forms.

The end of understanding, then, is justification. Problems about truth in religion will certainly engage us in the pages to follow. But it may turn out, and should not *a priori* be excluded, that truth is not separable from other measures of value—from consistency, righteousness, justice, happiness, satisfaction. In that case, we will be obliged to reckon with the interdependence of 'ethical' or 'aesthetic' with 'epistemological' questions. The prospect that a concern for truth should not be isolable from a whole complex of other human goals and ideals should surprise no one, except perhaps certain philosophers who have thought to give only the true-false test to human convictions and certain theologians who, rejecting this view, have concluded that the true-false test need not be given at all. As for our view, we may express it with a parable and an assurance. The parable concerns the cult of a great though little-known saint, one St. Michael the Microstepper, who (it is told) flourished in a long-gone century. St. Michael's great achievement was to have made a journey from Baghdad to Jerusalem, taking only very tiny steps—none over three centimeters in length. The conviction of this cult (it is said) is that life must be modeled on this prodigious feat (or, feet). Now, however, the Quest of the Historical Michael arises. Did he indeed make that journey, taking only such steps? Historical criticism, form criticism, and redaction criticism, followed by a New Quest, converge to assure the cultists that he did indeed do so. And still there are doubters who wonder whether they should set out upon Michael's way. . . . The parable shows that, when it comes to convictions, be they Michaelist, atheist, Buddhist, or humanist, truth is not enough. The assurance we give, though, is that even here truth does matter. (Even in our parable, one might ask whether it is true that we ought to model our lives on St. Michael's.)

We began this chapter by noting the confused variety of approaches to the understanding of religion, and the variety in religion itself. We have tried to show that this variety, not proper to religion alone but characterizing human convictions in many departments, presents us with problems to be solved as well as opportunities to be grasped. The problems that most interest us are the discovery and description of common elements among convictional communities and the development of a theory to provide a basis for the justification of convictions, especially religious convictions. Religious convictions, like others, are expressed fully only in the full range of actions of the person or community that is convinced by them. It is, however, the linguistic actions—the speech-acts—which are especially revealing of convictions and of whatever common elements are present to form the basis of interconvictional justification. Our method of investigation requires that we attend to the way the religiously convinced express their convictions in the full context of their utterance. So we must turn again to the variety of religious convictions, and thus to some particular religious speech-acts, to understand and to justify religious convictions. Before our work is done, we hope to show that it points directly toward a structure within which the many-sided task of understanding religion, justifiable or not, may be carried on.

2

To say that it is belief in the dogmas of religion which is the cause of the believer's intending to behave as he does is to put the cart before the horse: it is the intention to behave which constitutes what is known as religious conviction.

R. B. Braithwaite[1]

The language about which we are talking—the vernacular of the civilized nations of the Western world in the twentieth century—is a very young language. It is scarcely two centuries old. It is, therefore, a very particular language, related to a very specific civilization, and related to a very specific period in that civilization. But it is strongly connected with the evaluations, the beliefs, the convictions upon which that civilization has been built.

Willem F. Zuurdeeg[2]

So our conclusion is that for the religious man 'God' is a key word, an irreducible posit, an ultimate of explanation expressive of the kind of commitment he professes. It is to be talked about in terms of the object-language over which it presides, but only when this object-language is qualified; in which case this qualified object-language becomes also currency for that odd discernment with which religious commitment, when it is not bigotry or fanaticism, will necessarily be associated.

Ian T. Ramsey[3]

Rival Interpreters
of Religious Language

ALTHOUGH PHILOSOPHERS SINCE SOCRATES HAVE FOUND THAT many philosophical problems can be solved or dissolved if the language in which they are stated is clarified and subjected to an adequate test of significance, the remarkable advances in logic in the late nineteenth and early twentieth centuries (especially the work of Gottlob Frege and Bertrand Russell) and the analytical techniques developed by Russell and by G.E. Moore made the potential of linguistic philosophy seem virtually limitless.[4] Thus when Ludwig Wittgenstein published his *Tractatus Logico-Philosophicus*[5] (a title suggested by Moore) with an introduction by Russell, its strong claims for the efficacy of linguistic analysis created great interest and excitement both in the Anglo-American philosophical community and in Europe, where his influence was important in the development of the Vienna Circle.

In the *Tractatus,* Wittgenstein was understood to mean that the traditional problems of philosophy and their proposed solutions were based on an inadequate conception of the limits of significant language. Once one recognized what was necessary for language to be significant, he could see that these 'problems' and their 'solutions' were stated in language which failed to meet these necessary conditions, and hence were not significant. Thus the problems were not genuine problems but 'pseudo-problems' and the 'solutions,' though they had the grammatical look of statements and theories, were nonsense.[6]

The statement of the necessary conditions for linguistic significance was called the verifiability criterion of meaning; it was the central doctrine of the philosophers known as logical positivists, among whom the Vienna Circle philosophers were preeminent. On this criterion, there were two sorts of meaningful (or cognitively meaningful) statements: statements which made no empirical

19

claim at all but which were true simply because of the meanings of the words used in them, and statements which made an empirical claim whose method of verification could be specified in terms of certain empirical procedures. Statements of the first kind were called analytic, and those of the second, synthetic (or empirical). Sentences which fell into neither category might have a *kind* of meaning: they might be orders or commands ("Shut the door" or "Take up your cross and follow me"), they might be expressions of our feelings ("Yay, team!" "Good grief!" or "Hallelujah"), or they might be mixed cases: "The Senator is a demagogue" (which might be a mixture of "The Senator persuades people to follow him" and "The Senator? Ugh!"). But the philosophically and scientifically interesting meaning on the positivists' view was cognitive meaning: only to the extent that statements had cognitive meaning could they be true or false; only to the extent that they were true or false could they make claims or predictions, state theories or laws, or describe or report facts; only to the extent that they could do these things could they be fit objects of our belief. And the positivists drew an explicit conclusion from this doctrine: the characteristic and most important utterances of religion, as well as of metaphysics and ethics, were either disguised definitions, elaborate expressions of feeling, or completely meaningless.

The threat of positivism to many sorts of religious belief[7] is genuine and serious enough. If its conclusions are correct, most religious language is purely 'emotive'—the positivist word for language which merely expresses attitudes—and the 'beliefs' expressed in it are no more capable of proof or of being true or justifiable than "Yay, team" or "Hail to thee, blithe spirit" or "Yum, yum." Thus religious 'assertions' do not express proper beliefs at all, but attitudes which are, on the kindest view, related to genuine beliefs much as "Yum, yum" is related to "ice cream contains sugar." Even sophisticated theologians, long since used to the charge that their assertions were false, were shaken by the implied charge that they weren't asserting anything at all, not even falsehoods. And worst of all, there seemed to be something right about what the positivists claimed. If religious claims were compared even to very theoretical scientific claims, they did seem peculiarly inaccessible to verification, and no one could deny that an important function of much religious language is to express feelings and to evoke similar feelings in others.

Sophisticated believers could accommodate themselves to some extent to the positivist view. Strictly theological propositions like "Allah is God" or "God is one substance and three *personae*" (to mention two not likely to be expressed by the *same* believer) could be defended as definitions or consequences of definitions, with which they could compare such propositions as "Seven is a prime number" or "Force is the product of mass and velocity (F = MV)." With more reluctance, they might interpret reports of religious experience as straightforward autobiography: "I heard a voice speaking to me . . . and was not disobedient to the heavenly vision"[8] could be likened to "I heard the Captain's order and did as he commanded," or even "I heard the voice of my conscience and obeyed." But what of claims that God acts in the world, or that the world has certain determinate characteristics? Such talk is not analytic; its denials are not self-contradictions. Yet it is in a certain way unfalsifiable, cannot be checked. "God created the world" is said by theologians to be as compatible with steady state as with big bang theories; if it is, it can hardly be a straightforward alternative description of how the world came to be as it is. Is it then purely emotive, as the positivists believed? While this suggestion is implausible to the believer, it is difficult to give any sort of specific account of the particular attitude or feeling that "God created the world" allegedly expresses, without sooner or later reintroducing the problematic notion of God. Gratitude or reverence or feelings of absolute dependence require objects to be intelligible; one cannot for long be grateful or reverent except toward what somehow provides for us or awes us; one cannot appropriately depend unless there is that which is dependable. But attempts to work out theologies which preserved such religion while discarding God (or the term "God") ran into difficulties of their own; in any case, they seemed to grant the positivist all of his central claims.

Meanwhile, logical difficulties had arisen in the verifiability criterion which led to its virtual abandonment in the form which made it such a sure and powerful device for separating the meaningful from the senseless and, incidentally, for dismissing many of the most important (to the faithful) religious utterances. But the skepticism about the significance of these utterances survived the demise of logical positivism, becoming widespread even among those who were, or who would like to be, religious. The grounds for this skepticism were still substantially those stated (perhaps too stringently) by the positivists, namely, that there is simply no way of verifying such utterances. Whatever difficulties there were in stating the matter precisely, many people agreed that an utterance that cannot be verified in any way cannot really say much, if anything, about us or our world. How then could it be significant?[9]

Thus the positivists seemed (and seem) to many completely victorious on their own terms. If the meaning of an utterance was to be identified with its ability to describe or pick out some discoverable feature of the world apart from its utterer, then it seemed we must regretfully or gleefully conclude that many central religious utterances are indeed meaningless.

Several aspects of the method of the logical positivists, however, received heavy criticism. One of these was their style of separating sentences from the setting in which they were issued, thereby treating any possible meaning those sentences might have in abstraction from the concrete circumstances of their issuance. Thus, confronted with a random sample of religious utterances such as these:

A   "Lo, he over all things is watching"
B   "I take refuge in the Buddha"
C   *"Tat tvam asi"*
D   "Jesus said, 'One thing is needful'"
E   "Jesus opened the blind man's eyes"
F   "There is nothing"
G   "God led Israel across the Sea of Reeds"

the positivists would characteristically treat them all alike as possible bearers of meaning.

But such utterances could certainly be made by a variety of persons in a variety of cultures for many different purposes: they might be written or spoken, might appear in ancient texts or be heard on the lips of people today; these people might employ these words with or without themselves having religious intent; while ordinary adherents of religions might use one or more of them as information to children, or while practicing for a pageant, or merely to improve diction. And 'hearers' if any, might be attentive or indifferent, hostile or asleep.

Do such varied circumstances of utterance make no difference to meaning? Or if they do matter, which of them is primarily to be considered? the language in which the utterance (or inscription) is issued? the grammatical, syntactical, semantic relation of that sentence to others? the beliefs, intentions, feelings, the whole life of the speaker or the hearers? the state of affairs (outside utterance and speaker and hearer, and perhaps independent of them) in the world to which the utterance relates? the impact and effects of the utterance itself? The positivists were not indifferent to all of these, but they totally ignored some, and thereby missed the maturation of the philosophical seeds they had helped to plant.

There are other thinkers, however, who went beyond the positivists in these matters, attending to the aspects of language the positivists had denied or ignored. These more recent thinkers took full measure of the positivists' account of 'cognitive' language and generally accepted it as doctrine in their own understanding of religious language. They found in other aspects of language, however, ways of avoiding the usual positivist conclusion that religious language is meaningless. In this chapter we are going to consider the views of some principal post-positivist thinkers. Our aim is not primarily historical. Rather, we think each of these views embodies insights which any adequate theory must include and errors which any adequate theory must avoid. Hence, an understanding of these insights and errors will help us to formulate the speech-act theory we shall eventually propose.

I. Braithwaite[10]

In 1955, R.B. Braithwaite, a philosopher of science, was invited to give the Eddington Memorial Lecture at Cambridge, later published under the title *An Empiricist's View of the Nature of Religious Belief.* He began this lecture with the assertion that the verification principle of meaning is in complete accord with the contemporary philosophy of science. "The meaning of a scientific statement is to be ascertained by reference to the steps which would be taken to verify it."[11] However things might stand with that principle in the eyes of recent analysts, Braithwaite felt that it worked well for science. He acknowledged, however, that it seemed not to do as an account of the meaning of religious utterances, for these are neither straightforward empirical assertions nor scientific hypotheses nor logically necessary statements like the statements of logic and mathematics (the three classes which the supporters of the verification principle regarded as possessing truth-values).

One way of understanding and appreciating the special success of the verification criterion with scientific language (at least in Braithwaite's opinion) is to see that scientific language is used to describe, predict, report observation, and so forth. Given these uses, it is not surprising that being verifiable is crucial, or at any rate more important, for scientific language: of what use is a prediction that cannot be checked? To see the matter in this way, however, enables us to recognize a more fundamental account of meaning than the verification criterion provides. If the verification criterion is successful because it is based on the *use* of scientific language, that suggests that it is the use of language that is the key to understanding its meaning. And this is the conclusion that Braithwaite reaches. Thus "the meaning of any statement is given by the way in which it is used,"[12] which Braithwaite understands to be the teaching of the later Wittgenstein, can become the new measure of meaning.

Braithwaite next notes that, besides religious utterances, there is another large class of utterances which are not to be verified by the 'standard' methods: the class of moral utterances. How are moral statements used? Some philosophers had said that their use was to express feeling. But there is no particular feeling which is essential to moral utterances, however true it may be that they do (by the way) express feeling. What is indispensable to moral assertions according to Braithwaite is that they *declare the intention* of the asserter. Thus Braithwaite proposes a theory of moral language which is not emotive but in his term "conative." For me to say "Rioting in the streets is wrong" is to declare that, if the appropriate situation arises so that I have opportunity to riot in the streets, I *intend* not to do so. Of course not all intentions are classified as moral. What makes a given declaration of intention moral is its subsumability under some general policy of action. Thus if "I ought to give Barbara a book" translates as "I intend to give Barbara a book, and that is a special instance of giving books to scholarship students, which I ought to do, that is, intend to do as a general policy," then "I ought to give Barbara a book" satisfactorily qualifies as a moral assertion. The expression of the intention, and the background presence of a general rule, are the clues that language is being used as moral language.[13]

The central claim of Braithwaite's lecture is that characteristic religious "assertions" are to be understood in the same way as characteristic moral "assertions."[14] They are declarations of commitment—commitment to a way of life. They express the intention of the one who makes the "assertion" to follow that particular way of life. Once we acknowledge that such religious declarations occur in a larger system of religious utterances, we can see how they may express the intention to live the life associated with that system. Braithwaite offers the sample "assertion," "God is love (*agape*)." For a Christian to "assert" this is for the Christian to express his own intention to follow an "agapeistic" way of life. The expression of intention by the speaker *exhausts* the meaning of the utterance. Thus, although Braithwaite abandons the verification principle proper, he retains intact an empirical criterion of meaning. Intentions are empirically ascertainable; we all know that we can ordinarily discover whether or not a man has lied to us about his intentions, that is, whether his avowal of intention was true or false. Our intentions (unlike the God of Christian theism, who might by a non-Braithwaitian have been taken to be the referent of "God is love") are discoverable by empirical investigation. Of course, we do not always fulfill our intentions; due to weakness of will, or whimsy, or hardness of heart, or to external circumstances, we may and often do fail. Even so, we know what we mean when we say, "Jones intended to give her the book," whether or not the intention was fulfilled. And we may know ourselves to be correct in saying that about Jones.

Braithwaite now anticipates a first objection which will be raised against his account: on this view, do not all religious "assertions" come down to pretty much the same thing? For while Christian "assertions" might be said to be agapeistic, might not the same be claimed of Buddhist utterances? Yet surely the man who confesses Christianity does not *mean* the same as one who confesses Buddhism? The answer to this objection, says Braithwaite, is to be found in the stories which accompany religious intentions: the different accounts or tales which make up a part of the religious "assertions" of Buddhism, on the one hand, and Christianity, on the other. These are "straightforwardly empirical propositions capable of empirical test."[15] The Christian stories, for example, will in large measure be about Jesus and his followers. As such, they have to be either true (factual) or false (fictional) stories. Their function in religious language, however, is not to offer themselves as true, and their falsity does not lessen their effectiveness. Rather they serve as psychological reinforcement for the intention which is being expressed. Thus if the Christian says, "God is love" (which on analysis, as we have seen, means "I intend to live a life of love"), he will associate that expression of intention with the (factual or fictional, hence empirical) tales of Jesus' living a life of love, or St. Francis' living a life of love, tales which the believer need not entertain as true, but which he most surely does find reinforcing his own actual intention so to live.

Braithwaite cites Matthew Arnold, "that great but neglected Christian thinker," as the patron saint of his views.[16] Arnold's insight into the *imaginative* element in Christian belief, his discovery of religion as "literature" rather than as "dogma," is the inspiration for Braithwaite's talk about "stories."

Thus a man who utters a religious "assertion" is doing two things, the one "intentional," the other "propositional." "Intentionally," he is expressing his commitment to live in a certain way, an expression which will be tested by the life which he actually does live. "Propositionally," he is telling or alluding to a story, which he may or may not believe ("Jesus loved his friends," "Jesus rose from the dead"; perhaps "God is one substance and three *personae*"), but which functions psychologically to reinforce his intention so to live. The connection between the "intentional" and "propositional" elements is not linguistic or logical, however, but "psychological and causal." The (Christian) utterer of "God is love" is reminded of certain stories or associates his utterance with the stories and expects others in his community to do so as well.[17]

It is interesting at this point to compare Braithwaite's account of religious language with a hint thrown out on the topic by the Oxford moral philosopher, Richard M. Hare. Hare's view, expressed almost by allusion rather than exact statement in two brief essays,[18] is that religious views are a kind of outlook or interpretation placed upon the facts. He tells the story of a man who thinks all professors want to murder him. We take him around to see a number of professors, exposing them (as we suppose) as the harmless souls they really are. But what we take to be signs of the harmless drudge (stooped figure, chalk on coat, peering eyes) our man takes to be the clever concealment of their real plan—to murder him! Hare calls that in which we differ from the man afraid of professors his *blik* (a coined word). And Hare notes that, if this man has a blik, we have one, too. To be sure, his man's blik is insane, while our blik, we say, is a sane one. What Hare thinks is important to note is that though bliks differ, no difference about the observable facts need exist. Bliks are not factual; but they do make a difference—that man will flee all professors, or arm himself against them. We will not. Other instances of bliks may be the expectation that steel (and other substances) will retain in the future the properties it has possessed in the past (without that one we will not trust ourselves to steel elevator shafts); the belief that (in the words of the Psalmist) "the earth is weak, and all the inhabiters thereof: I bear up the pillars of it,"[19] to which an alternative (and equally non-factual) belief or blik might be, "Everything happens by chance." And it is bliks, Hare holds, which are the stuff of religious belief. If Braithwaite makes religious language primarily the expression of intention, Hare makes it primarily a matter of a kind of picture or conception to which we are committed. In the later Hare essay, this notion of commitment is depicted as possessing a greater logical complexity than Hare felt himself prepared to expound at the time of writing. On the one hand, religious believers in their utterances have sometimes taken themselves to refer to "supernatural facts." When they have done this, they have simply been mistaken, according to Hare. On the other hand, there is a certain way of viewing the facts which relies upon assumed principles, principles which are not themselves factual, but like Kantian principles govern what we experience and how we experience it. These ways, these principles, may vary, and in their variation may lie differences in religious as well as moral views.[20]

Hare and Braithwaite agree that typical religious utterances do not make claims about or describe the world independent of the utterer. Their meaning does not depend on verifying claims or descriptions. Instead, they say, we must look to the utterer's intentions and the life style which his religious utterances avow. Those who regard "God is love" as a claim about a natural or supernatural Being, or "God is one substance and three *personae*" as a description of that Being are victims of dogma. If such a dogma were correct, then religious utterances would indeed be meaningless. But the use of religious utterances is not to describe or assert or predict, but to avow, and it is that use which is the basis of their significance.

Braithwaite's theory of how religious language works is a brilliant piece of work, as remarkable for its brevity as for its clarity. The latter inevitably suffers from the former, however, and we must give attention to some matters which neither Braithwaite nor Hare has made clear. Braithwaite gives us only one example of a religious "assertion," namely, "God is love," which he says expresses a general principle, the intention to live an "agapeistic" life.[21] But Braithwaite does not make it clear whether "God is love" is *merely* the expression of an intention, or whether it is *also* the telling of a very brief "story" about God. Unfortunately, there are severe difficulties with either interpretation.

If, as seems more likely to us, Braithwaite intends "God is love" to be taken as a pure expression of intention, one whose exhaustive translation would be, "I intend to live agapeistically," then one sort of difficulty arises. This is that there is no imaginable reason for employing the sentence "God is love" to express *that* intention; nor is there any reason to analyze "God is love" as an expression of my intentions. Compare a lawyer's office whose door sign says simply, "Flats fixed"; there seems to be no reason for the lawyer to put out *that* sign, and no reason, based on the sign, to suppose a lawyer within. Granting, for argument, that the positivists were quite right, and that there is no way to say *anything* about God, nothing either factual or fictional, true or false, then it is not in the least clear why "God is love," *that* sentence, expresses or states anyone's intentions.

This may perhaps be seen more clearly by trying to extend the analysis, taking as fresh cases "God is wrathful," "God is lord of all," "God is omnipotent." Shall we analyze these as "*I* intend to be wrathful," "lord of all," "omnipotent"? That does seem counter-Christian; the traditional Christian view might explain that God's wrath makes appropriate my repentance; God's lordship, my obedience; God's omnipotence, my dependence. But on this alternative reading of Braithwaite those explanations are foreclosed.[22] While there are certainly linguistic problems in references to a transcendent God, there seem to be even more such problems for this type of utterance if all such reference is on principle excluded.

We can best illustrate this difficulty by imagining an agreed-upon code. In the code whenever a mate wants to express a desire for sex, he will say something about hunger or desire for food. So far so good. But suppose now he badly wants to express a desire for food itself? In this case, he can do it by saying, "Code's off. Let's eat—and I don't mean. . . ." In Braithwaite's analysis, the difference is that *there is no way to say* "Code's off"—no way to talk about even a fictional God.

But if we say instead that "God is love" is *not* a pure expression of intention, holding that such utterances can also tell a "story" about God, we are faced both with Braithwaite's apparent rejection of this reading, and with a fresh difficulty. For now "God is love" must be taken to mean not one thing but two things—and two things between which there is no linguistic connection, but only (according to Braithwaite) a psychological and causal connection. There is, for many speakers, a psychological and causal connection between "sugar" and "spice," too, but that is not a linguistic connection; it cannot entitle us to believe that when a speaker says one, he means the other. Think of the confusion that mistake would produce in everyday situations!

To be sure, Hare's account does not admit a similar refutation, but this is true because it is not at all clear what Hare's understanding of bliks really is. He does not define them, and their success depends upon this vagueness of meaning.[23]

As a consequence, we have to recognize that neither Braithwaite's nor Hare's theory can adequately account for the very sophisticated religious talk of a believer such as Braithwaite himself; and *a fortiori*, it cannot account for the talk of more conventional religious speakers. The difficulty arose from the too-exclusive concentration upon one of the dimensions of religious discourse—the declaration of intention—to the neglect of other important dimensions. What we clearly require is an account which is able to include not only the element of representation which the positivists, albeit negatively, emphasized, but also the element of intention and other affective elements which Braithwaite fastens upon. And perhaps there is something else, of more fundamental importance still, which must be included.

II. Zuurdeeg

A radically different perspective is presented by the Dutch-American linguistic philosopher of religion, Willem F. Zuurdeeg, who in 1958 published an account of religious language, *An Analytical Philosophy of Religion.*[24] Zuurdeeg had written his doctoral thesis on the ethical views of the logical positivists, notably Herbert Feigl. In Holland during World War II Zuurdeeg had belonged to the Dutch resistance, and had been puzzled, during that time of conflicting loyalties and ambiguous moral situations, by certain striking linguistic features in the conflicting claims of Nazis and anti-Nazis. How, asked Zuurdeeg, could such conflicts be described and analyzed by philosophers? In his account, Zuurdeeg employs the term "conviction." Although he begins by reporting the historical and common usage of the term, Zuurdeeg then gives it a technical sense for his purposes.

> We take the term "conviction" to mean all persuasions concerning the meaning of life; concerning good and bad; concerning gods and devils; concerning representations of the ideal man, the ideal state, the ideal society; concerning the meaning of history, of nature, and of the All.[25]

Since, on Zuurdeeg's definition, a "conviction" applies to matters of ultimate importance, being convinced is certain to be decisive in determining the sort of person one is.

Convictional language, language in which we express our convictions, is not "indicative" language, the language of science. Indeed, Zuurdeeg refrains from using the notion of a conviction "in any purely intellectual realm of discourse." But he also resists calling convictional language emotive, for that "draws too much attention to the subjective aspect of the conviction."[26] To avoid this overemphasis on the subjective, as well as to provide a positive account of convictional language, Zuurdeeg introduces a set of terms correlative to conviction: the *convictor* (that which overcomes or convinces) is "the somebody or something" which overcomes or convinces me—my god, my race, my Third Reich; the *confessional group* is that community, racial group, church, or party which shares my convictions and reinforces as well as corrects them. Moreover, I and my confessional group are overcome by a convictor in a certain context, a *convictional situation.* Christians would have as their convictor the God revealed in Christ, as confessional group the Christian church and their own branch of it, as convictional situation the historic Scriptures and tradition to the present, as well as the attitudes of parents, teachers, friends; an enlightened Frenchman might have as his convictional context the writings of Voltaire, Pierre Bayle, Condillac, and Comte, and a contemporary community consisting of his living friends and intellectual allies; and again a Communist might have the writings of Marx, Lenin, and Mao, with the party and the proletariat as the components of his convictional situation. It is also important to note that no man has merely one convictor—we have each been "overcome" by several convictors, which may form a hierarchy of power and importance for us, and this hierarchy in turn may be rearranged from time to time.[27]

Where would we expect to find confessional communities expressing their convictions? The church is an obvious place, but by no means the only one. Convictional language is found not only in the Apostle's Creed, but also, according to Zuurdeeg, in *Mein Kampf* and the *Communist Manifesto.* The first sentence of the *Manifesto,* "The history of all hitherto existing society is the history of class struggles,"[28] may appear to be an indicative claim, but in fact it states a conviction, which with others in Communist theory goes to make up a theology, an attempt to assess the significance of all human existence. There are not only overt religions such as Buddhism, Christianity, or Islam, but also crypto-religions with crypto-theologies such as Marxism. Even formal philosophical and metaphysical systems can be crypto-religions. If we so consider them, our assessment of the significance of the language used by Sartre, Russell, or Plato would have to change as well. For convictions are not the mark of religious believers alone—everybody has convictions. They appear for some in connection with religion, but for others they take shape as poetry, or in philosophy, or in connection with political belief.

Even sciences are affected by convictions. A "presuppositionless science" is not, says Zuurdeeg, a reality but an ideal which we ought to strive for, but whose realization is unattainable. Zuurdeeg argues that all sciences have been affected by the attitudes of their practitioners. This is most evident in the quest for a purely objective science of religion. It can be shown, Zuurdeeg believes, that the history of this science reflects its purely Western and Christian background, and this has caused distortion in the handling of non-Christian, non-Western religions.[29] The same can certainly be said for the writing of (scientific) history; for instance, the history of philosophy. The historian cannot get outside his own skin or his own confessional community. Physical scientists are able to pursue their investigations only because they have certain presuppositions; for example, that what is obtainable in the science is reliable information, is worth getting, and that the science in question ought to obtain this information in fulfillment of its obligations to the truth.[30]

Certainly this is not a weakness of scientific investigation, says Zuurdeeg. Though we must seek to free ourselves from irrelevant convictions, we are dependent upon relevant ones in more than one way. An instance is the aforementioned conviction expressed by the first sentence of the *Communist Manifesto*. Such a convictional claim serves indicative language by providing a program for critical scientific investigations of history. To what extent are the causes of the American Civil War more clearly understood if we apply to its origins the concept of the class struggle? The sentence in the *Manifesto* cannot give an "indicative" answer to that question or any other, but it raises a question not previously considered. Convictions thus serve a heuristic function. And often they do this by overcoming other convictions which had served to obscure that particular investigative possibility. The advance of the "indicative language," as Zuurdeeg might put it, is made upon the back of convictions.

Convictional language itself often appears to have indicative elements. Religious faith, for example, claims to deal with events which really happened, with persons who really lived, with a God who, it is said, really exists and really acts on history. In the religions of the biblical tradition (Judaism, Christianity, Islam), men speak of knowing God as well as trusting him. Here, then, appears to be a knowledge-claim, and that certainly seems to imply the presence of an indicative element. But Zuurdeeg holds that these appearances are deceptive. To be sure, convictions can clash with one another and thus have a certain indicative aspect. But the talk of religious people turns out at bottom to be liturgical and confessional; it is "repetition" of the convictional element in biblical language; it cannot be countered or falsified by scientific investigations; it is in a special sense "mythic."[31] The failure to recognize this mythic quality by taking religious claims indicatively leads to the assimilation of religious stories about the life of Christ, or of Buddha, or of descriptions of the classless society, to historical accounts of the life of Gladstone, or descriptions of the Trobriand Islanders. For the one who is not a member of the confessional community to do this is to misunderstand the language of the community. For one who is a member of the community to take its mythic language indicatively is to misunderstand not only the language but himself as well. For, according to Zuurdeeg, to express our convictions is to express ourselves.[32]

Thus, Zuurdeeg distinguishes between the *use* or *employment* of conviction language, on the one hand, and its acceptance as "Is-language" on the other. To "use" scientific language is quite in order. It is in this connection that "a characteristic of language ... generally accepted by analytical philosophers ... that the meaning of a language is equivalent to the rules of its correct use" arises.[33] Yet this rule cannot apply to the language in which we express our convictions. In the latter case, according to Zuurdeeg, to "use" the language is a kind of sham; thus Marx, Freud, and the logical empiricists have all exposed ways in which men "use" conviction-language to mask quite different goals, for example, the exploitation of their neighbors.[34]

Thus analysis of man's convictional language brings Zuurdeeg to an account of man as the speaking animal, *homo loquens,* man-who-speaks.[35] With indicative language (including its definitions and tautologies) man works as with a tool; he uses it. With convictional language man utters his hopes, his fears, his oaths, his judgments—that is, himself. A man cannot "use" his words if they are himself. Putting the matter somewhat differently, Zuurdeeg holds that man by speaking affects the world, inserts himself (his hopes, judgments, etc.) into it, establishes himself.[36] The balance of *An Analytical Philosophy of Religion* is given to an account of the principal modes of this convictional speaking: man's cosmologies, his metaphysical systems, the language of morals, and the language of religion are offered as instances of man at his proper but often curious vocation—the speaking of his convictions.

We now call attention to four interesting features of Zuurdeeg's account. In the first place, the notion of convictions cuts across the lines separating religious, ethical, and a variety of other sorts of convictions. Religion approached in this way is continuous with other sorts of human convictional enterprise. This feature of the approach might commend it in a period when religious studies are attending to non-Christian, non-Western religious expressions in a way that analysis tailored particularly to Christian faith could not serve. It also commends it at a time when our ideas of what religion is (what "religion" means) are in a state of evolution.

Second, Zuurdeeg's notion of convictions was attuned to the powerful role of convictions in human existence: the way in which men not only form, but are formed by, the convictions which they embrace. Zuurdeeg chose "conviction" to express the concept which he was examining because of its etymology: its root is the Latin *convinco,* "to conquer," not in the sense of military conquest, but of legal or argumentative triumph. A man convinced or convicted in this sense is a man conquered, overcome, by testimony which overwhelms him. Thus, a man's convictions go far to make him what he is; "we *are,*" said Zuurdeeg, "our convictions."[37]

Third, this notion comports well with our emphasis on the role of particular human communities (churches, political parties, communes, etc.) in the formation of religious or other convictional outlooks. Zuurdeeg seemed to imply that communities make convictions, but also that convictions make communities what they are.[38] Here, perhaps, is an opening not fully explored by Zuurdeeg for intercourse between philosophy of religion thus conceived and the sociology of knowledge. It is especially helpful to recognize that the convictions which form a particular person or group might stand in hierarchical relation to one another: A man may be "overcome" by Christian faith conceived thus and thus, but even more "overcome" by patriotism conceived in such and such a way,[39] and in the interaction of these lie interesting analytic possibilities.

Finally, Zuurdeeg, as a post-positivist, was sensitive to the difficulties which lay in the way of either asserting or denying that convictions are 'cognitive' in the way in which scientific beliefs are. This dilemma had been vividly expressed by the logical positivists, using the verification criterion of meaning. Zuurdeeg's ultimately unsatisfactory way out of the dilemma was to distinguish "indicative language" (of which the language of science was called a model) from "convictional language" (the language in which men expressed *themselves* by expressing their convictions).

Had Zuurdeeg taken the line that the only task of "convictional language" was self-expression, he would have had a view not unlike that of Bultmann;[40] however, with more fidelity to the actual content of religious utterance than consistency with his own distinction, Zuurdeeg held that when a religious speaker, confessing his conviction, says something like "God led Israel across the Sea of Reeds," he is not only indirectly letting us know about himself, but also purporting to tell us something about the Reed Sea crossing, Israel, and God.[41] Only, said Zuurdeeg, this "recital" of biblical history cannot be checked; it is just "repetition"; it is, in a sense of the term which regrettably Zuurdeeg never clarifies, "mythic."[42] Within the conviction which expresses it, it is simply impregnable; it cannot be impugned, checked out, or discarded as false whatever the evidence might be. We have no objective standpoint from which to judge convictions. In our terms, Zuurdeeg is a hard perspectivist.

As we appropriate Zuurdeeg's work, it is important, therefore, to note its limitations. It is not at all clear what Zuurdeeg means by "conviction." His definition is a topical one, yet it seems farfetched to claim that everything of which one is persuaded on certain topics (devils, for example) has convictional status in one's life, or that other things omitted by Zuurdeeg (for example, war and peace) do not have such status. Even if the definition were tightened, however, other serious difficulties remain. For example, it is far from clear what Zuurdeeg means or could mean by saying that we *are* our convictions. This cannot be an identity-claim (even if I am blond and am married to a redhead, my convictions are neither blond nor married to a redhead); is it then attributival? or causal? or metaphorical? The truth is, we cannot tell *what* this claim means in Zuurdeeg's use.

The principal difficulty in Zuurdeeg's account, however, stems from his confusing three different propositions: (1) that we are unable to justify our convictions in any way whatever; (2) that we are unable to judge convictional utterances from a standpoint of detached objectivity; and (3) that we are unable to distinguish "indicative elements" in religious utterance. Yet these are distinct, and have quite different claims to our assent. As to the third, we can accept it only if, like Zuurdeeg, we stipulate it. For in actual practice we will see that very many convictional utterances as employed by ordinary speakers *do* have an "indicative" or, as we should say, representative element. To the extent that Zuurdeeg ignores this element, his account of convictions is faulty.

Concerning the second, we again point out that there is a sense in which in Zuurdeeg's use it is true merely by definition. For if being detached and objective requires one to be convictionless, and if everyone has convictions, it follows that we cannot be detached and objective. Nevertheless, we do not think this claim is trivial. It embodies an important insight which is obscured by Zuurdeeg's broad imprecision about how convictions are related to other beliefs and about how language expressing convictions is to be understood and related to what he calls indicative language.

Finally, the first claim—that we are unable to justify our convictions in any way—seems different from the other two. It seems not so much trivial, or obscure, as simply unsupported. Of course, if justification were exhausted by scientific justification, or if there were no claims to truth made by convictional utterances, then it would take on a certain plausibility. If, however, those are false suppositions, matters are different. In any case, Zuurdeeg has given us no reason for thinking them true.

III. Ramsey[43]

Many believe that Ian T. Ramsey, formerly Nolloth Professor of Philosophy of Religion at the University of Oxford, and from 1966 until his untimely death in 1972 Anglican Bishop of Durham, England, made a definitive contribution to religious thought on the broader scale. However that may be, his work on religious language was certainly central to his total program, and we will examine only his contributions to this topic, assessing the degree to which they contribute to our own goals. His published work in this field is extensive.[44] However, much of this work was of an occasional nature, and Ramsey never finished drawing together his mature systematic thought on this and related topics. For present purposes, however, we can discern three central and recurrent theses of Ramsey's work. (1) First there is his claim that religious language grows from "religious situations," otherwise described as

situations of "cosmic disclosure," in which a "characteristic discernment" occurs and a "characteristic commitment" is made.
Since this is intended to account for the origin of religious language, in this discussion we will call it the *generative thesis*. (2)
Second, there is Ramsey's claim that religious language consists of
"models" whose function is to instruct the hearer to proceed
imaginatively in a particular way until (it may be) a disclosure
occurs for him. Since this is intended to show how the language of
religion functions in relation to the disclosures, we will call it the
functional thesis. (3) Third, there is his claim concerning the
testing of religious utterances: they are to be tested for their
"empirical fit" to the religious situations from which they are said
to rise and to which they are said to lead, and (governed by the
principle that we live in one world, so that religious experience
must be experience of just one Universe) they are to be tested for
their coherence and comprehensiveness *vis-a-vis* other utterances in
the stockpile of theological discourse. Since this is intended to
show the adequacy and appropriateness of a given religious utterance, we will call it the *justificatory thesis*. It is apparent that
these three theses concerning the genesis, function, and justification of religious language are related to each other; they are also
related to other Ramseyan doctrines concerning the unity of God,
the analogy between "God" and "I," the nature of perception,
and so on, but the three we have named comprise an integral
theory of religious language and we concentrate on them.

We begin with Ramsey's *generative* thesis. There are certain
situations, he holds, which are characteristically religious.[45] These
are situations in which a certain sort of "disclosure" or "discernment" occurs, and a certain sort of "commitment" is made or
realized. Not all disclosures, however, are religious. Disclosure
situations in general are those in which someone involved in the
situation not only perceives the empirical data which constitute
the situation, but goes beyond these to realize something in the
situation not described, or not adequately described, but in all
disclosure situations something is disclosed which is not restricted
to "observables."[46] Ramsey was endlessly resourceful in providing
new and often entertaining examples of ordinary, or non-religious,
disclosure situations. Indeed, on one view, these ranged over such
a wide variety of logical types that it is difficult to say exactly
what it is that they have in common.[47]

One frequently recurring Ramseyan disclosure situation is the
gestalt pattern, in which a bundle of data are seen first as mere

bundle, and then as a recognizable image[48] —for example, a poster, first discerned only as colors, lines, dots, intensities, is then seen to form a portrait or a landscape. Another example frequently employed is from mathematics: a regular polygon of given radius and n sides is to be changed by increasing the number of sides; as the number increases without limit, the notion of an n-sided polygon gives rise to the notion of a circle, which can (thus) be defined as a regular polygon of an infinite number of sides.[49] In both the gestalt example and the mathematical example, there is a sense in which the intended notion (portrait, circle) is fully presented by the constituent elements, but in another sense the former is "more" than the latter. This appearance of 'more' is a necessary feature of disclosures.

Another sort of Ramseyan situation yielding a discernment is one in which persons stand in a formal or institutional relation to one another, whereupon, because of some occurrence or other, these persons are then "disclosed" to one another in a more human or personal way. Examples are a courtroom scene in which the prisoner stands before the judge to be sentenced, only to be recognized as the judge's boyhood friend, or a formal academic tea at which some embarrassing or "revealing" event—someone spills punch on the dean's wife; someone bends over and a garment seam rips wide open; all the lights unexpectedly go out—causes the situation to lose its frigid formality as, in the shared predicament, persons become human for one another. At a certain point "the ice breaks, the penny drops, the light dawns," and discernment of persons as persons occurs.[50] These latter examples seem to depend upon the widely shared capacity to view ourselves and others at a variety of levels of immediacy and self-involvement. They provide a bridge to what is for Ramsey the sort of ordinary disclosure which provides the nearest analogy to religious disclosures, namely the disclosure of "I": "Can we not all recall a primitive state," he wrote,

> where we talk of ourselves in terms of proper names such as 'Neeny,' where these are wholly restricted to our public behaviour. Even at this stage we are of course aware of ourselves. My point is that at this stage we have no language to fit. We use of ourselves a word 'Neeny' which others can use in precisely the same kind of way. But when we later use 'I' significantly of ourselves, it is because we recognize it as being used as an indicator word by others for themselves, relating to their public behaviour and more, and we recognize that we ourselves want

to talk precisely of that, of 'Neeny' and more, and so of
'I' . . . So we become aware of ourselves as we become aware of
an environment transcending observables.[51]

Ramsey clearly associated the awareness of the self as more
than observables, signaled by the use of "I," with moral situations,
and the latter are frequently to be described as religious situations
also. In moral situations, the element of commitment, already
present in some degree in the previous examples of disclosure,
comes into its own.[52] In the mathematical examples, there was
implied a commitment to visual concepts and mathematical
axioms which made the respective disclosures possible. The personal disclosure examples involved some degree of commitment to
the persons involved in the situations. But in moral situations a
total commitment of far wider scope than the personal examples
and of far greater demand than the mathematical or visual ones is
required. "Duty" is for many a "key word" in moral situations,
and its characteristic demand is total and unyielding.[53] Yet the
disclosure of duty, like the disclosure of geometrical figures, of
friends, and of self, arises from and is grounded in empirical
situations. "Duty" is the "more" of an empirical situation.

Disclosures involving persons and disclosures involving morality
bring us to the threshold of religious disclosures.[54] These are
disclosures concerning the entire cosmos which evoke from those
who experience them total commitment. Ramsey held that "belief
in God arises when there occurs a disclosure of such a range and
extent that it might be called 'cosmic' ";[55] the examples he gave
(ranging across religions and cultures) can best be considered after
we have introduced the second Ramseyan thesis.

In singling out disclosures, relating the several sorts to one
another, and calling attention to this feature of religion, Ramsey
performed a valuable service, we believe, to the religious community in which he shared. We are far less certain how to evaluate the
claim that religion or religious situations are to be *essentially*
characterized by the occurrence of disclosures, or to appraise the
(generative) thesis which holds that all religious language arises
from, reflects, or is used to evoke such disclosures. While there is a
trivial sense in which all this is true enough, the sense in which
experience and discovery (which together might be called "disclosure" or "discernment") appear in every human enterprise, we
cannot understand Ramsey in this sense. Rather he made the exact
claim that a certain kind of disclosure (which he called "total")

distinguishes religion and generates religious language. Now, how are we to know whether this is true of the Sikhs and the Siwash, or (to take Ramsey's favorite examples) of the Nuer and the many kinds of Christians?[56] Can "disclosure" even account for the many strands of religion which appear in biblical history? for Saul among the prophets? and for the religion of the author of Ecclesiastes? and for the shrine at Beth-el? and for the ecstasies of the first-century Corinthians? Is Ramsey's generative thesis an insight into the nature of all religion, or does it constitute a stipulative recommendation for the understanding of religion, a recommendation from a highly sophisticated Parson Thwackum?[57] The fact that we cannot answer this question, and that, as far as we can tell, Ramsey has not done so,[58] epitomizes one of our difficulties with the generative thesis. Another difficulty can be made more clear after we have explained Ramsey's *functional* thesis, to which we now turn.

In *Models and Mystery,* Ramsey said that the problem of being articulate about the mysterious, though characteristic of religion, is also characteristic of science.[59] While what is discerned in religion is ultimately a mystery, so is what is discerned in science. In both cases, a strain is put upon language to speak of what cannot be expressed in straightforward, ordinary ways. And in both cases, there is recourse to "models" in order to manage the linguistic difficulty. Ramsey refers to Max Black, who distinguishes two kinds of models used by scientists: scale models (for example, the Bohr atom) and analog models (such as the formulas of chemistry).[60] Now the former, says Ramsey, are of no value in religion. The analog model, however, which Ramsey renames a "disclosure model," is the characteristic mode of religious language.[61] God may be said to be a strong tower, a father, a shepherd, and a king; in this way each of these expresses a particular discernment-commitment. Now it is important that such models be recognized not only as indicators, but also as imperfect (or "odd") indicators. The model must therefore indicate in what way God is towerlike, or shepherdlike, or fatherlike, and also in what way he is not. To meet this need, says Ramsey, we must employ "qualifiers." These function as instructions to the imagination, saying in effect: start with that model, but modify it, develop it in *this* direction. Moreover, Ramsey argues, the use of such qualifiers as "eternal," "infinite," "ultimate," "transcendent," constantly remind us that no development we make will be wholly adequate; none will remove the mystery. Thus we badly misunderstand the "instruction" if we take it to be equivalent to an ordinary term in the language. "Almighty Father," when spoken of God, is not just in series with "father," "strong father," "stronger father," "stronger-yet father." The God characterized as "Almighty Father" is not a member of that series, not even the most powerful member. "Almighty Father" is rather the instruction to expand the qualification of "fatherhood" until a discernment occurs to which an appropriate commitment can be attached. At that point, when the light dawns, the qualified model has done its characteristic work.[62] Similarly, the assertion of the Nuer tribe that "The twin is a bird" leads to the discernment that in respect of God or Spirit, twins and birds (as well as cucumbers and oxen) have a like symbolic function.[63] Once again, language provides a model, in this case clearly a paradoxical one, to provoke a discernment.

Ramsey's functional thesis is that it is such qualified models which are the stuff of religious talk, these and not, say, first-person avowals or straightforward descriptions or moral commands. It follows that all religious language has either a hidden imperative or hortatory character, implicitly instructing the listener to proceed down the lines of reflection suggested by the model employed until a characteristic disclosure occurs. How then would Ramsey handle such a traditional utterance as "God led Israel across the Sea of Reeds"? Clearly such an utterance must provide a model which has been qualified to the point of evoking a disclosure, on Ramsey's view.

What disclosure might this be? Let us return to the age when Israelites told one another of the events of their coming to the new land. We can imagine a number of stories being told about the journey: "Our ancestors drifted into this part of the world." But that might seem false; so inadequate as to be a contradiction of the truth. "Our tribal leaders led our ancestors here," may be the next account. But that may seem still inadequate. So the next story is tried: "The prophet Moses led our ancestors here." That comes closer. Moses was a sacral figure, a man of divine power. The story, then, has more of the meaning which it needs to have; it is less inadequate. But some would feel it inadequate still, it may be, and would say "*El* led our forefathers to this land." Is it the case that now the light will dawn; that the significance of the story about entering the new land will be disclosed to the speaker and hearers? If so, the story has done its work. A straightforward 'story' is told, but in telling is changed by the use of 'odd' terms:

"the prophet Moses"; "El" (which we translate "God"). It is crucial to the success of such language that it *not* be taken in straightforward ways; crucial that if the question is then asked, "But who is *El*?" there be no straightforward answer, as there would be if the question had been "But who is Aaron?" Rather the answer will call for further suitably odd language, further 'stories,' further models suitably qualified, until, it may be, a disclosure occurs for the listeners.

Note well Ramsey's insistence that the stories may not work. There is no one story in the chain of disclosure-stories which guarantees success; if the hearer doesn't 'get it,' the only recourse left to the speaker is to tell other stories, until, if at all, such a disclosure-point is reached for the listener.[64] If however this seems to make religious language too subjective, we can remember that Wittgenstein made some similar remarks about 'getting' ostensive definitions,[65] and Lewis Carroll some very clever ones about 'getting' logical inferences.[66] But if there is no flat guarantee that a given person will follow a logical inference or understand an ostensive definition, we may not be too disturbed that on Ramsey's view religious language provides no flat guarantee that the hearer will experience discernment in connection with a given disclosure-story, either. Religious language runs the risk of failure, but perhaps no more than does all language.

This brings us into position to say a little more about the generative thesis. What is the relation between disclosure and commitment in religion and in religious language? Ramsey's understanding of the matter is that these properly arise together; one who enjoys a religious disclosure will properly have a religious commitment as well. The commitment without the discernment is bigotry and idolatry; the discernment without the commitment is insincerity and hypocrisy.[67] But Ramsey also thinks that the nature of religious language is to function by presenting models which, when suitably qualified, express and evoke the religious disclosure. Presumably, then, the same models express and evoke religious commitment as well. But how this occurs is hard to say. If I know that my mother has been kind to me, I know that gratitude is in order. Kindness and gratitude are related logically. I can learn (and teach) both what counts as maternal kindness and what counts as filial gratitude: her care for me in childhood, for example, and my care for her in her old age. But what is the case with the 'discernment' connected with the model-utterance which says that God is infinitely kind? This does not, on Ramsey's account, entail the claim that God has done or will do any particular kind act, or series of kind acts. What, then, is the appropriate commitment for such a discernment? Is there anything in a (Ramseyan) disclosure which could itself answer that question?

The difficulty is that the elusive nature of the models seems to break down the ordinary connections between disclosed quality (in this case, kindness) and evoked commitment (gratitude), and we are not sure where to find new connections.[68] Ramsey tells us that religious language will treat kindness, or any other term, not as an ordinary term doing ordinary work in the ordinary way, but only as a "disclosure-model," to be qualified until the desired disclosure occurs. But when that happens, will the new 'kindness' any longer be connected to the old 'gratitude,' or even to some new 'gratitude'? The answer, which must come from Ramsey's theory of models and their functioning, seems to be that we cannot say that it will not be so connected, but we cannot say that it will, either, and therein lies the trouble.

If commitment without appropriate discernment is bigotry, won't any total commitment to such an elusive disclosure as that of the kindness of God be bigoted *per definitionem*? And on the other hand, won't the absence of such commitment be prudence and never hypocrisy? To avoid these consequences what is needed is some logical—not merely psychological—account of the linguistic relation between the two, in this case, between disclosure and commitment. Ramsey's theory, like Braithwaite's, cries out for such a connection but does not provide it. We remark that such an account need not eliminate 'mystery,' nor reduce the objects of religion to the objects of the dinner table or the hardware store, but it must include a clearer statement than we have here of the logical grammar of religious utterance.

Turning again to the functional thesis, we must ask why it is that *all* the language of religion must consist of analog or disclosure models? Assuming for the moment the general linguistic adequacy of both kinds of models, why may not religious language consist of picture models as well? Ramsey is severe in his strictures against Karl Barth for thinking that there are "supposed facts which the words [of theology] picture," holding that this leads Barth to an intolerable dualism, to two worlds of facts.[69] But, neglecting the question whether this 'two-worlds' ontology is what Barth intends, surely some religious speaker might indeed believe in, and meaningfully talk about, another world of facts than the everyday world. At least Ramsey gives no linguistic, as opposed to theological, reason to deny this possibility. Indeed, it seems that every religious speaker sometimes speaks in straightforward ways and is at these times liable in his religious talk to be straightforwardly mistaken, just as those who speak of facts are liable to be mistaken. Ramsey himself acknowledges that besides the qualified models (whose role we do not deny), there are in religious speech certain "key-words," such as "God," or "Spirit," which are the "irreducible posits" of the system.[70] If these, why not still other non-models, or at least non-analog-models, in religious speech? The functional thesis requires adjustment at least at this point; religious talk cannot consist of models and qualifiers alone.

This brings us to the question how, in Ramsey's theory, religious language is to be judged not merely possible, but appropriate, and hence to the *justificatory* thesis. Ramsey has been hastily criticized by some for neglecting or even denying the descriptive or representative role of religious language.[71] However, we have just seen that this criticism cannot stick. Unlike Braithwaite, and far more clearly than Zuurdeeg, Ramsey has attended to the descriptive and referential role of religious talk, even while making it clear that the 'facts' religion is interested in are a different sort of facts than empirical ones.[72] On the other hand, Ramsey firmly rejects the possibility that religious language can be verified in the way in which, as he sees it, assertions deduced from generalizations in empirical science can be verified. Such verifiable deductions theology "cannot and must not provide."[73] The reason Ramsey gives for this is theological: if verifications were possible, then God would be a manipulable object like the objects of scientific study; "God would have become a scientific concept."[74]

How, then, are we to decide what religious talk is preferable? A given case always begins for Ramsey by noting a particular cosmic disclosure. Since cosmic disclosures are not available on demand, this may seem daunting, but on Ramsey's view they are certainly frequent enough to yield the phenomena of religious talk. If a given disclosure is articulated at all, it will be paired with a given model. The model is now to be compared with all other available models. We can be confident, Ramsey holds, that all these models aim at one object, since in cosmic disclosures we confront just one Universe, which in each disclosure is apprehended as a whole. Thus we "develop discourse from each model only with a constant eye on other models . . ."[75] It is even more important that the model shall fit the empirical circumstances which give rise to it—thus model-talk about 'love' of God must *fit* the empirical human circumstances which led to this talk.[76]

It is not easy to nail down Ramsey's notion of "empirical fit."

> The theological model works more like the fitting of a boot or a shoe than like the 'yes' or 'no' of a roll call. In other words, we have a particular doctrine which, like a preferred and selected shoe, starts by appearing to meet our empirical needs. But on closer fitting to the phenomena the shoe may pinch. When tested against future slush and rain it may be proven to be not altogether watertight or it may be comfortable—yet it must not be too comfortable. In this way, the test of a shoe is measured by its ability to match a wide range of phenomena, by its overall success in meeting a variety of needs. Here is what I might call the method of empirical fit . . .[77]

The fitting of a boot suggests a high degree of personal taste; on the other hand "empirical fit" is also like the fit between a detective's new-found clue and the theory on which he is operating at the moment:[78] this clue fits the theory that the archdeacon not the curator was the murderer; that one does not.

In any case, if the language the religious speaker "builds out" from models which display "empirical fit" is based upon as many models as possible (but how is this determined?), if it is as "consistent, comprehensive, coherent, and simple" as can be, then, in Ramsey's view, it will conform "closer and closer to the language which a believer uses about God."[79] In other words, the language of Christian believers in God *does* possess "empirical fit," *is* consistent, comprehensive, and so forth, and is therefore justifiable, or very nearly so.

Clearly, this thesis of Ramsey's is theistic and specifically Christian. As it stands, then, it does not meet the broader, more abstract demand for a theory of how, in general, religious talk (or convictional talk in general) may be justified. But if we generalized Ramsey's justificatory thesis to cover the testing of atheistic and non-Christian religious talk, would it prove serviceable? The trouble is that we cannot be sure how such an extrapolation should go in order to fulfill Ramsey's intentions. Certainly his work contains, as we have seen, numerous hints for the broadest-ranging account of religious language and for its justification. Particularly attractive is the suggestion that, besides (somehow) fitting the facts, appropriate religious talk will be "consistent, comprehensive, coherent, and simple." Regretably, however, these hints are not worked out in such a form as to fulfill the goals mentioned at the beginning of this chapter. We want, as Ramsey might have put it, a map of the entire terrain of religious utterance.

Summing up our examination of the portion of Ramsey's work we have surveyed, we find the generative thesis interesting but unproved, the functional thesis stimulating but incomplete, and the justificatory thesis cast in a form which does not meet the broader need for a general theory of justification. Nevertheless, Ramsey comes nearer, in two ways, to meeting the standards of an adequate general theory of religious language than any other recent worker in the field, for he takes seriously the referential-representative intentions of religious speakers, and he comes nearer to showing the correlation between religious and other kinds of everyday speech. We think he fails to show how the 'factual' component of religious talk is necessarily attached to its self-involving aspects, and we think he fails to explicate the single most important element which makes religious utterance seem odd or strange to non-religious listeners (and vice versa)—its convictional basis. He fails, that is, to reckon with the way in which communities of believers, whether the Irish Republican Army, or the participants in a congress of physical chemists, or the worshippers of God in Christ, each share a special set of profoundly held assumptions and beliefs which make them the persons they are, control the shape and meaning of what they say, and thus define the problem of the justification of their language and their beliefs.

Ramsey enthusiasts might hope that his admirable insights and his considerable industry could be salvaged to perform this task as well. They might hope that on the bases laid down by the generative, functional, and justificatory theses, a general theory of language encompassing convictional pluralism could be erected. While we take a less sanguine view, we do expect that these Ramseyan theses may form a part of a general theory which draws on Braithwaite and Zuurdeeg as well but which is laid down on rather different lines.

* * *

Since our own work began, that of the post-Wittgensteinian philosophers of religion (we refer to Malcolm, Anscombe, Geach, Winch, Rhees, Phillips and others) has blossomed forth and has justly received considerable attention in the literature. Perhaps the most interesting of these for present purposes is Dewi Z. Phillips.[80] Like ourselves, Phillips says that there can be no adequate account of religious belief which does not pay close attention to the believer's understanding of what he means by what he says; moreover this meaning is not personal or private to any one believer but is embodied in the tradition or way of life of those who share a religious language. Like ourselves, he holds that neither philosophers nor anyone else can make a religiously neutral or external assessment of central religious claims; that is not a possible philosophical task. Phillips also insists that "religious languages games" are not isolated from the rest of life.[81]

On the other hand, Phillips seems absorbed with a single notion of religion which we suspect is no more adequate to the full range of religious speech than are the special theories associated with Ramsey and Braithwaite. Further, Phillips seems to think that logically there can be no questioning of the criteria religious speakers employ—it is simply unintelligible to demand the justification of these criteria.[82] Throughout his work Phillips appears to struggle with a tension or inner contradiction between this invulnerability of the grounds or criteria of religion (hard perspectivism) and the continuity of religion with life (soft perspectivism) which he also insists upon.[83] Since we intend to develop our own defense of soft perspectivism and to demonstrate the inadequacy of hard perspectivism generally (see especially chapter 6), there seems no point in providing a detailed criticism of Phillips and those who agree with him in this regard.

A different sort of explanation is required for our passing over the work on language done by certain European hermeneutic theologians and their American disciples. We refer to those for whom "language event" or "speech-happening" *Sprachereignis* or *Wortgeschehen*) is a key term and who have been strongly influenced by the language theories of Martin Heidegger—notably Ernst Fuchs, Gerhard Ebeling, and their American interpreter Robert W. Funk.[84] Insofar as these names define a particular tendency in Protestant Christian theology, our own task requires no more special attention to them than to any other theological tendencies in Catholic, Judaic, Buddhist, or Muslim thought—that is to say, none at all. Insofar as they reflect a special theory about religious language, however, we are in principle concerned with that theory. As we read the hermeneuticists, we find them saying many things with which we are inclined to agree. We say "inclined," because

their linguistic questions are raised within a framework so different from our own that we find it difficult to state any exact
agreement or disagreement. To illustrate the difficulty, notice that
when they refer to the work of J.L. Austin they display disastrous
misunderstandings of his work,[85] and we imagine that any brief
attempt of ours to characterize Heidegger would be equally disastrous. This does not mean that *rapprochement* is impossible. But
to attempt it would require another book instead of the present
one.

So our position *vis-à-vis* the post-Wittgensteinians and the post-
Heideggerians is different: the latter are, so to speak, our distant
European cousins, somewhat strange and often unintelligible to us
but apparently with similar interests which might be developed on
closer acquaintance; while the former are more like rival siblings in
the family of philosophical analysts. Our work has grown from
neither. It does depend on those we have examined in this chapter,
one of whom, Zuurdeeg, stands in the existentialist European
tradition. In most respects our understanding of language depends
even more upon the theories of J.L. Austin, and we now turn to
the exposition of his work.

3

So far, however, we have scarcely begun in earnest: we have merely felt that initial trepidation, experienced when the firm ground of prejudice begins to slip away beneath the feet.

John L. Austin[1]

If you feel that finding out what something is must entail investigation of the world rather than of language, perhaps you are imagining a situation like finding out what somebody's name and address are, or what the contents of a will or a bottle are, or whether frogs eat butterflies. But now imagine that you are in your armchair reading a book of reminiscences and come across the word "umiak." You reach for your dictionary and look it up. Now what did you do? Find out what "umiak" means, or find out what an umiak is? But how could we have discovered something about the world by hunting in the dictionary? If this seems surprising, perhaps it is because we forget that we learn language and learn the world together, that they become elaborated and distorted together, and in the same places. We may also be forgetting how elaborate a process the learning is. . . .

Stanley Cavell[2]

A Speech-Act Theory
of Religious Language

THE HOPE OF FINDING THE SEEDS OF A THEORY OF RELIGIOUS
language in the work of the Oxford linguistic philosopher John L.
Austin may strike some as comical, for Austin never devoted
himself to religious language as such, and his sardonic *obiter dicta*
on religion did not tend to inspire a surge of confidence in the
breasts of the faithful. Moreover, many have supposed that the
doctoral dissertation of Donald D. Evans gleaned whatever could be
harvested in the field of philosophy of religion using Austinian
tools. In reality, Evans' work on Austin concentrates upon the
notion of 'performative' language, recognizing only in a brief note
that Austin in his culminating work had abandoned the performative and had developed instead the theory of speech-acts.[3] So
while on the one hand the account we are about to give of
religious language represents Austin's own views no more than did
Evans', on the other hand we do hope to provide a foundation for
the analysis of religious language starting from the latest and most
considered views of Austin and his successors.[4] Concretely, this
should permit us to give a satisfying account of the convergence of
historical, sociological, and linguistic factors in any significant
utterance, thereby advancing beyond the theories described in the
previous chapter. We propose to set out an account of speech-acts,
to apply this to sample utterances, one non-religious (non-
convictional) and one expressing a religious conviction, and then
to examine these results as critically as we have the work of
others.

I. Speech-Acts

Austin was a philosophical iconoclast who took a certain pleasure in overturning what had been considered central doctrines in

49

philosophy in his day and in disregarding the received dichotomies of philosophical thought. Thus it is not surprising that he should have begun his systematic explorations of language by attending to forms of speech which refused to fit into traditional linguistic categories and in any case were generally regarded as trivial by analysts. Suppose I say "I bid one heart" when it comes to my turn to bid in a game of bridge. One way to understand my utterance, one which had commended itself to some philosophers, was to take it as a description of myself, a statement about me. Such an interpretation would assimilate "I bid one heart" to "I have one heart," or "I have one kidney." That seemed, though, a wrong-headed view of the matter. If "I bid one heart" is a statement, it is either a true one or a false one—but even to ask which it is seems to miss its point, as it is certainly to mistake its role in the game of bridge. So long as we maintain traditional dichotomies, however, denying that it is a statement seems to imply either that it is meaningless (which it certainly isn't), or that it is some sort of command, or an expression of feeling, which seems equally to miss its point in the game.

What then is that point? Clearly, to bid one heart! Then, suggested Austin, let us call it, not a statement, nor a command, nor an expression of attitude—but a *bid*. Thereby we recognize that when I say "I bid one heart" (it being my turn to bid in a game of bridge), I have *done* something, namely, bid one heart. Having tried this, it is easy to multiply examples of utterances which exhibit the same intimate relation between saying and doing. Thus if the judge, while performing his function, robed and on the bench, says to the prisoner in the courtroom, "I sentence you to thirty days in jail," he has thereby *sentenced* him, not described sentencing (or expressed a feeling or a wish). And if your physician says, "I advise you to exercise daily," he has *advised* you, certainly not described you or your regimen. And so with many other such utterances in this form: consider "I pronounce you (man and wife)," "I pray that (my soul may be delivered)," "I invite you (to my house for dinner)," or "I resolve (to pay off my debts this year)." Austin first dubbed utterances of this kind "performatives," and set out to find the characteristics which distinguished them from the apparently non-performative, true-or-false utterances which had received so much attention from philosophers and which for contrast Austin called "constatives," for example, "That barn is red."

Austin found, however, that the performative-constative dichotomy broke down upon examination.[5] What had seemed to be two classes dissolved into only one. For he could find no characteristics which would unfailingly distinguish his new class of performatives from the old class of constatives. At one point he had suggested the "hereby test" for performatives: an utterance was performative, according to this test, if it could be put in the form "I hereby (warn, sentence, bid, etc.). . . ." Thus, "I hereby bid one heart," "I hereby promise to pay you five dollars," and "I hereby sentence you to five years" all make good sense, and the "hereby" does not change that sense but functions to show explicitly what would be true even if the "hereby" were for convenience omitted—that *saying it is doing it.* Therefore, the utterances even without the "hereby" were seen to be performative utterances, and the verbs "sentence," "bid," and "promise" were performative verbs.

So far, the test works. But what about the verb "state"? Take any statement, such as "I am a citizen of Washington." If we change the utterance to "I state that I am a citizen of Washington," it remains the same statement, and so does "I *hereby* state that I am a citizen of Washington." But if "state" is performative, the same must be true of "assert" also, yet these are the paradigmatic non-performatives. So the "hereby" test failed to work. The same thing was true of every proposed test: both the purported classes were liable to be unhappy in utterance if the facts did not support them, both were dependent upon the context or circumstances of the speaker as well as his intentions, both could occur in identical grammatical forms. What had been hoped for from the distinction was not realized. The 'performative' distinction neither separated the class of utterance to which "true/false" applied from all other classes; nor did it separate utterances which could be felicitously or infelicitously uttered from all others; nor did it divide utterances into two mutually exclusive classes of any sort.[6]

The collapse of the performative-constative distinction, while at first glance representing merely the failure of one more hopeful theory, in fact opened the door to a more promising approach. Beginning with the observation that performatives were a saying which was doing, it had been possible to describe the various ways in which this doing could go wrong, or be subject to challenge, or fail. But if performatives were indistinguishable from the others, all utterances could be usefully treated as kinds of action, having the sorts of linguistic liability and linguistic asset which performative acts had been seen to possess.[7]

To call language a kind of action will not be very helpful unless we can say what we mean by that. The philosophy of action has come in for considerable recent discussion,[8] and philosophers will see what path we perhaps incautiously take here, among several possible ones. Let us begin with a non-linguistic story: the body of a heavily padded human, marked in large numerals "43," is somehow attached to an inflated, elliptical object. Man and object are seen to move into a group of similarly padded but differently numbered humans; after a time, the movement slows and stops. Already, we have before us a number of different senses of action. In the broadest of these, we can describe the motion of man plus object as his (or their) action; this sense corresponds to describing any physical motion, say of pool balls on a table, as 'action.' Again, attending to the fact that '43' is self-propelled, we can speak of *his* (physiological) movement as action, without so far intending to discriminate between. this sense of action and the action of his heart in beating, or of his sweat glands in secreting. Next we come to a more interesting sense in which '43' has acted—he has moved across the ground (cf. drawing in a deep breath or raising his head), but this sense interests us here only because it leads to the next.

Suppose now that we say, "43 was slanting off tackle." That is significantly different both from breathing, or digesting lunch, but also from raising his head, drawing a deep breath, or moving about. What we have done is to put 43's movements into the context of a game, with the consequence that there are ways in which his actions can be successful or go wrong. The notions of "off tackle" and of "slanting" cannot be explained without referring to the game of football, so that the assessment of 43's run will require a knowledge of both the rules of the game and the aim of the team playing the game, which is to win and not lose. We can illustrate this by noting circumstances in which we would not say that 43 slanted off tackle. He would not have done it if (a) he had been playing a different game, say one in which there are no tackles; or (b) if he had not been a player in this game; or (c) if he hadn't had the ball, or had fumbled; or (d) if he had been tackled before he got to the line.

If, however, difficulties like (a) to (d) do not arise, we may also be able to attribute another action to 43: making a first down. That can be true only if the run comes off. But it requires that other conditions be satisfied as well; certain yardage must be covered, and there must be official recognition of his success, which in turn rests upon certain well-known objections not having arisen or been sustained—penalties incurred, end of the game, or the like.

Again, whether 43's action was successful or not, he will perhaps delight, dismay, encourage, or disappoint various spectators, cause bets to be won or lost, money to change hands, statistical records of team and player standings to change, even coaches to be hired or fired. These results are not provided for in the rules, nor are they the point of the game, but it is significant that it is moves in the game, not mere physical movement, which have these effects. It is also significant that they are effects on people who understand the game, at least in the sense of knowing that there are sides, knowing what counts as succeeding, and so on.

We wish to focus upon the last three senses in which 43 has acted: he has (1) *moved*; (2) thereby, and under the circumstances, *made a move* in the game; (3) thereby, and because they knew the game, *had an effect* upon players, spectators, and perhaps others.

Now let us shift to a verbal situation and, guided by Austin, note the ways in which saying something is action. Consider the man in the striped shirt with the players. His mouth opens, his chest heaves, sounds come forth. This may seem to be of a piece with heartbeats and breathing until we specify that Striped Shirt moved his jaw, issued the sounds. But this becomes interesting, in turn, if we (1) acknowledge that Striped Shirt has *said something* (cf. 1 above), has, we may say, performed a *sentential act.*[9] If further we ask *what* he said, we are inquiring for some recognizable words appearing in a recognizable sentence (in some recognizable language) which will specify the sentential act he has performed. Suppose he said "Time out." If so, this is so far no different from what the alumna in the stands does in explaining to her son, "Time out," nor from what the son does in echoing his mother's explanation by saying "Time out." But we recognize that the referee has not only said something but also thereby made a move in the game—he has (2) *called time out.* Austin referred to this second kind of action as an illocutionary act;[10] we will simply call it a *speech-act.* Striped Shirt has inserted his words into the situation and made a difference. Time out has been called. Whereas what the alumna did by inserting her words into the situation (her speech-act) was explaining, not calling, and what the son did (his speech-act) was repeating, not explaining. (3) Once again, other persons and other states of affairs are *affected* by the referee's act in the game. (This is even more evident in the case of a penalty assessed by the referee.) And these effects, too, can be attributed to the referee, though in some cases not to him alone. Austin calls the act by which such effects are produced the referee's *perlocutionary act*—he disappoints or delights, decreases or increases the sales at the concession stand, causes bets to be won, the score to be changed, the statistics to be compiled differently than if he had not done what he did. Though, of course, there are cases in which he might not do any or all of these. In general, action in sense 3 is dependent on action in sense 2, and 2 is dependent on 1; whereas there can be sentential acts (1) without speech-acts (2) (we can just say sentences over like pupils in a reading class), and there can be speech-acts (2) without perlocutionary acts (3) (in such cases there would be no effects to be listed).

It may be objected by now that our comparison of the notion of speech action to acting in games, while it may do for certain ritual or social patterns of conversation ("games people play"), is an inevitably reductionist treatment of utterances which express religious or any other central human convictions. To treat these as moves in a game is already to misunderstand their import. But this objection would reflect a misunderstanding of the point of the preceding paragraphs, which seek to show, if only by a simple example, that as actions rise in grade to the level of meaningful human utterance they necessarily rise also to a setting in complex human structures (languages, linguistic institutions) and occur in connection with complex human practices in such a way that their meaning presupposes these structures and practices. It is not our intention to claim that the significance of all such structures and practices is on a level with those of organized sport, but to show how meaningful action is based upon the social world in which it plays its role. Our main point may be succinctly summed up thus: *Saying something, talking, speech in the full sense that saying something is a way of acting meaningfully, is to be understood in terms of the crucial significance of the speech-act* (Austin's "illocutionary act"), rather than in terms of the sentential act or the perlocutionary act.[11] This is to be our guiding principle in the present search for the significance of religious utterances.

Now the speech-act theory can serve us as the foundation for a theory of language only if it can help us account for those aspects of language whose omission we have criticized in earlier theories, while it nevertheless retains their insights. We propose to investigate this possibility by stating the conditions which must be fulfilled for the successful completion of two particular speech-acts. We expect these to be complex enough to reflect the various aspects of meaning we have suggested and yet allow for the evident capacity of large numbers of people to speak a language. Now rules are often best understood by noting what would violate them, so we will ask what an English (for convenience, but any other natural language would do as well) speaker must do to make a non-defective, faultless, or happy *request* and then, a happy (religious) *confession.*

This choice of samples may strike some readers as revealing a fatal indirection in our work. Should we not rather deal with 'statements' and 'religious statements,' thereby confronting the central difficulty: the 'cognitivity' of religious speech? To raise this objection in this way, however, is to display a basic misunderstanding of Austin's work in breaking down the misplaced barrier between statements and all other forms of speech. In discarding the performative theory, Austin was discarding the 'statemental' (or, as he might have put it, the "constative") theory as well, and the latter was the more significant discard. Nevertheless, the statemental theory dies hard[12] and for legitimate although misplaced concerns. We share the concerns and therefore wish to place them within a more adequate (speech-act) theory of meaning. To make this clear it may be helpful to say more about the sometimes misleading term "statement."

In a rough and ready way, the vocabulary of our language, or any other natural language, will employ certain verbs to designate certain speech-activities—blessing, promising, suggesting, advising, objecting, begging, answering, stating. But these categories are not always mutually exclusive, nor equally precise. Thus in *telling* someone something, I may be advising, or ordering, or objecting. "Tell" is a more general class of speech-act, which, according to circumstances, may or may not be specifiable in more exact ways: when you told me to get a new secretary, were you advising me or ordering me? But "state"—like "tell" and "say" and (sometimes) "assert"—can be used in this more general way also. This more general and historically more recent use of "statement" has been employed by traditional grammarians, who distinguish statements from questions and commands and again by those philosophers who employ it as a synonym for "sentence" or for "utterance," or more narrowly for any sentence or utterance which is true or false. Sometimes, on the other hand, philosophers have used "statement" to mean an abstract entity, the content or 'proposition' which might be expressed by an indefinite range of sentences or utterances. (In this sense, the same statement is said to be expressed by sentences which translate one another in two or more languages.) And there are still other technical philosophical uses, but we can comprehend these only in terms of the ordinary uses.

Returning to ordinary speech, we note that "statement" and "state" are sometimes used in an older and more restricted sense, which is suggested by their etymology (from the Latin *stare*, *status*, to stand). In this sense, statements are speech-acts issued in relatively formal circumstances by persons who have reason to be informed on the subject of the statement, and consist in setting forth (generally in the interests of or even at the request of the hearer) the matters about which the speaker is so informed, generally within certain restrictions as to content and style. Thus a prisoner of war may state his name, rank, and serial number, trespassers may be required to state their business or move along, and a participant in an argument may state his case. These instances remind us that those making statements are presumed to have special access to the subject matter of the statement—the serviceman is presumed to know his own name, rank, and serial number; the trespasser but not the Pinkerton guard can state the trespasser's business (though the Pinkerton guard may be called upon to state his own suspicions); we state the other man's case in an argument only after we have heard it, and then normally subject to correction. They also remind us that not everything belongs in a statement, though certainly something other than facts may belong there: Thus one may state a claim, state an argument, state conditions, state limitations. "Just state the facts, ma'am," is probably not designed simply to limit the policeman's interogee to *facts;* rather it is designed to limit her to facts of which *she* has direct knowledge—to what she knows to be facts, and can therefore *state,* as opposed to her surmises and hypotheses.

We may test this understanding of the ordinary and strict use of "statement" by noting some natural limitations in the language. We do not say "state" whenever we are dispensing facts, for I can *admit* this fact, and *advert* to that one, and in neither instance will "state" do the required work. Nor can we always use the verb "state" in speech-acts where "say" is called for: the believer *says* his prayers; perhaps he *offers* a prayer; but he does not *state* his prayer. When the reporter is called to take down the suspect's statement, it is understood by the experienced that certain matters are to be set out in the resulting document—matters concerning which the suspect speaks from the 'privileged' position of his firsthand knowledge, and which bear upon the subject matter at hand. His 'statement' will be recognizable as such only if it observes, within reason, these limitations. In this sense all of us can, and regularly do, *say* far more than we *state;* our statements are a weightier and a sharper-edged fraction of our talk. Clearly the question of what in the religious realm someone is in position to state is closely related to the question of what in that realm he is in position to know to be true. But this is very different from saying that all that is true, or even all that he knows to be true, can be stated.[13]

It is in this light, we think, that the following passage in Austin's essay "Performative Utterances" is to be understood:

> Suppose for example you say to me 'I'm feeling pretty mouldy this morning'. Well, I say to you 'You're not'; and you say 'What the devil do you mean, I'm not?' I say 'Oh nothing—I'm just stating you're not, is it true or false?' And you say 'Wait a bit about whether it's true or false, the question is what did you mean by making statements about somebody else's feelings? I told you I'm feeling pretty mouldy. You're just not in a position to say, to state that I'm not'. This brings out that you can't just make statements about other people's feelings (though you can make guesses if you like); and there are very many things which, having no knowledge of, not being in a position to pronounce about, you just can't state. What we need to do for the case of stating, and by the same token describing and reporting, is to take them a bit off their pedestal, to realize that they are speech-acts no less than all these other speech-acts that we have been mentioning and talking about as performative.[14]

Austin's point here is not that one cannot ever make statements about other people's feelings, for that claims can be made about feelings even by the 'feeler' himself is evidence that they are not *completely* private, and what is in principle not private may in practice become public. Rather what Austin sees to be possible is that some circumstances may arise in which although we are there and can speak yet we are *in no position* to make a statement about another's feelings—and a chance meeting in the hallway seems to be such a circumstance. I can't in the normal run of things state what your feelings are this morning simply because I've walked past you in the hallway.

This notion of being in position may bring into focus the difficulty in treating religious utterances such as A to G (chapter 2) uniformly as statements, even though we may concede that such utterances have cognitive content. Inability to state is a commonplace of everyday life. The difficulty may be physical (drunkenness, or aphasia; or consider the circumstances in which one could state, "I am now gargling vigorously"), but these are generally surmountable. The inability may be due to the privileges or circumstances of the speaker's life. Although I can surmise, I cannot state what the British prime minister wore to bed last night, since I was not there—but someone who was can perhaps state that he wore pink pajamas, and I may then be able to state that on the other's authority. The president's physician cannot state, is not in line to state, current U.S. policy in some Lebanese crisis, while the president and the secretary of state are and can. Or the inability may be one based on the moral certainties of the case: thus in some Oscar Wilde play, a frivolous fop may say, "Madeleine, I love you passionately. Marry me, do, do," when we know that the fop is not passionate about anything, so that his utterance is not a falsehood but a misfire, a giant bark from a Pekingese pup.[15]

We begin to see, then, what difficulties might be involved in a genuine religious statement, and to ask what circumstances might justify classifying a given religious utterance as the speech-act of stating. Can there be, within Christianity or Judaism, *statements* about God? We remember the theological caution in the presence of mystery which led Israel to avoid even the nameless name of her God. We recall the theological tentativeness of the Greek Christian Fathers, and (to shift to our own time) we remember that Buber said God could properly be only addressed, never expressed. If there is in these traditions nevertheless much talk about God, we must ask whether this is not confession, or praise, or explanation, rather than statement. For in their view of the matter, no human person is ever in position to make statements about the biblical God. Never, because in the tradition which acknowledges this God, nothing counts as getting into position to make statements about him, and obviously outside it nothing does. The gargler cannot, while gargling, make statements about gargling because he is too close to it. I cannot make statements about the prime minister's pajamas because I am not close enough to his bedroom. The president's physician cannot make statements about U.S. policy because he is not in the line of responsibility. In the strands of Jewish and Christian tradition which we have just recalled, it might be said that believers cannot make statements about God because God is too remote ("God is in heaven, and you upon earth"—Ecclesiastes 5:2) or because he is too near ("In him we live and move and have our being"—Acts 17:28). If on the other hand there is a strand in these traditions which holds that such statements can be made by some in virtue of a special position of participation or of faith which they occupy, we will shortly single out that position in specifying the conditions for confession. Perhaps in the eyes of some that will come down to the same thing as examining the conditions for a (special, religious) act of stating, and if that is true, we will be content. We think we have said enough to indicate how our starting point differs from that of the 'religious statement' school of language analysts.

II. Requesting and Confessing[16]

A certain diner, A, while sitting at table with others says, "Please pass the bread." Now let us ask what has happened, what must have happened, if A's utterance is counted a *happy request*? How do we know that A has not only made sounds or issued some words but has thereby, in these circumstances, successfully and happily asked that the bread be passed?[17] We will list the conditions for happily requesting in summary form and then offer some explanation of each of them.[18]

1. *Preconditions.* The speaker (in this case, A) and some hearer know a common language (in this case, English); both speaker and hearer are conscious and free from relevant physical impediments so that speaker's sound-production and hearer's hearing of speaker are normal.

2. *Primary conditions.*

    2.1 The speaker issues a sentence (performs a sentential act) in the common language.

    2.2 There is a convention of the language to the effect that this sentence is a way of (performing the speech-act of) requesting.

3. *Representative or descriptive conditions.*

In issuing this sentence the speaker describes or represents a possible future state of affairs with sufficient exactness that it can be identified as the requested state of affairs.

4. *Affective or psychological conditions.*

4.1 The speaker wants the requested state of affairs to come to pass.

4.2 The speaker's intention in issuing this sentence is to use the language's convention for requesting (see 2.2) and he intends the hearer to understand (by his use) that he is so using it.

4.3 The hearer on the basis of the issued sentence takes the speaker to have the requisite wants and intentions just listed (see 4.1 and 4.2).

4.4 Neither the speaker nor the hearer foresees that the possible future state of affairs (see 3) would come about or has come about in the ordinary course of events, that is, without speaker's sentential act.

To return to our old analogy, the *preconditions* are related to the speech-act in somewhat the way in which, in football, the requirement that the players and officials shall be on the field and functioning is related to making a move in the game (slanting off tackle). While the preconditions are the most constant of the sets of conditions we have specified, they are not invariant for all classes of speech-acts. Some speech-acts require no hearer (cursing? practicing speaking? cheering?). It might also be claimed that some religious speech-acts (e.g., prayer) require no human hearer and within some contexts no hearer at all. These facts indicate that the preconditions are not necessary conditions for the faultless performance of *every* speech-act and that the precise relationship of the preconditions to successful performance of a particular speech-act must be determined case by case, involving non-linguistic (for example, theological or scientific) considerations as well as linguistic. Nevertheless, it does seem correct to say that without the existence of hearers and a common language there would be no such things as speech-acts to begin with. Given the common language and its conventions, speech-acts which dispense with one or more of these preconditions become possible.

As we shall see, there is no *a priori* way to say which conditions can be dispensed with; we must know what other conditions are met and which speech-act is in question. Given the presence of other conditions, any one might be dispensed with; given the absence of others, any one condition might be necessary for a given speech-act. That we must admit 'non-linguistic' considerations may seem regrettable, but it also seems inevitable. As we indicate later (and as Austin and Quine, in their different ways, showed) the search for the purely linguistic or the irreducibly logical apart from a particular context seems doomed to failure.

The condition we have called *primary* is one which we were once disposed to call the essential condition for the performance of a speech-act.[19] Yet bizarre cases can be imagined in which the primary condition is not sufficient, and extreme circumstances in which it is not necessary, for the performance of the act of requesting. The positive point to note is that not just any sound (see 2.1) or just any sentence (see 2.2) can normally be used to make a request: the range of possibilities may be wide, but it is not boundless. "Bread, confound it!" will not normally count as a *request,* nor will "Please *fine* the bread" count. The trouble·with the latter is that we don't know what it means; that is, we have no bread-fining convention, though one can imagine a world in which we had that and not a bread-requesting convention. There are many ways of getting the bread: Mr. A might wire electrodes to a subject's elbows and close the circuit; he might hypnotize some-one and instruct him to pass it on a signal, say the ringing of a bell; he might order someone to pass it, threaten him if he did not pass it, or audibly speculate on how it would be if he had the bread. Any of these might result in his getting the bread, and some of them have some things in common with requests, but none of them are requests for bread. What they fail to be and what a request must be is a sentence whose utterance is a conventional linguistic device (a device recognizable by speakers of that lan-guage or dialect) for making a request. Only in that case can its utterance be the performance of a speech-act of requesting.

If someone objects that 2.2 is circular, defining a linguistic act in linguistic terms, this should be admitted: the circle could be made less obvious (to the careless) by circumlocution; it can be avoided altogether, however, only at the greater risk of obscuring the conventional character of the illocutionary act.[20]

There may be speech-acts which involve no reference to or representation or description of anything, though we are hard-pressed to think of examples: only in certain circumstances do we greet or thank someone,[21] and clearly requesting does have a *representative* or *descriptive condition,* as do appraising, pardon-ing, and, as we shall see, (religious) confessing. For requesting, the requirement is that A must make it reasonably clear *what* he is requesting, and the requested state of affairs (the bread being passed) must be a possible one, which means that there must be bread available, someone who can pass it (all the hearers not helpless paralytics), and the bread must not already be in A's hands, if his request is to be a happy one.

By this time, the point of the search for the conditions of a happy, or successful, speech-act, as opposed to a merely possible or minimal one, should be coming into focus. For if someone objects that saying "Please pass the bread" while holding the bread, the only bread, in your hands is *some* kind of request, we would grant that this may be true (though the burden seems to be on the objector to say what such a speaker is up to). But we would add that such an act would not work well linguistically; hearers would be puzzled, or suppose that they had misunderstood, or perhaps take it that the speaker did not know what he had just said. Now such responses are indications that all is not well linguistically, while our conditions taken together set out the broad range of cases in which linguistically all *is* well. Under these conditions, though all may not be well dietetically or morally or socially,. A's utterance is linguistically happy, and that is our present concern.

If this point is kept in mind, the remaining, *affective conditions* can be briefly explained. As in the other conditions, it is important to remember that they will differ for different speech-acts: sincerity, for example, seems appropriate enough an affect for stating and promising but is not a linguistic requirement for requesting. The relevant condition in the latter case is that A must want the possible future state of affairs referred to in 3 to come to pass. The strength of his desire, however, is not to be measured by his 'sincerity,' but only by what is necessary for the total success of the act—want it enough to accept and not refuse the bread when it is passed. (To refuse it would be to incur such a linguistic reproach as, "But you *said* please pass it.") Mr. A may want other things as well—all the bread he can ever get his hands on, the undivided attention of his hearers, perhaps the moon, but those wants do not go to the happiness of his request.

The next condition shows the way in which the speaker's intentions are woven into the fabric of his action. The correct description of these intentions (4.2) shows the necessity of steering between the Scylla of supposing that happening to say words in an approriate order counts as a happy request (for in fact, if he didn't intend to say those words, he will have to make some excuse to those who heard and acted upon them) and the Charybdis of supposing that intentions count for everything, so that it doesn't really matter which words were spoken or in which order or that it doesn't matter whether Mr. A intended to be taken as requesting (suppositions so extraordinary that we should have to invent fantastic stories in order to illustrate them).[22] Making what we intended to say the absolute determinant of what we have in fact said would have the general effect of opening too wide a loophole for speakers, in more weighty situations, to wiggle out of what they have said—welsh on bets, break promises, and slander their neighbors with impunity.

The next condition, called "uptake" (4.3), is simply the recognition that utterance involves a receiver as well as a sender, and calls attention to the necessity that the hearer grasp A's intentions and wants as a result of the employment of the convention. And the final, negative requirement points up the hollowness of requesting what is taken already to be the case.

If we have succeeded in our purpose of setting out the conditions for one type of utterance (in this case, a request) and relating them to one another, it will be seen that affective, representative, and primary illocutionary forces are not competing rivals for the bearing of meaning in an utterance, nor are they mere conjuncts, so many assorted apples, oranges, and pears in a bowl. Rather the representative and affective conditions make for the meaningfulness of an utterance whose primary condition (in this and every such case) is that it belongs to the possibilities of the language, as a possible (conventional or rule-governed) move within that language. Representation (description, reference) is certainly not eliminated, but neither is it given a favored hierarchical status. Austin felt that earlier theories were mired in the 'descriptive fallacy'—the view that the proper business of words was to make (verifiable) statements, whose virtue was to be true and vice to be false. Others have spoken of a 'performative fallacy,' presumably an overemphasis on the conventional aspect of language. We hope to avoid both errors. If the utterance of a sentence under a certain convention is primary, it is only because such conventions constitute the language and make *linguistic* meaning possible. That descriptive or representative conditions are often necessary reflects the fact that language is not a self-contained activity but comes to grips with a *world* which language alone cannot replace. And the affective conditions arise from the fact that language is the instrument of *persons,* for whom desires, intentions, beliefs, and so forth, have central significance. On special occasions any of these conditions could be unfulfilled and a request could still be made. But this is only to say that we can understand the exception to a rule well enough—as long as there is a rule. We can understand an enjoyed or sought-after punishment as nevertheless punishment, even though it breaks the (general) rule that punishments must be unwanted, but we so understand it only because it is the exception and we know it. Sometimes, of course, the exception becomes the rule; language does grow and change. But it does not grow without starting from rules, nor without making new rules as it develops new forms.

Some may feel, however, that our linguistic account of A's speech-act is defective. What of the changed situation at the dining table, what of the active roles of his hearers, what of the whole sweep of consequences of his speech-act? While these may be trivial in the case of "Please pass the bread," that does not make it an unsuitable example for our inquiry. We note that even "Please pass the bread" may have astounding consequences. The bread may be poisoned or, less dramatically, someone may have resolved to leave the table if A asks for bread just one more time. And so on. The trouble with talking of consequences lies in just this indefiniteness: while it is possible, as we have shown, to set out the conditions for a successful (illocutionary) speech-act, there can be no successful formulation of all its possible consequences. One act may cause another, and causal chains go on and on. Our attention centers on the speech-act proper since our interest lies in discovering what can (rightly) be said and what can (happily) be believed. One point, however, should be made with care. We must distinguish the reaction of A's hearers which is *essential* to his request from that which is merely produced by his request (its perlocutionary effects). The former reaction (see condition 4.3 above) was called by Austin "uptake."[23] Uptake can be distinguished from the perlocutionary effects in the following way: if without the effect in question, it is questionable whether the utterance is entitled to be called a request (or if it is taken as an order or a complaint) then we are talking about uptake. Requests are requests *of* someone; there must be uptake for any request to have been made. On the other hand, felicitous requests do not need to be honored or fulfilled—A can request the bread without getting it, as every beggar knows. We note, too, that where the normally central features of the illocutionary act are missing or unknown or distorted, an observer may use what would normally be perlocutionary effects as tests of what sort of speech-act has been performed. For example, if some hearer hands a speaker some object which satisfies him and which elicits gratitude, we may classify the speaker's earlier unheard or indecipherable utterance as a request, plea, demand, or petition. But in singling out, with Austin, the illocution or speech-act proper, we are choosing that way of viewing language which contains the key to justifiable utterance and so the key to justifiable (religious) convictions.

Now we will apply the method we have just demonstrated to a religious utterance. From the samples A to G listed in chapter 2, we choose G "God led Israel across the Sea of Reeds" on the grounds that it is from a tradition with which most of our readers (and we ourselves) are somewhat familiar, and that it will bring up most of the problems we want to discuss. It is not self-evident that G as it stands is a speech-act nor is it self-evident that it is religious. For one could merely say or write those words (as we have in preparing this page), thus performing a sentential act but so far not a speech-act. Furthermore, a variety of speech-acts might be issued via that sentence: a historian of religions might use these words to relate the traditional belief of the ancient Hebrews, just as we might say, "Ceres blessed the crops of the ancients" to report *that* tradition, without ourselves being believers in Ceres' bounty. Or again these words (or rather their equivalent in an ancient language) might have been used by a Hebrew of the time of Exodus, say Moses. Or in a different way by one of Pharoah's charioteers. Or, again differently, by a later chronicler or psalmist. As before, we must locate the utterance, find its setting or story, in order to discover its force.

Let us say that G is used by a Christian or Jewish teacher today: call him Aleph. With the utterance of G he is confessing his faith in the past providence of God as he teaches his class. We shall regard such a use of G as one genuinely religious case.

As before, we will ask what has happened if Aleph's utterance is properly to be classed a *happy confession*. We will list the conditions for happily confessing in summary form, with explanations following. The numbers will correspond as nearly as possible to those in the requesting case.

1. *Preconditions.* These are identical with those for the requesting case (see page 59).
    2. *Primary conditions*
       2.1 The speaker issues a sentence (performs a sentential act) in the common language.
       2.2 There is a convention of the language to the effect that this sentence is a way of (performing the speech-act of) confessing.

We explicate 2.2 as follows:

2.21 In issuing this sentence the speaker takes up or maintains a certain stance, to which he is thereby committed.

2.22 In issuing this sentence, the speaker displays, i.e., witnesses to, this stance.

3. *Representative or descriptive conditions.*

In issuing this sentence the speaker describes or represents the relevant state(s) of affairs with sufficient exactness to make it possible for him to take up that stance (2.21) and to display it (2.22).

The relevant state(s) of affairs will vary from confession to confession. In our story, Aleph's G requires:

3.1 In a certain historical context, a certain event (being led across the Sea of Reeds) has occurred to a certain people (Israel).

3.2 This event is attributable to the God acknowledged in this context.

3.3 This God exists.

4. *Affective or psychological conditions.*

4.1 The speaker has a certain affect, namely awed gratitude, and in issuing this sentence conveys his possession of it to the hearer.

4.2 The speaker's intention in issuing this sentence is to use the language's convention for confessing (see 2.2), and he intends the hearer to understand (by his use) that he is so using it.

4.3 The hearer on the basis of the issued sentence takes the speaker to have the requisite affect (see 4.1) and intentions (see 4.2), and he takes the speaker to have displayed or witnessed to the stance (see 2.22 and 3).

To seek the *primary condition* for confessing is to inquire what is involved in being a confessor, what one must do to confess. On our analysis, the primary elements are stance-taking and witnessing. By "stance," whose synonyms are "outlook," "position," and the like, we mean the entertaining (as true and important) of certain alleged facts, the embracing of certain pervasive theories about what matters in life, the hoping of certain hopes, the adoption of certain roles in certain communities, and the undertaking of certain patterns of behavior with regard to those facts, theories, hopes, and roles. The stance of Aleph is that of one who remembers and is heir to the storied crossing of the Sea of Reeds and who therein is committed to God and his fellow-heirs.

Thus if, having issued G, it is put to Aleph that he certainly doesn't *act* like a believer, he may, with consistency, either defend his behavior as misunderstood by the objector or plead weakness of will. If however he replies, "So what? Never mind how I live; I'm just telling what I believe," then linguistically something is wrong. Either Aleph does not know what a confession is, what his words (normally) mean, or his intentions were mistaken by his hearers (he was, perhaps, a historian not a confessor). The point, we emphasize, is a philosophical and not a theological one. It is like the situation in which A, told that there *was* no bread, angrily replied "So what; I said *pass* it." Our concern is not with his manners but his intelligibility. What could he mean, or what, in the case at hand, could Aleph?

Aleph's is one possible stance, but there are others which may also be embodied in confessions: an ancient Egyptian might confess, "God" (or "Jah") "led Israel across the Sea of Reeds, but I'll still serve the sun-god Ra," or perhaps "Ra drove Israel away, across the Sea of Reeds," while a Promethean modern might confess "God led Israel across the Sea of Reeds, yet I defy Him to tamper with my independent life." Our point in these perhaps farfetched examples is that merely and even sincerely to *say* the words of G is not *eo ipso* to take up or even to understand Aleph's stance; we must learn what Aleph's stance is from Aleph and his community. In that community there is something which those words cannot but mean, something they necessarily mean.

The other primary aspect of confessing is witnessing—the term which we believe most nearly does justice to the signaling quality which coheres with stance in the act of confessing. The witness is called, not to lecture or to argue, but to testify. He tells us not so much what he thinks as where he is, where he finds himself. We may catch the difference between the reporter and the witness by remembering the characteristic work of a Pascal and of a Hegel: Pascal sets out to show us where he finds himself; on the basis of what he shows us we can infer something about the way things are, the way the world is. Hegel on the other hand sets out to tell us how it is with the world and more, overall and in general, and from this we may infer the stance in which Hegel finds himself: Hegel is by intention a philosophical reporter; Pascal, again by intention, a philosophical witness. Again, this point may be illustrated by imagining that when Luther at Worms said "Here I stand," he was misunderstood as reporting his location in the cathedral: "I'm over here, Sir, by the north transept. Were you looking for me?" But that would make more than one mistake: not only a mistake about the sense and reference of the speaker's words, but also a mistake about the kind of speech-act he was performing. Luther was not describing or reporting; he was confessing. And confessing entails bearing witness, not only taking a stand but showing it, which is different, as we have said, from stating it.

Have we captured the force of confessing? We may test our understanding by reference to the forefather of Western literary confessions, St. Augustine. The *Confessions* constitute a sketch of the landscape of reality with which that convert to a new set of convictions found himself confronted. He begins with praise to God: "Great art thou, O Lord, and greatly to be praised."[24] He then continues with an account of his own personal history from infancy through the adventures and perplexities of his young manhood to the conversion which set his subsequent life's direction. There is the admission of sins and the expression of intense regret. He reflects upon the possibility of knowing God, upon the nature of time, and upon the ideas of creation, sacred scripture, and church. In all these ways, Augustine is giving account of the setting in which he takes his stand, his horizon; he is taking up that stance and thereby affirming it, and he is exercising the loyalty (to God, to church) which setting and stance require of him. If we turn to the *Confessions* of Jean Jacques Rousseau (1712–1778), again there is personal history, again there is the self-searching attempt honestly to know the true meaning of the personal past, again the author confronts a certain landscape and takes his stance with respect to it. The common features of these works, in some ways so diverse, focus on their self-involving quality—the writing is not merely *about* the author, as some autobiographies manage to be; rather the confession *shows* us the author in action, attempting to give a faithful account of what shapes him. Thus the act of confessing involves, both in this literary genre and in our own account of confession, the appropriation of a place, a taking up of those commitments or loyal ties which are seen to be appropriate to the place, and a self-involving display of these.

Thus a confession such as Aleph's points inescapably to a context which is taken to be real. We recognize that not every Jew or Christian employs G as does Aleph to celebrate a real crossing of an actual sea under divine guidance. Their confession of G might still be happy but it will be so under a different set of conditions for happiness. Whether or not it is Jewish or Christian to do so, it is possible for confessors to hold non-historical, as well as non-theistic, religious convictions. We have chosen the conservative and traditional faith of Aleph as our illustration both because Aleph represents a large number of actual believers, past and present, and because this illustration shows clearly how the analysis must take account of every dimension, whereas confessions with a suppressed or diminished representative aspect might not.

The central feature to note in this case or any other is that the *representative condition* is just what is required for the fulfillment of the other conditions. In Aleph's case, the Israelites must as confessed have crossed that sea; this event must be placed within a wider stream of biblical narrative, here called the "context" of the event; God, the God to whom the context refers, must be God, must exist. Note in particular that the happiness of Aleph's confession on its representative side depends *on these conditions* and not merely on his belief in them; for example, if Aleph, depending on older Bible versions, confessed that it was the *Red* Sea which Israel crossed, his confession, as Aleph's community now knows, would have been in that regard unhappy, Aleph's sincerity and blamelessness notwithstanding. Sincerity is not a sufficient condition of happy confessing any more than of happy requesting.

As with the Red Sea, so with a God who acted in this case, and who therefore acts in Israel's history and in world history; if this is not the way it is, Aleph's confession is unhappy as it stands. But how are we or how is anyone in this pluralistic world justly to say that these conditions are or are not fulfilled? Here we seem to have run directly into contested convictional ground. Here the hard perspectivist would have us back away, unable from any perspective other than Aleph's to say what would count as satisfying these conditions, while the non-perspectivist would perhaps say, let science (or philosophy, or common sense: in any case let *my* view) settle the matter, thus proposing, it seems to us, that we sail our inquiry right over the dry land in a miracle of transconvictional justification greater than the parting of the seas at the Exodus.

But what other way can we propose? We admit that the answer is not easy, and we will be occupied for the rest of this book in giving our full reply. Yet some preliminary things can be said here, and others when we discuss the affective conditions for the happiness of Aleph's G.

The sorts of problems which are here intertwined in the evaluation of Aleph's utterance may be roughly labeled historical, hermeneutical, theological, and something must be said about each. At the outset, the historical problems seem most straightforward. Was there a crossing of the Sea of Reeds by a people called Israel? Let us suppose that 'objective' historical inquiry, at least in the decade in which Aleph issues his confession, tends to answer that there were at the relevant time tribal movements of Semitic peoples from the region of the Nile toward the eastern desert and beyond. But G requires much more than this. These "movements" are taken, within the biblical context represented by G, to have been a deliverance, a redemption, the rescue of a people from servitude in order that they might serve a holy and righteous God. Is it appropriate for Aleph's community to take its ancient confession as the interpretation of this 'objective' claim? Can the 'inner' history of the community thus coalesce with the 'outer' history of detached scholarship?

Theologian readers will recognize in the 'inner/outer' distinction the language of H. Richard Niebuhr, who, wrestling with a similar problem, thought that 'inner' history (defined as 'our' history, or as the history of persons) must be sharply distinguished from 'outer' history (defined as 'their' history, or as the history of things or objects). Yet he also thought these two accounts referred in some way to the same realities and might usefully correct one another.[25] While this last claim seems to us correct, for reasons we will later give, it appears that Niebuhr made two mistakes, though these come down finally to one. He spoke as if 'inner' and 'outer' history could be sharply distinguished in the first place, and he spoke as if 'outer' history was not shaped by human goals, drives, and convictions just as is 'inner' history. If we can doubt the God of Israel who is said to preside over Israel's self-confession, asking whether her self-understanding is not fallible, we can equally doubt the god of scientific historiography, asking whether that muse does not slumber or sleep. Yet we draw from these double doubts not hard skepticism but a less dogmatic caution: the testing of a biblical outlook on history is sure to be slow and full of pitfalls for the rash confessor (or the rash professor).

Even the optimism implicit in the last sentence, however, is overstated, and for this reason. The context of biblical thought lying behind G is a world of narrative whose leading actor is God himself—a God who acts in a world of action. But the hermeneutical question is this: does it still make sense, today, to say, as G presupposes, that God acts in history? How can God act in history? Notice that the form of this question (and not merely the answer it seeks) is historically conditioned, being in part a function of our modern cosmology. This is not to say that the "how?" did not arise before modern times. It did arise in antiquity, and again in medieval times, where we find theologians at pains to provide explanations of the acts of God, explanations given in terms of the cosmology which they had inherited from Aristotle. The dawn of the modern era, however, brought with it a new cosmology (Galileo, Kepler, Copernicus, Newton), and it became difficult to say how God, who as Jews and Christians regarded him was neither the universe nor a part of the universe, could be said to 'act' in the universe. The interesting possibilities were in principle four: (1) one could cling to the old cosmology in spite of the changing intellectual climate; (2) one could accept the new cosmology but continue to talk of God's acts in the old ways; (3) one could accept the new cosmology and give up talking about God's acts; (4) or one could find new ways to describe God's acting and (therefore) a new way to describe God himself. The first, or reactionary/rebellious route was taken by some. Perhaps the real point of the Catholic Church's condemnation of Galileo is to be found in the (understandable if hopeless) attempt to hold on to a *particular* way of being able to talk about what God does. That way, as it turned out, was not a live option. The second or accommodating route became what we know today as theistic orthodoxy. God was said to act in the world by providence (ordinarily) and by miracle (extraordinarily). The trouble was that the traditional theistic account (as we find it, for example, in a philosophical theologian such as Samuel Clarke, 1675–1729) left an unclosable logical gap between the theistic God and the world in which he was supposed to act, the Newtonian world. For it was never made clear how an otherworldly God could affect a this-worldly world, a world which ran on Newtonian principles very well by itself.[26]

The third view arose about the same time as the first and second, was apparently more logical, though less interesting in the religious sense, and was dubbed *deism*. On this view, God did not *act* in history. He started the world and would end it with a final judgment, but in between the world was on its own. Deism removed the problem of God's acts from the current scene, however, only by the expedient of reinstating the same problems at a temporal distance—in connection with history's beginning and end, where once again God must act and where therefore the

logical problems inexorably reappear. The fouth alternative belongs especially to the nineteenth and twentieth centuries. In it,
the notion of God is reconceived (as by Spinoza, Schleiermacher,
or Whitehead) with a view to providing a sense of "God acts"
which is compatible wtih modern cosmology.

The historical conditioning of "How can God 'act'?" then, is
not only a function of a changing cosmology, but also a function
of a changing theology—that is, a changing conception of God.
Logical consistency and grammatical correctness are insufficient
conditions for the intelligibility of G. It must make sense in terms
of the cosmological and theological understanding available at the
time of its utterance.

Perhaps we can make this point clearer with an example. Men
have long spoken of the "rising" and "setting" of the sun. On the
geocentric view of the ancients, the sun, moon, and stars 'really
rose' and 'really set.' A changed cosmology, however, produced
another account. It is the earth which moves, men said, rotating
on its axis; the sun's motion, then, is 'apparent motion.' Once that
fact was fully accepted in a culture, it became possible to speak
again (or still?) of the rising and setting of the *sun*. "Sunset"
remains in our vocabulary after all. Now, however, a new analysis
is offered on demand: "When we say 'The sun rose' what we mean
is. . . ." The child who has learned the terms "sunrise" and "sunset" has more to learn about astronomy but not about proper
English. But there may also have been, for some speakers at least,
an intervening time, between the passing of the old theory and the
widespread acceptance of the new, in which it was felt that "The
sun rose" was simply an unacceptable way of speaking.

Now, with the appropriate changes, it is the possibility of just
such a difficult time for a certain form of speech (and we do not
here judge whether the time is temporary or permanent) that we
contemplate in specifying the present linguistic condition. Does
Aleph issue G in such a historical context, at such a time in
history, that an important part of its representative aspect, requiring that we be able to assign some sense to "God acted here," is
(in this time) impossible? If so, G is unhappy in this respect.[27]

There may be some who are impatient at this point. "Let's cut
all the chatter about speech-acts and felicities and theories of
religious language," they might say: "Get down to brass tacks. Is
there any God, or isn't there? If you think there is or isn't, give
your reasons, and I'll look into them. If you can't say, why bother
with all this business? Why bother with *anything* else until that is
settled?"

To such a position we are truly sympathetic. Only, we will all ask, which *is* the present condition (3.3)—true, or false? Our object has been to note the way in which *possible* and *happy* speech-acts must mirror reality; we believe, in other words, that the present inquiry, so far from being beside the point, is a direct journey in search of the answers that our brass tacks critic wants— or rather it is a tour book saying what such a journey must be like. What we are seeing for a special case here, and will argue in detail within, is that there is no such journey which ignores the convictional communities to which Aleph, and we, and Brass Tacks, each belong—no non-convictional road to the truths around which our convictions cluster.

Briefly to illustrate this, consider the objection to our view which goes as follows: "I've no particular problem with statements about God. I can state flatly that God doesn't exist. And I can do it because of the modern scientific worldview." If for "modern scientific worldview" we substitute "modern philosophy" or "logical incoherence in the concept of God" or "the course of human history" we will have represented the views of very many convinced atheists. Only now, as the term "convinced" suggests, we will have stepped across a convictional line separating those of Aleph's tradition from certain of those outside it, and will thereby have raised, though in a different way than for Aleph, the question what makes the atheist's 'confession' (or 'statement'—let him choose the term for the moment) a happy one—how may *it* be justified? And we know no shorter route to the answering of his question than the one we are already pursuing.

That is to say, it appears to the present writers (whose religious beliefs differ radically on the issue) that because of the convictional nature of the particular belief in question (the existence and nature, and leave us with the same difficulties, as does G itself. To put the point in the terms we have been employing, it seems that for a member of Aleph's community, and certainly for anyone fulfillment of certain of the representative conditions of G directly, save by means of utterances which partake of the same logical nature, and leave us with the same difficulties, as does G itself. To put the point in the terms we have been employing, it seems that for a member of Aleph's community, and certainly for anyone else, happily to make the straightforward assertion that the representative conditions of G are all fulfilled (including the condition that God did in fact lead Israel across the sea, and therefore that God does indeed exist) he must issue a speech-act which is itself a confession, or (what comes to the same result) this 'straightfor-

ward assertion' can only be issued by one who is in position to
make such a confession. And this is not the tautologous point that
only those believe that God exists who believe that God exists, but
is the rather richer one that such assertions *happily* occur, *can*
happily occur, only in connection with the rich involvement in
stance, in commitment, and in appropriate affect (yet to be
discussed) which make up the happiness of G.

The *affective* or *psychological conditions* for Aleph's G are
noticeably more complex than those for a request at the dinner
table, and partly because of that complexity, here we are even
more willing than elsewhere to be corrected by anyone who can
show that we are mistaken. We will however give our reasons for
listing those we do, and will particularly note, as before, how the
affective conditions interlock with the primary and representative
ones (so that changing the others may not be as simple as some
religious revisionists might suppose).

Awed gratitude is itself an affect of a rather high order of
complexity and sophistication. Everyone has wants (to name the
chief affect of requesting), but gratitude, humility, awe, and their
convergence in awed gratitude are the outcome of a long development in the world to which Aleph belongs. But why awed gratitude here? For certainly we are not suggesting that this is the only
affect appropriate to religion—joy, dread, hope, guilt, detachment,
fear, ecstasy come to mind at once, and all of these *may* characterize the confessor of G. But the requirement of awed gratitude may
be explained by noting that if Aleph shows, or is taken by all
hearers to show, either by his attendant behavior or by the manner
of uttering G itself, that his attitude is not in fact awed gratitude,
G is thereby exposed as unhappy in utterance. If, for example,
when challenged by such a reply to G as: "Then why act so
ungrateful to him?" Aleph replies: "I don't believe all that ba-
loney about God; I'm just teaching Religion 101," his consistency
is saved, but now our story about him must change; he is not after
all in uttering G confessing his faith. Or if the conversation goes,
"Then why don't you seem at all grateful to him?" "What's
gratitude got to do with it? I'm just stating a fact," Aleph would
here be showing, given our original story, that he does not understand *what* he has said, does not understand the affective force of
his own utterance, does not know what his words (in this case)
mean.

A word should be added about Aleph's "conveying" his possession of the affect via his utterance (see 4.1): we do not mean that

confessional speakers should tend to histrionics; rather we mean that it is normal, expected, and conventional for these words of confession to imply that the speaker has just such an attitude, and thus abnormal, unexpected, and deviant for the speaker to lack that attitude.

The evidence for awed gratitude as the appropriate affect of G can be found by consulting the tradition in which we have placed Aleph. Among the Psalms we find those which celebrate the mighty past acts of God, such as Psalm 105:

> Then he led forth Israel with silver and gold,
>   and there was none among his tribes who stumbled.
> Egypt was glad when they departed,
>   for dread of them had fallen upon it.
> He spread a cloud for a covering,
>   and fire to give light by night.
> They asked, and he brought quails,
>   and gave them bread from heaven in abundance.[28]

Now this Psalm begins with an injunction which sets its tone throughout: "O give thanks to the LORD."[29] In other words, the recital of the mighty deeds of God which follows is viewed as cause for gratitude and, as the use of the tetragrammaton (in our versions represented by capital-letter LORD) shows, gratitude in which God is exalted and the worshipper accordingly stands in awe. Thus the gratitude he is called to express is humble or awed gratitude.

Of course this might have been an isolated occurrence; however an examination of the whole Psalter shows that whenever the theme is the mighty, saving acts of God in Israel's history, the characteristic feeling-exhortations are to thanks (*hodu*), blessing (*baraku*), and praise (*hallelu*). Of these three, the *hallelu* is a call to sound the note of praise—the exaltation of God and the abasement of all else before him; the *hodu* is a summons to thanksgiving, that is, gratitude itself, and the *baraku* calls for a combination of these two elements of praise and thanks: "the term [*barakah*] is to be understood as an ascription of *praise and gratitude* for blessing received. . . ."[30] To be sure, other affects as well are proposed and expressed and evoked in these 'psalms of recital,' but the others vary; ours is constant. What we have called awed gratitude, then, was for the psalmists who shared in the formation of Aleph's tradition the natural affective accompaniment of their confession.

But what can be argued for the tradition's beginning can equally be argued for its later stages. In the early Christian period there arose in the worshipping communities a liturgy which became central, its origin being attributed to Jesus himself. A characteristic feature of this liturgy was a central prayer which *recited the wonderful works of God* both in creating the world and in guiding his people on a journey through history, a journey which included deliverance from Egypt, and which finally led to the coming of the Christ, who "on the night when he was betrayed took bread, and when he had given thanks, he broke it,"[31] as the prayer goes on. The function of the prayer was to recite and celebrate God's saving acts; thus it is like G. But the name of the prayer and of the whole liturgy of which it formed the central part, was the eucharist, i.e., the thanks giving.[32] Again the note of awed gratitude sets the affective tone for the recital of God's deeds.

Finally one might give attention to contemporary Jewish worship. In the Kiddush, the prayer of consecration at meals in pious Jewish homes and now also a part of the Friday evening service of many synagogues, the Exodus from Egypt is recalled:

in love and favor Thou hast given us the holy Sabbath as a heritage, a reminder of Thy work of creation, first of our sacred days recalling our liberation from Egypt.

And this prayer begins and ends with the Hebrew words "Blessed art Thou, O Lord our God."[33] What we have is again an expression of awed gratitude to God—in the first instance for the Sabbath, but behind that, for the "liberation from Egypt" which the Sabbath recalls. Alongside this we may mention the Passover Seder service. Here the ritual is introduced with the Four Questions, whose answers point to the meaning of the Passover meal as a memorial of the Exodus. Then there comes a midrash on Deut. 26:5–8, reminding the hearers of the mighty deeds of God in the deliverance. To this midrash is attached the Dayyenu, a hymn or chant which singles out those deeds one by one:

> Had he given us their substance
>   but not torn the Sea apart for us
>   Dayyenu
> Had he torn the Sea apart for us
>   but not brought us through it dry
>   Dayyenu
>
> . . .

> Had he satisfied our needs in the desert for forty
>> years but not fed us manna
>>> Dayyenu.[34]

What then is "Dayyenu"? It means "for that alone we should have been thankful" or more literally, "it would have been enough for us." Humble or awed gratitude, occurring just where we would by now expect it. Not only here, but also in the great Hallel

> O give thanks to the Lord
>> for He is good
>> for His mercy endureth forever[35]

and indeed throughout the whole Seder, the tone is that of deep and humble gratitude for God's deliverance of his people. Thus, if Aleph remains in the tradition which gives his G both its point and its particular sense, his confession expresses awed gratitude.

The remaining affective conditions are parallel to the requesting case, including the requirements for intention (see 4.2) and uptake (see 4.3), and though they possess intrinsic interest, they need not detain us now.[36]

Now see what follows from this analysis. Aleph cannot *happily* confess that God led Israel across the Reed Sea unless he is in position to do so. To be in position is among other things to possess the affect we have called grateful awe. Without that attitude neither Aleph nor anyone else can in this sense confess what God has done. The outsider cannot happily make that confession (without becoming in the act an insider to Aleph's confessing community), but the outsider cannot happily deny that God has so led Israel, either; not without meeting the affective conditions for *that* utterance, which are not the same, but which would themselves require some particular getting into position for felicitous utterance (and this is true whether it is a rival religion— "there is no God but Ra"—or irreligion—"secular atheism is the only honest outlook"—which undergirds the denial). So far, we seem to be led toward a hard perspectivism.

On the other hand, there are the representative conditions (see 3.1, 3.2, and 3.3) to remind us that confessing stance and witness (see primary condition 2.2) together with awed gratitude (see affective condition 4.1) are not sufficient to make a confession happy. I can, like Don Quixote, take up my stance against the evil giants which threaten us all. If, however, the giants are in truth windmills, my stance will be comic, however noble it may be as well. No one can say that Don Quixote has not taken a stance, has not confessed. But no informed Sancho Panza can say that Quixote's confession was a 'happy' one if the representative conditions are unfulfilled—that is, if the giants are not giants. Indeed we are now in position to see just the degree to which the representative condition must be fulfilled in order for the confession to be happy—namely that degree which is required by the assumed stance itself. In other words, the speech-act requires that a certain state of affairs shall prevail if the act is to be happy, but the demand is not a tyrannical one; there is some margin for error in representation in every speech-act where representation is involved. It does not matter, for the happiness of G, whether "Israel" is five thousand or five million strong; nor does it matter how 'transcendent' or 'immanent' the God referred to in G may be, provided only that he can be identified as the God of the Israelite tradition in which G stands. We may with good reason be interested in such matters, but that interest lies beyond our concern here.

What does matter is the intimate interdependence of affective, representative, and primary conditions for happy utterance, the interconnection of language structure and persons and whatever else there is beyond both. As to the issue between perspectivism and non-perspectivism, we will address that in chapters still to come. That issue will not be settled, however, save by constant reference to the actual structure of language, a structure we have seen revealed in speech-act analysis.

III. A Critical Review

It seems natural to ask whether the understanding of religious language developed in the preceding section can be applied to the analysis of utterances outside Christianity and Judaism. The most satisfying sort of answer would be to repeat the exercise, taking as illustration an utterance drawn from another religious tradition. Now it is no part of our intention to offer such an exhaustive demonstration, but we will summarize the conditions for happiness of another of our samples A through G, namely F, "There is nothing." We will suppose this to be spoken by a Buddhist mystic in order to explain the third *Jhāna* of Buddhagosa's mystical path.[37] This permits us to reassert that none of our samples need be issued as confessions: we can envisage injunctions, self-committals, disclosures, and still others, while our present example is an *explanation*. Here in compressed form are its conditions:

1. *Preconditions:* same as before.

2. *Primary:* speaker issues a sentence which counts as a convention-employing attempt to explain, i.e., to relate that which hearer does not understand to that which he does.

3. *Representative:* A mystical state occurs with sufficient reliability to call for and to sustain explanation; this state apprehends a truer 'picture' of the world than that of the previous *Jhāna,* and this 'picture' is blankness—all is washed away. Non-mystical 'pictures' of the world are therefore in an important way false.

4. *Affective:* The speaker wants the hearers to understand the mystical state, its appropriate world-picture, and the true status of the apparent world; he has the corresponding linguistic intentions; he is so understood and so taken by some hearers, for whom the 'picture' of blankness is evocative of the speaker's point.

It is interesting that if as we stipulate here F is *explanation,* then the affect appropriate to the mystical state (detachment?) need not be possessed by the speaker himself in order that his speech-act be happy, whereas if a more strongly self-involving speech-act is issued, say by one of the disciples who after meditation *testifies* attainment of the Third *Jhāna* by issuing F, there would be stronger affective demands. However, even if an explanation is issued by a non-mystic, it carries *representative* freight unless suitably qualified. One such qualification would be for the explainer to say, "This is the explanation a *mystic* would give of the Third *Jhāna.*" These sorts of points are of course fully explicable only in a full account such as we have given for G above. In a less formal way, we will explore other convictional speech-acts, including some which employ some of A through G, in chapter 4; we leave to the interested reader the (not inconsiderable) task of working out others for himself.

We plan now to bring against ourselves the sorts of criticism we leveled at our immediate predecessors in the analysis of religious language: Braithwaite, Zuurdeeg, and Ramsey. We acknowlege the possibility that we may neglect weaknesses we share with any or all of the three, but hope that the spectrum of analysis we have chosen may be broad enough to minimize that perspectival flaw in our analysis.

A fundamental objection to Braithwaite was that he emphasized one side of religious language, the conative or affective, to the neglect of all else. By now it will be clear that our three-dimensioned analysis of speech-acts (primary, representative, affective) is intended to correct that flaw. On the other hand, we faulted Braithwaite for failing to show how the stories in his account were connected linguistically with the intentions. A similar flaw in Ramsey was the inexplicability of the connection between discernments and commitments. Can a like weakness be found in our own account? We think not; we have at least offered evidence and argument to show that there are not three meanings in A's request or Aleph's confession but rather three sorts of force or three dimensions, all of which must be present if there is to be *one* fully meaningful utterance—if there is to be one happy meaning. In one way, we are strongly indebted to Braithwaite: he brought home to us how inseparable are the central meaning and the affective force of many religious speech-acts. We think our account of Aleph's G reflects that insight.

The chief debt we owe to Zuurdeeg, on the other hand, has been his emphasis upon the centrality of convictions, and that emphasis will come to the fore in the next chapter. We brought two charges against Zuurdeeg's theory of religious language; first that he made "convictional" language immune to any confrontation with "indicative" language (religious language thus immune to the language of science), and second that his account was intolerably imprecise or vague. As to the first, we think that Zuurdeeg's notion of convictional language is mired in hard perspectivism, and we recognize that that is a charge non-perspectivists will by now be bringing against us. We must defer our argued rejection of non-perspectivism in general to chapter 5 and our full argument against hard perspectivism to chapter 6; at this point we can only claim without showing it that our own theory falls into neither category. If such a tactic of delay opens us also to the charge of vagueness, we must so far plead *nolo contendere,* or hopefully ask for a postponement. We might be charged in an opposite way, instead, with making our account of language (modeled as it is upon Austin and Searle) *too* precise or rigorous to fit the rough and ready expediencies of everyday religious utterance. Our best defense against that is to note again that not all utterance in daily life is felicitous—and yet it is still utterance. We *have* allowed for the infelicitous cases.

While it is Ramsey's theory of religious language which on the whole we admire the most among the three for its balance and insight, our own account differs from his both in intention and in method, making comparison and contrast somewhat difficult. We have already mentioned Ramsey's failure to show a link between discernment and commitment and our reaction to that flaw. Ramsey, walking in the footsteps of Schleiermacher, assumed that all the sorts of religious utterance, Christian and other, were (insofar as they were religious) alike; in that sense he took an 'essentialist' position concerning religion. We have not intended to do this, so if our method of analysis turned out to be uniquely suited to Jewish or Christian sorts of religious utterance, this would be in our eyes a defect. In fact, however, our account is in no special way limited even to 'religious' utterances but will fit other sorts of convictional utterance, political or economic or cultural, as well as those religious sorts which have no representative force at all (cf. *"Om"*).

Finally, we objected that Ramsey's "disclosure" or "discernment" theory of representation was too narrow to account for all religious representation, even though it seems strikingly apt in some cases. Even Ramsey had to allow for basic "posits" or "key-words" which did not seem to fit into his "qualified model" theory of representation.

In this regard, we too seem to have failed, because we seem to have no *theory* of representation at all, while at the same time we incautiously hold that valuations such as true and false do clearly apply to some religious utterances—God either did lead Israel across the Sea of Reeds or did not. And in this we differ not only from the positivists (who held such claims not false but meaningless) but also from all the post-positivists we considered in chapter 2, for they in effect conceded that point to the positivists.

But should we not be able to say in general what we mean by calling such a claim false or true; or should we not at least be prepared to say which is the case in our sample utterance?

In response, we remind our readers that we disagree with one another on the latter question, and we expect that our readers disagree in similar ways. But we believe that we have come upon an understanding of why that disagreement is (in the short run) inevitable, while not (in the long run) invincible. Such disagreement is lamentable to the extent that we might have hoped for a simple and clear test by which to vote utterances such as G in or out. It will seem to some readers that what we have been saying *must* be mistaken. How can there be an utterance that makes a claim of truth whose truth is hidden by the very conditions of its happy utterance? Isn't it just obscurantism to entangle questions about the truth or falsity of an utterance with questions about the commitment or stance or attitude of the utterer? Surely (the question now becomes rhetorical) questions of fact cannot be so confused with questions of stance, of *value,* as we have made it appear?

To such complaints, as we have said, we are quite sympathetic. Indeed, it appears that Austin's term for characterizing the point of view behind this protest, "descriptive fallacy," is not quite the one we need. For "fallacy" suggests that the one gripped by these expectations about getting the facts straight (and thus unreceptive to this part of our account) is making some *logical* mismove which has stultifying consequences. That however is not the way we find the so-called 'descriptive fallacy' arising. Rather the descriptivists (and we in our descriptivist moments) are captivated by a picture, see things in a *certain* way. The picture here is of a world of 'facts,' independent of us and (perhaps) of each other, facts the description of which would tell us the whole truth about the world. In such a world, whatever was a fact, whatever was true of the world, could be described or stated. If we don't have the right statement, the full description, we must simply try harder: attend to new arguments, gather more facts, and so forth. What can't be stated or described is just what can't be the case.

What remedy have the authors for such a state of mind? We certainly do not mean to repudiate the descriptivist's concern with truth and falsity—we are as concerned as he is to say what is true about the world. But if it turns out that the representative, primary, and affective elements of our utterances are intertwined as it seems to us they are, then saying what is true will sometimes truly be an elusive goal. The history of convictional controversy (political and social as well as religious) seems to offer reasons for believing that just collecting facts or thinking up new arguments (important as such tasks are) is insufficient to resolve such controversies. To that extent, at least, the picture of the world which captivates the descriptivist seems to be an incomplete one. And insofar as our more complex pluralistic picture accounts for these difficulties in arguing about convictions, it seems to be a better picture of reality—truer to the facts, if we are still allowed the expression.

Ramsey's account of religious discernments allows for one way of getting at what he might have called (but did not) religious 'facts.' We think that the full range of religious language or of convictional language generally cannot be as simple as Ramsey makes it; the adequate account must allow for more kinds of (possible) 'facts,' more ways of 'knowing,' than can be embraced by any single philosophical theory of representation we know of.[38]

Yet that is not to say that all these ways will finally be equally satisfactory. Thus we are reminded of our standing promise (chapter 1) to show that fully to understand the speech of convictional speakers is to learn whether what they say is *justifiable*. Clearly, our analysis so far has not fulfilled that commitment. For we have found Aleph's confession embedded in the language frame of his community in such a way that we can neither fully understand it nor find it adequate or inadequate until we attend to that wider frame, the whole set of religious convictions in which it is embedded. We must now turn to exploring that wider set.

4

If the formation of concepts can be explained by facts of nature, should we not be interested, not in grammar, but rather in that in nature which is the basis of grammar?—Our interest certainly includes the correspondence between concepts and very general facts of nature. (Such facts as mostly do not strike us because of their generality.) But our interest does not fall back upon these possible causes of the formation of concepts; we are not doing natural science; nor yet natural history—since we can also invent fictitious natural history for our purposes.

. . .

Grammar tells us what kind of object anything is. (Theology as grammar.)

Ludwig Wittgenstein[1]

It is the erotic sense of reality that discovers the inadequacy of fraternity, or brotherhood. It is not adequate as a form for the reunification of the human race: we must be either far more deeply unified, or not at all. The true form of unification—which can be found either in psychoanalysis or in Christianity, in Freud or Pope John, or Karl Marx—is: "we are all members of one body." The true form of the unification of the human race is not the brothers, Cain and Abel, but Adam the first man, and Christ the second man: for as in Adam all die, even so in Christ shall all be made alive.

Norman O. Brown[2]

How Are
Convictions Justifiable?

WHAT A MAN CAN HAPPILY SAY, INDEED WHAT HE CAN SAY WITH any meaning whatever, is intimately related to his action and to the way things are ('the facts') and to his (affective) participation in both of these. His action, because speech itself is a kind of action and because our acts affect one another; the way things are, because speech-acts typically have some sort of representative force relating them to the existing world; the speaker's (and hearer's) affects, because they engage both of these. Thus the happy speech-act is not the grammarian's grail that our preceding technical inquiry may have suggested to some; rather 'happiness' in speech-acts *is* closely related to the happiness of the speaker in the world; to inquire about the speech-act is to inquire about the state of the speaker in his situation, and thus about the situation too.

I. Convictions

The speaker, Aleph, was a man of religious belief, and in every case he would be a man with some beliefs. It was this very fact which gave rise to our linguistic inquiry when (in chapter 1) we indicated the connection between beliefs and talk. These are not two disparate or disconnected sorts of human phenomena; what we believe and what we say are tightly connected. Now, however, we are in far better position to see how this is so. What a man believes is expressed in what he does but most clearly in that special form of doing which constitutes his speech. If he says nothing (which is so extraordinary as to require minimal attention here), or lies or is insincere (less extraordinary), we all have ways of detecting, interpreting, and dealing with these modes of verbal behavior, for they are logically dependent upon the normal mode, which is saying what one means, thinks, believes. Even if most of the time, or all the time, a particular speaker speaks ironically, or hypocritically, or deceitfully, his speech is fully intelligible if and only if we measure his irony, hypocrisy, deceit, against straightforward speech, so that in those cases, too, belief and speech are inseparable. Aleph's speech-act (his confession) is an expression of Aleph's belief; it is indeed a *confessio fidei*.

Are we enunciating a startling doctrine of linguistic philosophy, or rehearsing a truism? Perhaps this is one of those cases, so interesting to philosophy, in which the commonplace seems startling because it has been overlooked or even denied. In any case, one very important consequence follows: *the conditions for the happy utterance of a speech-act are also the conditions under which the belief(s) expressed by that speech-act are justifiable.* Suppose Mr. A, at a table where there is no bread, believes the Yorkshire pudding to be a loaf of bread. If then, requesting, he says "Please pass the bread," his request is unhappy because its representative condition cannot (then and there) be satisfied. Note however that his belief, too, is 'unhappy' and for the same reason—there is no bread; the Yorkshire pudding is not bread; his belief is mistaken. Similarly for Aleph: his belief that Israel crossed the Reed Sea, or that God led Israel, will if mistaken make his speech-act, G, unhappy, and the belief, so far as it is mistaken, is an 'unhappy' belief.

Note that it is no more true of beliefs or similar mental states than it is of speech-acts that their 'representative' failures (such as failures in description or reference) are the only ways they can go wrong. We have treated speech-acts first and at some length because their more public character makes these possibilities more evident in them, but beliefs and the like (attitudes, intentions, hopes, and so forth) are also subject to a wide range of flaws. Let us refer to beliefs alone for the time being, since they are crucial in the work ahead, and recall some ways in which, paralleling speech-acts, beliefs can go wrong. Most important, a 'belief' can simply fail to be a belief at all by being some other mental state or act instead, so that we have misnamed it a "belief"; or it may be a mere jumble or confusion. These failures may be compared with the failure to fulfill the primary condition of a speech-act—the failure to use an appropriate linguistic form. Thus "Bread pass please the" hardly qualifies as a request, or any other speech-act, if the language in use is English; correspondingly the 'thought' designated "Bread pass please the" is not a belief; no one thinks *that*, and it is hard to say what the "that" is; it is not a wish or a desire or a feeling; either. Likewise, some other words or even G in the mouth of a person with a different stance than Aleph's may not express a *confessional* belief but a guess or a supposition instead.

It hardly need be pointed out that a similar parallel exists between the affective conditions for the happiness of a speech-act and the affective conditions for the happiness of a belief which that speech-act expresses or to which the belief corresponds. If the utterer of Aleph's G is not a man of grateful awe in the measure demanded by his speech-act, his act is affectively unhappy. But the same is true of the (confessional) *belief* that God led Israel across the Reed Sea: happily to believe this is to feel one way and not another, just as to say it happily is.

Thus with a few appropriate changes, the apparatus of appraisal which applies to utterances applies to beliefs and thoughts as well.[3] To be able to understand what a man says is to be able to understand what he thinks; the unhappiness or the happiness of what he says or can say shows the justifiability or the unjustifiability of what he believes, also.

It follows that for any belief, there are a certain number of possible challenges which might arise, roughly those which could arise in connection with the issuance of the speech-act expressive of that belief. Of a belief which can meet such challenges, we will say that it is a *justifiable belief*; of one concerning which (some of the) possible challenges have arisen and been met, we will say that it is in these respects or in that degree a *justified* belief; of a belief which has been challenged by and has met every such possible challenge, we may say that it is *fully justified*. The process by which challenges are met or responded to is the process of *justification*. This process (and connately the achievement, also called "justification," which results when the process is carried out) will be of central interest to us in the pages ahead. Here we emphasize that while "justifiable," "justified," and "justification" are important terms for us, they are not technical terms on which we have a copyright. Like most of the terms we use in the present work, they are ordinary words used in their ordinary ways and are thus not employed with special precision. Our goal is to be plain about what constitutes the justification of belief in the ordinary case, not to erect special or arbitrary standards of success.

At this point the most important fact to note is that the

challenges to one's belief which can arise are evidently limited in number. We recall the three 'dimensions' or 'forces' in terms of which speech-acts can be assessed—the primary, the representative, and the affective. We have just seen that a similar grouping is possible respecting beliefs.[4] However the three-fold scheme was itself only an arrangement, whose purpose was to order the conceivable challenges to a given speech-act (in A's case, "There isn't any bread," "You're not asking, you're ordering!" "It's right in front of you, dear," etc.) conveniently. The responses to these challenges, rather than any particular arrangement, constitute the clearest means of showing the point, the thrust, the *meaning* of an utterance. If these challenges do not appear or if they are met satisfactorily, we have clear evidence that the issuing of the speech-act is happy.

This dependence of meaning and happiness in speech-acts upon a limited number of conditions is paralleled by the dependence upon a like set of conditions for determining the meaning and the happiness—or, as we shall usually say in their case, the justifiability—of beliefs. Indeed, so direct is the parallel that it would be boring for us to repeat the exercise of chapter 3, this time attending formally to the belief(s) expressed by Aleph's speech-act rather than to that act itself. Nevertheless, there was a point in attending to utterances first. For in their case, some matters became clear which would remain obscure if we attended to beliefs alone.

Take the notion of justification, just introduced afresh. How well justified does an important belief have to be in order for *us* to be justified in accepting it as our own? At one extreme, we are tempted to answer "Not at all. I have a perfect right to think my own thoughts, to believe as I please." Yet that temptation clashes with another, more precisian, urge, which wants to answer "Infinitely well! There *is* no limit, no requirement is too great, no doubt too small, to entertain." Here the parallel with language may be profitably invoked. For similar temptations to latitudinarianism and puritanism may arise in the question "How happy must a speech-act be?" and here too we may be tempted to answer with either the precisian "Infinitely happy" or the latitudinarian "I have a right to say whatever I please." But we have just seen that neither of these is fair to the linguistic facts. We can't say just anything (though we can indeed say anything *sayable*), and what we can happily say is subject to fairly definite and (in principle) satisfiable tests. If a man has done what we all do when requesting bread (or thanking his helper, or advising his neighbor), it does not matter, linguistically, what else he may or may not thereby have done. If the (enumerable) challenges are not applicable, that's all there is to be said.

Now we can compare this account with one for the parallel case of beliefs. While, to be sure, a man is entitled to his own thoughts, this may express no more than the self-evident truth that only he can have *his* thoughts. Or, perhaps, that there is no practical or morally acceptable way that we can stop him from thinking his thoughts. In fact, of course, he cannot believe just anything, for his 'belief' may not be *belief* at all, as we have noted above. Or it may be in various ways unsuitable, in which case, although he (so far) believes it, the possible challenges show the ways in which it is untenable and in need of revision. Suppose Jones reports to us his belief that the dean (known to be an upright man) is actually an arsonist. "Why do you believe that?" "No reason, I just think he is." "Well, have there been any suspicious fires lately?" "No." "Has he behaved strangely?" "No." "Are you possessed of past records, or some psychological data about the dean, or something else the rest of us do not have?" "No, nothing; I just think he is." But even a hunch requires some circumstances which make it appear an appropriate hunch, and if Jones is honest about having no reasons *at all*, then his belief is patently inappropriate, perhaps even unintelligible—a belief to which he has no right.[5] Note that it is not merely the *announcement* of his belief which is unhappy. We say "You shouldn't say that," to such a person, but we do so, in this case, on the ground that he has no right to that belief. Of course we have chosen an easy, if extraordinary, case in which the belief is of a slanderous character, so that challenging it seems important. It does at least illustrate, however, that beliefs are not unchallengeable any more than speech-acts are.

The other parallel also applies: the demand for justification cannot be an unlimited one in the case of beliefs, either. If my belief is a suspicion (that the dean is an arsonist, or that the milk is sour), it need have no more reason for happily existing than suspicions normally require (need not be already proved, need not be self-evident, need not be widely accepted). If we know how to recognize ordinary, *bona fide* suspicions, we are also in position to reject the spurious and to identify justifiable or justified ones.[6] As in the case of speech-acts (cf. accusations, promises, requests), the conditions for believing, and for happily believing, are limited in number, and can normally be listed, even though in practice no one happens to list them.

If, once a challenge has appeared and been examined, one is not confident that the conditions are satisfied, or is persuaded that they are not, he will be able to say that the belief in question is (to that degree) unjustified, even though it had been his own. On the other hand, until such a particular challenge does arise, there is no reason to suppose that the beliefs one holds are fraudulent, or defective, or bogus, any more than one would normally suppose that whatever he *says* is inappropriate, false, or unintelligible. To be unjustifiable is, we repeat, to fail to meet one or more of these conditions for happily believing, and the task of justification is that of responding to *actual* claims that one or more of the conditions is not met, or to *actual* doubts that it is. Justification is a response to challenges, and these challenges are both limited in number and definite in content.

Now an important clarification must be introduced. We have spoken of "challenges," and this term seems to suggest that the difficulties with speech or with belief come from outsiders, with the speaker or believer always playing the role of attorney for the defense, while someone else attacks what he thinks and says. In fact this is an inadequate portrayal of the real situation. Sometimes, to be sure, it is someone else who points out my faults in speech and thought. Very often, however, it is I who first doubt whether what I said is what I meant to say or should have said, while unexpressed beliefs can hardly be challenged save by this route. Even external challenges have no effect unless we ourselves see that they have some merit. It is our own experience, our own standards, then, which often call into question our beliefs, and the 'challenge' most often takes the form of an internal dialogue.

This internal dialogue, however, is made more intense by two external factors. One is that it is a rare thing for a man to have any totally unshared beliefs. Many of our beliefs are shared by most people; some beliefs are so widely held (that sky is blue, that grass is green, and that water runs down-hill) that we may spend a lifetime without meeting anyone who cares to challenge them in any way. We are accustomed to and generally dependent upon the sharing of many elementary beliefs. The other factor to be mentioned is that some of our most important beliefs are nevertheless *not* shared by all, and we know that they are not. Indeed, we know that besides our own community of belief-sharers, there are other belief-sharing communities which may doubt, challenge, or by their very existence even threaten important beliefs we do hold. These two factors—that of community and that of pluralism—are of great importance in justification, and we must say more about them.

First, however, let us narrow the range of beliefs to be discussed. We would speak of beliefs like Aleph's—but like Aleph's in
what respect? His utterance expressed a religious belief, yet it is
difficult or impossible to delimit the class of 'religious beliefs' in
any satisfactory way; "religious," like "religion" escapes any
straightforward definition, as we said in chapter 1. Besides, we
shall have to decide what to do about *ir*religious beliefs, which
clash with religious ones and thus are logically similar to the latter.
Further, not *all* beliefs on religious topics are either very important or very interesting. The importance of Aleph's G is not
merely that it is religious, but that it holds a special place among
the utterances and beliefs of those who accept it. G, we may say,
is a *convictional* utterance, and the belief(s) which it expresses are
Aleph's *convictions*.

Here, then, is the special sort of belief with which we are
concerned. Convictions *are* beliefs, and they do bear a special
relation to the rest of our beliefs and to ourselves as well. "We are
our convictions," said Zuurdeeg. We now have a more exact way
of speaking about these central elements in our thought (and
speech) and can explain the definition of convictions we offered in
chapter 1. Convictions, we said there, are persistent beliefs such
that, if X (a person or a community) has a conviction, it will not
easily be relinquished and cannot be relinquished without making
X a significantly different person (or community) than before.
Convictions, then, are a class of beliefs, to which the considerations we have made about beliefs in the preceding pages—their
intimate relation to speech-acts, their liability to the flaws and
capacity for the success or happiness which speech-acts may have,
and their corresponding links with the speaker-believer and the
world in which he lives—all apply. This is the exact sense in which
"we are our convictions" can be taken: a sense in which all our
beliefs are immediately related not only to the world but also to
ourselves.

Further, we see the senses in which convictions are 'important'
beliefs and thus more central to the lives of their holders than are
their other beliefs. For one thing, they are *persistent*. "Persistent"
does not merely mean continuous or long-lived. Being persistent
implies the capacity to resist attack, to overcome, to continue in
the face of difficulties. I may have held a belief all my life,
unchallenged, only to discard it the minute some evidence of its
falsehood or any other sort of unsuitability is presented to me.
Such a belief is therefore not a conviction. On the other hand, I
may have acquired a belief only yesterday, but if it is in fact

persistent in character—that is, the sort of belief which I *will* cling to in the face of difficulties, maintain against doubts within and adversaries without—and if it meets the further condition of a conviction, then, new though it is, it is already my conviction, though I may not yet have recognized it as such.

Now there may be persistent beliefs, stubbornly held, which nonetheless have no *significant* role to play in the lives of their holders, but these, failing the second of our criteria, will not qualify as convictions. By "significant" beliefs, we mean those which exercise a dominant or controlling role over a number of other beliefs held by their believers, or those which govern (or correspond to) broad stretches of their thought and conduct. Every belief is related, at least prospectively, to one's conduct: for example, one will be disposed to identify it as one's belief, or to conceal one's possession of it. Some beliefs, however, are much more decisively related to the lives of their owners than this. We have explored in some detail just such a belief in our examination of Aleph's convictional speech-act, G, in the previous chapter. That speech-act, or the belief which it expresses, is happy only if in identifiable ways Aleph's (other) words, and Aleph's other, non-speech deeds, correspond to it. Further, these other words and deeds are of great moment in his life. If, for example, he fails to live a life of awed gratitude in face of God's historic act of deliverance of his people, Aleph's belief is unhappy as a conviction. Beginning to live a life of awed gratitude (or ceasing to do so) is a good instance of a significant change in the sense proffered in the paragraph before last.

What would be an instance of a belief which fulfilled the first, but not the second, criterion, that is, one whose change was non-significant for the believer? Suppose a man believes himself to have been born in a certain city and state where he remembers living in early childhood. Suppose that his belief about his birthplace is supported by what he regards as good evidence—a birth certificate, a parent's word, the beliefs of others whom he trusts. Now someone tells him he is mistaken; he was born across the state line. He is distrustful of the new claim, as we all are when persistent beliefs are challenged. He doubts, he argues, he resists. Finally, he is shown overwhelming new evidence of his birth in another state and given a reasonable story to explain his previous misinformation—parents who for such and such good reasons lied to him, forged the birth certificate, etc. Reluctantly, he changes his mind. His persistent belief is finally abandoned, replaced by a new one. Yet he is in character and action very much the man he was before. He has only acquired new information (including new information about his parents' veracity), perhaps a new practice for answering place-of-birth queries on questionnaires, but nothing more. His belief about his birthplace was not, in the required sense, a conviction, for its change produced no significant change in him.

Our claim is not that beliefs about God's dealings with Israel are necessarily convictions, while beliefs about birthplaces cannot be. We can imagine non-convictional views about God (though perhaps these require a changed sense of the term "God"); alternatively we can envision circumstances in which a belief about a birthplace is indeed convictional; that is, one which is not only persistent but which also affects the character and attitudes of the holder in such a way that changing the belief would mean a changed person.

Let us concede, however, that it is not always easy to recognize 'significant' changes. For one thing, there may be marginal cases. Some ethical beliefs, though persistently held, play only a peripheral role in the lives of their holders, and these may be beliefs associated with religion as well. Indeed one of the characteristic problems of religious ethics in a changing world is the religious community's difficulty in dealing with beliefs which are of marginal importance for contemporary life and faith but which are maintained as if they were central. A little reflection upon the beliefs of a community, or upon the reader's own, will show that these lie in a spectrum ranging from most to least important. It may be questionable in a given case whether the change of a tenacious belief somewhere in the spectrum is correlated with significant character change, but this is not a grave difficulty for the notion of convictions here advanced. For there are similar borderline cases in many definitions.[7] That we generally, or normally, are able to identify cases of significant change of conviction is shown by the fact that we talk about such a change as a "conversion," or perhaps of the significantly changed one as "seeming a different person." Such expressions bear witness to the sort of change we have in mind when we say that convictional changes are significant changes in persons.

Now, however, we must acknowledge a more radical difficulty raised by the definition of convictions we have proposed. Not everyone will agree on these cases of 'significant' change. Take the case of Aleph, the hero of chapter 3. If Aleph should painfully but

truly relinquish his faith in the God of Israel, give up his conviction about God's leadership of his people in the archetypical
exodus, cease to live under the shadow of that numinous event, we
can imagine that, nevertheless, *someone* may say, "That's a trivial
matter; not a very significant change at all. All this business about
gods and miracles and providence in history—quite immaterial to a
man's life; a little more superstition here, a little less there, but it's
six of one, half a dozen of the other." While on the other hand,
our counterpart may regard our story of the man who gets a new
belief about his birthplace as an inescapably convictional occurrence: "Blood and soil—that's what makes us what we are!"

Our point is that to count a change as significant involves a
judgment which may itself be convictional. While our example
may be a bit forced, still one must recognize that those of vastly
different views from his own might see the world, and what
matters in it, so differently that neither Aleph's change, nor the
conversion of St. Paul, nor the Protestant Revolt against Rome,
nor the enlightenment of Gotama would count in his eyes as
convictional. No matter what is changed, something is sure to
remain the same, and it is always logically possible that what
changes will seem to someone insignificant (although we shall
argue later that not every consistent opinion on what matters can be
maintained in practice). It follows that while our definition of
convictions is conviction-neutral (or nearly so), its *application* can
be affected by the convictions of the applicant. This must be
recognized; it is one of the complexities with which pluralism
confronts us.

We have just noted the topical neutrality of convictions. They
can be beliefs about whatever their holders are convinced about—
gods, devils, the social security system, or the sanity of their
neighbors or themselves. It is clear that convictions may be disput-
able (and disputed); it should be made clear that they may be
undisputed (or even indisputable). Some philosophers in examining
beliefs and systems of belief have emphasized distinction between
knowledge and certitude, but convictions are likely to include
both beliefs which the holder is said to know (have evidence for,
be able to defend) and those of which he is said to be (merely)
certain (feel sure about). Moreover, convictions will sometimes be
the conclusions of reasoned arguments and based upon evidence.
But the premises of such arguments may themselves be the convictions of the arguers, even presupposed ones of which the holder is

hardly aware. There is no guarantee that a man or a community will be aware of each conviction that is operative; in fact we can be as mistaken about what our convictions are as we can about almost anything else. (It does not follow from this that we *must* be mistaken, or that ordinarily we will be, or that we could be mistaken all the time.)

Convictions, then, are a varied class of beliefs, a fact which should not surprise us. After all, in the way we have shown, we *are* our convictions, and we humans are a varied lot ourselves. Some of us think things through; others act and live intuitively, in the main. Some of us have many convictions, others only a few. Some of us are deeply involved in convictional communities; others are lone wolves, convictionally speaking. Some seem to have acquired settled convictions long ago; others (especially the young) are consciously in process of convictional formation.

With so many things to be considered any general principles of justification may be hard to come by. Against the difficulties, however, we must weigh the desirability of achieving our goal. While convictions may be obscure, varied in character, and determinable only on grounds which are themselves partly convictional, they are nevertheless central to the lives of their holders and affect even non-convictional beliefs. Thus the justification of convictions may be difficult, but so much rests upon the results that the difficulties must be somehow confronted.

We have already hinted that the convictions of a community or of an individual are related to one another in a variety of ways. Thus the justification of any one conviction is not likely to be achieved without regarding its relation to other convictions embraced by the same community or the same believer. If the question is whether Aleph justifiably believes that God led Israel across the Sea of Reeds (or whether John Jones is justifiably convinced that there is a Communist master plot to take over the world, or whether anyone should be convinced that the scientific method is a reliable source of truth), one must attend not only to *that* conviction but to others which are a part of the wider set of convictions of the holder. We must at least consider whether the conviction in question is dependent upon others in the set—and therefore its justifiability dependent upon theirs. In any case, it is noteworthy that convictions do not occur in isolation; they are found in their holders along with other beliefs, some of which are, in the usual case, also convictions.

II. Conviction Sets

Let us attend a bit further to this clustering phenomenon, to see how it affects our task. For convenience, we will refer to the set of all convictions held by a person as that person's *conviction set* and to the set of all convictions held in common by members of a community as the community's (shared) conviction set. Of course, it may be that not every member of a convictional community (whether it is the Roman Catholic Church or the Society of Friends) shares *all* the important or central or defining convictions of the community. In such cases, we may still refer to the community's conviction set, meaning the set of beliefs which are persistently and significantly held by representative or key members of the community, its teachers, or elders, or authoritative leadership cadres. Thus the community as a community could not relinquish these beliefs without being significantly changed.

Since our own inquiry is aimed specifically at religious convictions, it may be useful to designate that subset of Mr. X's convictions (or community R's convictions) which are religious as X's (or R's) *religious conviction set*. However, our previous strictures concerning definitions of religion and religiousness hold here also: we had better not rely too heavily upon our ability to discriminate, in practice, religious and non-religious convictions. Fortunately it is not crucial, for present purposes, to be able to do so.

One aspect of cultural pluralism is that persons normally belong to a number of overlapping convictional communities, a fact with important consequences for the justification of convictions. The conviction set of a given person may include subsets shared with several communities—he may be at once a union member, a Baptist, a Democrat, an American, and a white racist; or at once a college professor, a health food faddist, an atheist, and a Slavophile. (That each of these is among other things a *convictional* community would of course require evidence.) What usually happens, Zuurdeeg suggests, is that the sometimes agreeing, sometimes conflicting convictions connected with these several communities are held by the individual hierarchically—that is, where X's nationalist convictions and his Catholic convictions conflict, one subset will tend to dominate his life, thereby reducing the force of the other subset.[8] Evidently the interrelation of a man's convictions may be a complex business, and there is no guarantee that anyone will manage the resultant conflicts easily or well.

To illustrate the complexity of relations among convictions, let us consider a model much simpler than the one just referred to. Let us provide the believer of the previous chapter, Mr. Aleph, with a religious conviction set having five member convictions. One of these will be the now-familiar

G   "God led Israel across the Sea of Reeds."

Let us further specify Aleph to be a Christian, whose remaining religious convictions are:

D   "Jesus said, 'One thing is needful,' "
E   "Jesus opened the blind man's eyes,"
J   "God was incarnate in Jesus of Nazareth,"

and

T   "(This) God exists."

Consider first D. To see how it may function convictionally let us recall its source in a story found in the Gospel of Luke. Jesus, in the story, visits the household of the sisters Martha and Mary. While Mary sits at Jesus' feet to listen, Martha is, in the winsome archaism of the King James version, "cumbered about much serving," and finally complains that Mary should be directed by the Master to help her, but Jesus instead says, "Martha, Martha, you are anxious and troubled about many things; one thing is needful. Mary has chosen the good portion, which shall not be taken away from her."[9] To investigate the religious employment of this story in Christian history would be a task similar to the investigation of the role of the Reed Sea crossing story. We will not attempt such an investigation, merely noting that the Martha-Mary story has sometimes been taken as an injunction against a busyness in life which causes the busy one to miss the main point, life's true meaning. Let us say that Aleph takes the story this way. Thus when he finds himself distracted by the whirl of events, annoyed, anxious, his perspective distorted, he is disposed to remind himself (and perhaps others as well) that "Jesus said, 'One thing is needful.' " This reminder expresses D, his conviction. Often, of course, it will be shortened in his speech and memory to the simple "One thing is needful." Aleph finds in that reminder a redirection to purposefulness and confidence as he faces his day's affairs. Another man might have had another motto: "Take it easy," or "Cool it," or "Observe priorities," or perhaps "Trust God for everything," but it is important not to obscure the differences between any of these and D.

To say that D is his conviction, and thus not *merely* a motto, is

to say that Aleph holds it persistently and that its change would
be a significant change in him.

Now the same sorts of points that were made about D can be
made about E "Jesus opened the blind man's eyes." Here, too, the
origin is a story in Christianity;[10] here, too, let us stipulate that by
this saying Aleph is reminded of one of Jesus' mighty works, which
he takes as a sign of the role which Jesus may play in his own life and
in the lives of others. Jesus is the enlightener, the dispeller of
moral and spiritual darkness, the restorer of *vision*. Full explication would show the function of this conviction in Aleph's life by
describing the sort of occasion on which he is prone to recall and
act in the light of E, and the conditions under which he can
happily embrace it (compare the discussion of G in chapter 3).

It may be objected that D and E are not themselves Aleph's
convictions; they are at best reminders of some conviction or
other. They are perhaps like the little signs which some men put
over their desks: "Smile!" or "Think!" These latter cannot be
convictions for the reason that they are not full-fledged beliefs;
though as mottoes they may remind their owners of real beliefs.
On this view, E would remind Aleph of something like "One
ought to expect new insight in the course of his life." Is not
something like this, rather than the over-particularized D or E, the
real candidate for convictional status for Aleph? This objection
seems to us misguided. While "Think!" and "Smile!" may not be
beliefs, "Jesus said, 'One thing is needful,' " is.[11] Thus D *can* be
Aleph's conviction. What the substitutes like "You ought to observe priorities" lack, and D and E have, is just the peculiar flavor
of such a belief. Lacking it, they miss the role which D and E can
play in the life of a believer. Wilfred Cantwell Smith, the historian
of religions, relates an episode on a journey in the Himalayas
which is instructive here. He finds "a humble fruit-seller," weigh-
ing out his oranges by means of a simple pan scale and (for
weights) three rocks said to equal two pounds—for the fruitseller is
too poor to own metal weights. "He was far from any possibility
of having his dealings checked; and there was no external measure
of his honesty, which I found was sustained rather by a verse from
the Qur'an which runs 'Lo! He over all things is watching.' " How
poor a substitute for the fruitseller would have been a generalized
platitude ("One ought to be honest"). No, his conviction was that
God watches—or more exactly it was these words of the Qur'an
themselves.[12]

Still, the objection has its point, too. Sophisticated religious believers have often sought to eliminate or de-emphasize the rough-edged immediacy of particular convictions like D and E, substituting for them broader general principles which the rational found more easily applicable to all situations and which did not depend on controversial historical claims. Not "Jesus said . . . " etc., but the precise "One ought to observe priorities." So the latter may become the form of the community's conviction. And yet in communities where such 'logical' refinements are widely adopted, haven't the faithful often become insensitive to the poignant demands of particular situations—situations upon which the concrete examples of the religious tradition, in all their particularity, might have reflected much light? Part of the point in the recent struggle over 'situation ethics' has been the discernment, by moralists and plain men, that general principles often fail in practice to convey the ethical urgency which the situation requires. The prophet Nathan's "Thou art the man" to King David, applying a story of greedy sheep-stealing to the marriage bed,[13] lacks explicit generalization, but it has provided a thousand generations of tempted men with a forceful particular conviction. [14]

Aleph's third conviction, J "God was incarnate in Jesus of Nazareth," confronts us with a conviction at a different level of generality from D or E. It provides Aleph with some understanding of the importance of D and E and perhaps other stories: these words and deeds of Jesus are crucial because in them *God* was working. It provides him also with a theoretical explanation, or a condensed version of an explanation, of the power and the purpose of Jesus' action. Potentially, J offers an explanation and summary of an indefinite range of further particulars as well. We will call it, then, a *doctrinal* conviction, or sometimes, when the context permits, simply a doctrine. The Christian doctrine of the incarnation, as is well known, is open to a wide range of theological interpretations, and we do not intend to invent for Aleph a new interpretation or even to provide the details of an old one for his case.[15] Instead we content ourselves with noting that in Christian tradition J need not refer literally to a particular event or set of events, such as the events of the Christmas story as described in Luke's Gospel. When events like the Christmas story acquire convictional status in Christian minds, they may function merely as particulars (logically parallel to D and E) rather than what we are here technically calling doctrines.

To exemplify the distinction between particulars and doctrines, we note that within Christianity the former are often the stuff of

popular devotions and serve as the texts of sermons, while doctrines are characteristically the building blocks of theological trea-
tises. Thus when Thomas Aquinas says, "But in the state of
corrupt nature a man needs grace to heal his nature continually, if
he is to avoid sin entirely,"[16] he is enuciating what was surely his
belief, was probably his conviction, and as a conviction is on our
classification a 'doctrine.' The same classification would be made
of Friedrich Schleiermacher's "The Redeemer assumes believers
into the power of His God-consciousness, and this is His redemp-
tive activity."[17] These are in their level of generality characteristically doctrinal.

We may make clear the relative distinction between these two
levels of convictions, and at the same time display some of the
practical difficulties of such a classification, by raising the question about the role, in Aleph's set, of G "God led Israel across the
Sea of Reeds." Grammatically G is similar to J, and this may
incline us to classify it as a doctrinal conviction. Were we to
provide Aleph with a richer set of convictions, these might include
particulars which could be subsumed under G. For example, "God
told Moses to lead Israel," "God opened the waters of the Sea,"
"God destroyed the pursuing Egyptians," might stand as particulars to G as D and E stand to J. As matters now stand, however, G
seems to refer to a single event or a class of events, constituting
the Reed Sea crossing, and it seems natural to classify it, with D
and E, as a particular conviction. Indeed we might supply Aleph
with a doctrine to preside over G; something like "God guided
Israel's history." Besides G, other potential particulars would
include "God led Israel forty years in the wilderness," "God led
Israel into the Promised Land," and "God gave Israel prophets and
priests." What becomes evident is that the particular/doctrine
distinction is, like over/under or to-the-left/to-the-right, a relative
one, admitting of variable application and possibly requiring still
finer distinctions in practice.

Moreover, there are higher levels of generality than our 'doctrinal' level. To see this, consider the fifth of Aleph's convictions: T
"(This) God exists." Even if Aleph is inclined to express his
convictions freely, this last may seldom rise to his lips. It is, we
shall say, a presiding conviction. In this case, the presiding conviction, T, is presupposed by J and G, but not all presuppositions of
convictions are convictions; and certainly not all presuppositions
of non-convictional beliefs are of convictional rank. In each case
the test of convictions must be applied afresh: they are, to repeat,

persistently held beliefs which their holder cannot relinquish without being significantly changed thereby.

That T presides over J and G explains the point of our parenthetical "(This)." It is precisely the God of J and G whose existence T affirms. Some may feel that "God" in Western thought is so clear a term that "this" is somewhat precious, over-nice (hence our parentheses); our own view, however, is that "God" without further designation may not be precise enough to show the connection we have in mind.[18] There is a rough parallel between the relation of D and E to J, and the relation of J to T. As in the earlier case, holding the lower-level conviction (J) seems to call for holding the higher-level one (T), while the converse is not true. But we have to reckon here also with the paradoxical possibility that a believer might hold J and deny T, even though J apparently presupposes T. He might do this because he regards "exists" as an unworthy way to express the 'existence' or being of God (cf. Paul Tillich), or because he does not in fact believe in the divine existence however described but does still find "incarnation" the most appropriate way of expressing something special or extraordinary about the role of Jesus, or perhaps because he is just inconsistent, an unstable but not impossible case.

We have now briefly described a religious conviction set whose member convictions may be found within the Christian tradition. Conviction sets may be much more elaborate than this, or they may be even more fragmentary and less connected between members. In any case, it would be an empirical question, how nearly the actual sets of actual communities and men displayed the schematism of particular, doctrinal, and presiding convictions here described. That the schematism is not completely without merit may be seen by the examination of the convictional structure displayed by such a document as the American Declaration of Independence. One will find in that instrument possible particulars, among them:

> The present King of Great Britain . . . has called together legislative bodies at places unusual, uncomfortable, and distant. . .

> He has dissolved Representative Houses. . . .

> Giving his Assent. . . . For cutting off our Trade. . . .

That these were in fact particular convictions of all or some of the signers of the Declaration is a historical thesis, to be tested historically. The same is true of the possible *doctrinal* convictions of the signers, for example:

> whenever any Form of Government becomes destructive of these ends, it is the Right of the People to alter or to abolish it. . . .

> A Prince whose character is thus marked . . . is unfit to be the ruler of a free people. . . .

and of possible *presiding* convictions, such as:

> all men are created equal. . . .

> they are endowed by their Creator with certain unalienable Rights. . . .

Whether the last are indeed of highest rank, or might better be classed among the doctrines concerning Nature's Creator whose existence was itself an (unstated) presupposition of the framers, is partly a matter for classification, partly for historical inquiry. In any case, borderline classifications are likely, and situations in which finer subclassifications may be required, just as there may be disagreements about the classification of the familiar sentences just quoted.

What seems important in the schematism is not its exactness in application to our examples, but the disclosure of the heterogeneous logical relationships of the several convictions contained in typical sets. For this means that the question of justification must attend both to the varied character of the convictions themselves, and to the variety of the involved relationships between convictions. With regard to the latter, we are far from having exhausted the complexity of these relationships in even so artificially simplified a set as Aleph's. So far, we have noted that his convictions might usefully be arranged according to their levels of generality. If now some conviction, say, D "Jesus said, 'One thing is needful,'" is *expressed*, the happiness of the resultant speech-act depends, as we have seen, upon conditions which might include, for example, the *loyalty* to Jesus to which the speaker, Aleph, is thereby committed, the *genuineness* of the reported saying of Jesus (did Jesus in actuality say that?), and the *intent* and attitude of Aleph in issuing his utterance (can these words be the speech-act which he intends to issue? what speech-act does he intend?). In other words, all the conditions which earlier (chapter 3) we grouped under the heads primary, representative, and affective will

be at stake. And, with the proper adjustments, Aleph's conviction, his convictional belief, is subject to these very conditions. If
Jesus said that one thing was needful, these words have special
import for Aleph, given his attitude to Jesus. They are to some
degree and in some way paradigmatic for his life, his singleness of
purpose, his attitude to the task of the day and to the busy whirl
of life around him. To make "in some way" specific, to understand the primary force of his speech-act (and the 'primary force'
of the conviction it expresses), would require a fuller specification
than we have yet undertaken of Aleph's view of Jesus. It would
require knowing the types of situations in which he can find his
conviction applicable; behind these lies the sort of "Jesus" whom
Aleph contemplates. We have seen (J) that his Jesus is the incarnation, the human presence, of God. Exactly what effect has that
doctrine upon his understanding of D? And what else does he
believe about Jesus? Is his Jesus an ascetic? a revolutionary? a
social reformer? In sum, we should require Aleph's "perspectival
image"[19] of Jesus, in order to know how that picture affects the
force of D.

Note then the interdependence of particulars D and E. The
Jesus who spoke (D) is on Aleph's reckoning (we may assume) none
other than the Jesus who acted (E). And among the conditions
for the happiness of each of these convictions are the loyalties,
attitudes, deeds of Aleph himself. How intricate an account it
would be which only took cognizance of all that was involved in
the tension and interaction of D and E! D demands of Aleph in
many a situation a certain detachment, while E demands in perhaps the same situations a certain intense expectancy. What will be
the vital balance between detachment and expectancy, between D
and E? If we recall the space required to set out in summary form
the affects, states of affairs, and commitments demanded by a
single (convictional) speech-act, G, how much more will two in
combination and perhaps in conflict require? And what if Aleph
had not two but two score such convictions? Then the calculus of
the adjustment of their several demands would become too long
for the telling. Like Tristram Shandy, it might take two days of
writing to describe one day of living. But for Aleph, as for
Tristram Shandy, it is the living not the telling that is crucial.

The upshot is that, while for analytic purposes it was necessary
to consider the implications for Mr. Aleph of his single conviction,
expressed in his single speech-act G treated in isolation, when it
comes to the assessment, the evaluation, of a particular life or

style of life and the convictions which form its backbone, it would be a fruitless task to attempt to assess the worth of any conviction in isolation. The convictions in Aleph's set do not occur in isolation; they cannot (normally) be tested in isolation; thus they are not accepted or reformed or rejected in isolation. The justification or rejection of convictions, we see, must often consist in the justification or rejection of *sets* of convictions, of conviction sets, which will stand or fall in interdependence and not one by one.

In the practical order, it must now be apparent, conviction sets as we understand them are seldom deductive systems or theoretical constructs. If they possess a unity, it is rather first of all the unity of their coinherence in the organic unity of a community of persons. Neither logical interdependence nor any other single explanatory feature will account for the occurrence of particular conviction sets. Logic, to be sure, is not debarred. The notion that some convictions preside over others suggests that logic has a role to play in most sets. But it may be associations of a contingent historical nature, or overt or subconscious emotive force of the sort explored by attitude research, or combinations of these and other, unnamed, elements, which bind our convictions together. We cannot, in general, say what these must be; they are surely as varied as life itself. What we can, definitionally, say is that the glue which binds convictions into a single set is their mutual relation to the life of the person or (normally) the life of the community in which he shares. The unity of conviction sets is the rough but vital unity of shared life.

Why is it said that conviction sets normally belong to communities, not individuals? Zuurdeeg, we remember, held that convictions implied convictional communities,[20] but this seems to have been for him not so much a philosophical or a linguistic inference as a shrewd observation of the human scene. To see what sort of necessity may lie behind this observation, let us once more consider an old objection to our procedures. "You have spoken," the objection goes, "as if it might be quite difficult to sort out the meaning and force of Aleph's five convictions in their interrelations. However, you have underestimated the difficulty. The task is not merely complex, but hopeless; not simply a large task, but an impossible one. It is impossible because we can never surely know one another's thoughts or meanings; they are inextricably private. Aleph means what he chooses to mean, but who are we, who are you, to say what that is?"

Our response to such skepticism has been to invoke the public and convention-governed nature of language and of thought as well. Neither we nor he may at a given moment know what a man thinks or means, but he can find out, and so can we. The assurance that this is so lies in the nature of language itself. We were in position to say what Aleph meant by G because G arose within a community, within a religious tradition. Note further that the community which provided the context of the utterance was not merely a religious community, though it was that. It was also a linguistic community, not in the sense that it was confined to or defined by one of the natural languages (English, Hebrew, Chinese), but in the sense of using one or more of the natural languages in common ways in order to form and express its shared beliefs, including its convictions. It was precisely this communal feature of Aleph's (and of all) speech which made it possible (in chapter 3) to determine the force of G and test its happiness in utterance.

If this is the case, we may now see that linguistic communities as just described are convictional communities as well: that some convictions must be shared to give form to the community, and even private or rebellious convictions of members of the community can be understood only in view of their connection with the communal matrix from which they diverge or dissent. Therefore by speaking of convictional communities we do not imply that all persons therein must have identical conviction sets, nor that any two personal sets will be identical. Our convictions are what we are, and we humans are not merely or totally alike. Moreover there are (as far as the present writers know) no irreversible convictions—all may be challenged; each may be modified under pressure; any may in the extreme be overthrown. But when we later consider the possibility of convictional rebellion (chapter 6), it will become clear that even the rebel can understand himself, or be understood, only in terms of that against which he rebels. (One rightly distinguishes, for example, Catholic atheists from Jewish atheists.) It is just the existence of such linguistic-convictional community which makes the understanding of Aleph's five-member conviction set possible.

Aleph's own set need not, perhaps rarely will, be simply identical with the community's shared set. Even in his departures from the common store, however, the meaning and justification of his set are dependent upon the meaning of the common set. Since each of Aleph's convictions acquires part of its significance from all the other members of his set, and since every member of his set depends for its understandability upon the language of the community, we cannot understand Aleph, or justify his set of convictions, save by reference to the community to which he belongs. If he participates in more than one community, then we shall have to consider each. The understanding and justification of Aleph's convictions, then, are dependent upon the understanding and (as we shall see) the justifiability of the community's convictions. It is the community which is logically prior, however keen may be our interest in the individual and his personal faith.

III. Pluralism and Justification

If there were only one convictional community, the human race, or if we lived, as perhaps men once did, in a community so isolated that the convictions of outsiders made no impact upon us, we might have little more to say on this topic. As matters stand, we are just arriving in position to state and to investigate a central problem of the justification of convictions. This is the plurality of convictional communities. Today we can neither ignore communities other than our own, nor, given the imbedding of personal convictions in communities which generate the meaning and determine the conditions of the possible justification of a set, can we easily justify our convictions in universally satisfactory ways if the challenge to our convictions comes from a rival community.

Convictional differences are at once more serious, and harder to adjudicate, than other differences of belief (for example, differences of opinion). They are more serious because convictions are themselves more serious. They are more difficult to adjudicate because they are intertwined with our own lives and the lives of the communities from which we spring. To judge them within convictional borders is a kind of self-judgment—a notoriously difficult task which may yet fail to satisfy our convictional opponent. To judge them *across* convictional borders seems either question-begging and presumptuous, or logically questionable: the former if we ignore the special problems involved, the latter if we acknowledge them.

How, then, are we to understand those whose convictions differ from our own? And for that matter how is any one of us (or any one community among us) to know that his own stance is justifiable, his own conviction set is right? Confrontation with these questions is likely to produce either dogmatism or cynical indifference—yet both dogmatism and indifference are to be seen as temptations rather than as solutions of these hard problems. Still, we must recognize that even to ask these questions in this form is rather different from the way in which some philosophers of religion have approached their task. These philosophers have assumed that at least they themselves (and perhaps their readers) have attained a grand cosmic neutrality, far above the strife of the systems. With their clean, convictionless slates they would set out on the quest, inviting the open-minded to come along and promising that at the end of the road there would be inscribed on their tablets nothing but the truth impartially discerned. Those who are satisfied with such a tale are not likely to have come this far with us, for we have made it clear that we possess no such higher neutrality, nor have we expected it in our readers.

Our approach implicitly challenges those who are blithely confident that their own conviction set is the only worthy one. To see my convictions *as* convictions is not to see that they are wrong, but it is to acknowledge the nature of my attachment to them, and thereby to be open, if only a crack, to understanding how someone else may see the world differently. Let us illustrate this from the contemporary debate about belief in God. In a perceptive essay, Paul van Buren suggests that there is something rather odd about the demand that the talk of people who talk about God, or who "have trembled in a situation which they might later describe as being 'in the presence of' the gods, or God," should be explained in terms of the way people generally talk about other matters.[21] Perhaps there just *are* differences in men, in the experiences they have, and perhaps the experiences of these few are not to be accounted for in terms of the general experience of mankind, or spoken of in ways which coherently report that more general experience. And, if we acknowledge this, should we not be prepared to take another step? To concede that not all human religious experience is the same, that just as there are those who do not engage in religious talk, so are there those who do not employ certain *kinds* of religious talk? Some (Augustine, Tillich) place the emphasis upon man's sense of limitation—his finitude, his guilt, his loss of 'meaning' in life—while others experience a sense of wonder rather than of limitation. "It is not *how* the world is, that is the mystical, but *that* it is," says Wittgenstein.[22] But van Buren comments that Wittgenstein was one of the minority, "one of the strange ones." He adds, "the decisive point to be made is that some men are struck by the ordinary, whereas most find it only ordinary."[23]

Now, asks van Buren, if some of us are "struck" when others of us are not, why should "contemporary secular man" become the measure for understanding his religious counterpart? Why in the world should we be interested in trying to justify religious language to this hypothetical man? How, for that matter, is he going to justify *his* language to the religious man? Isn't the issue between them precisely over what constitutes a justification? Will it do to say that there is a third way (the true way?) which sees both how the religious and how the non-religious see the matter? But if that were a way of seeing, would it not be *just* a third way of seeing, alternative to the other two as they are alternatives to one another?

> It seems to be the case that there is no alternative to seeing things *as*. Every seeing is 'seeing as.' Depending on our purposes, what we wish to accomplish, the context, and many other factors, we shall have what we call grounds for seeing a situation in one way rather than in another. But seeing the 'ordinary' as extraordinary, as a cause for wonder, is no more and no less in need of justification than seeing the 'ordinary' as ordinary and as something to be taken for granted.[24]

And so there can be no more important a problem for theology than "that of sorting out the ways in which we do justify for ourselves and to each other our ways of seeing, our perspectives, our (to give them a more honorific title) metaphysical beliefs."[25]

Contrast that 'theological' enterprise with the much easier task of discovering the conditions for happiness of a belief or an utterance in a community in which we all participate. Take our diner A's speech-act requesting the bread, for instance. In that case, we were careful to specify that there existed a linguistic community or sub-community, speakers of a dialect in which *certain* words (though not invariable, not indifferently chosen either) counted as the performance of that speech-act. A couldn't[26] say just anything and be counted as requesting the bread. And of course a linguistic sub-community implies a communal ethos as well and a community of custom and institution, making any given practice (such as requesting or passing) possible. To put the matter another way, the practice of requesting is both a linguistic and a cultural institution, and the two are inseparable; *glossai* and *ethnoi,* languages and peoples, belong together and serve in defining one another. Ethos works with language to specify the conditions of happy bread-requesting.

The reason we could specify so firmly and confidently (though not without considerable effort) the conditions of the happy performance of A's speech-act, the reason we could know whether the conditions for happiness *were* in fact fulfilled, is that the community to which A belonged is like our own—*is* our own, if we temporarily disregard the line between fiction and fact. We know directly the bread-requesting convention; it is our convention. Nor perhaps do we know anyone who lacks such a convention, anyone who construes the world of food at table radically differently than do we. If we do, a fresh problem at once appears. The reflection required to solve the problem, "What must we say, and what do, in what circumstances, in order to request the bread?" is then no longer the introspective what-we-would-say-when of ordinary language analysis, but (as J. L. Austin's investigations implied) becomes a task of quite a different order.[27]

We can see this shift of emphasis in the quest for happiness conditions in Aleph's utterance, "God led Israel across the Reed Sea." Aleph was specified as belonging to a community to which not all of us belong. Even if someone does belong to Aleph's community or one like it, he is very likely conscious of the pluralism involved, conscious of others who do not belong, and of linguistic obligations to those others. Why is it that the very statement of conditions for the happy performance of Aleph's speech-act seemed more dubious than those of A's? And why would the claim that those conditions are or are not in certain circumstances fulfilled seem more dubious still? What is there *odd* about Aleph's utterance?

We can say at the outset that it cannot be the novelty of "God led Israel across the Reed Sea," or of the very practice of religious confession. Both are very old, much older than the Christian era, much older, then, than the intellectual and spiritual tradition in which we live. Nor will it do to say that such confession is an exotic specimen in our culture, an Eastern import, in the way that (in 1975) joss sticks or temple bells are. On the contrary, some form of that confession is one of the foundation stones in the formation of Western culture. Many have suggested that the trouble is the use of the strange word "God," neither name nor common noun, which is the cause of our sense of discomfort or uncertainty. To be sure that word (or its predecessors in other tongues) has itself been there as long as the confession has been, or longer. Yet there is some merit in the suggestion that it is the strange "logic of 'God' " which is the scandal and stumbling block.

If however we follow the insight of more recent analysts, and our own in the preceding pages, we will prefer to say that the difficulty in understanding Aleph's utterance and appraising its happiness lies precisely in his convictional distance from us, or from others in our world, or in both of these. When a linguistic practice is one employed by everyone who speaks a language, there is relatively little difficulty in knowing what its conditions-for-happiness will be and in knowing to all intents and purposes what counts as the fulfillment of those conditions. One knows these things merely by knowing the language and culture in which the utterance is heard. For centuries men have confessed as Aleph confessed and have been understood and approved or challenged, the challenges directed mainly to the circumstances of the speaker, *his* fitness to utter those words, *his* being in position to utter that speech-act. But as a culture becomes more pluralistic the status of the convictions conveyed in an utterance may shift from "generally accepted" to "disputed" or "accepted only within a sub-community," and then we have the sort of circumstance which makes the process of examination for happiness similar to that in Aleph's case.

Ideally, how might this problem of pluralism be overcome? If conflicting sub-communities were members of a single overarching community, then the standards of the larger community (mankind?), subscribed by both sides, might serve as a convictional court of appeal. Indeed, it is partly by such means, we believe, that the perspectival fragmentation of the world may be mended. But we cannot with confidence indicate this procedure until we have fully examined the obstacle created by convictional pluralism. For example, what if a smaller community (or a single man) chooses to challenge the prevailing assumptions of the world-community itself? Can we say that the convictions of the challenger *must* be justifiable in terms of the challenged convictions? Surely it is not self-evident that in every such case it is the challenger who is wrong? But this is no hypothetical situation— prophets, reformers, and revolutionary leaders have always been a minority, as the phrase *Athanasius contra mundum* reminds us.

One way to avoid the problem is simply to deny the necessity of adopting *any* conviction set. Why not be content (even delighted) with beliefs of a more limited, *ad hoc,* and provisional nature? But convictions, as we have said, are those beliefs which are central to the character of a person; a change in them would involve a change (would, indeed, *be* a change) in his character. So what would it be like for a person to have no beliefs which occupied this central role? It is not perfectly clear that we could survive without *any* convictions. Are not such beliefs as that I am the same person I was in the past, that some of my present experience is non-illusory, that I know my friends and they me, and perhaps others still more elemental, such as that nature is in general predictable and that our talk must be in general consistent, actually both necessary to our kind of existence and themselves convictions?[28] Thus, we can make a fair case for the proposition that the very concept of a person requires convictions, since to be a person is to have the sort of persistence through time which convictions alone provide. Again, some have argued that to be rational one must have some one principle which organizes one's choices. Such a principle would surely be convictional.

But apart from these subtle, difficult, and controversial arguments, there is a straightforward objection to doing without convictions, or making out with only as many as survival seems to require. Our eighteenth-century predecessors would have called it a moral objection, an objection in terms of the kind of life such an abstinence would produce. To lack all persistent and central beliefs is, simply put, to lack character.[29] Not just laudable or virtuous character, but any character at all. To be religious or sensual, ambitious or greedy, malicious or kind, radical or conservative, is (among other things) to have the sorts of beliefs we have called convictions. Lacking them, one may sporadically perform particular acts of kindness or cruelty, do conservative or radical things, act piously or irreverently, but these will be only reactions to particular circumstances, not expressions of settled or identifiable character.[30] One is thus, in a way, the victim of these circumstances, just as a boat having freeboard but no sail or anchor is the victim of every chance wind. We grant that life can be led in this way, or, rather, that one can be led by life in this way. But if one still doubts whether such a life is satisfactory, let him consult Plato's *Republic* or *Gorgias,* where there are vivid portraits of men who always do as they wish, yet never get what they want. Nor is this merely an unfortunate but accidental fact about these men. For the man without convictions does not know what he wants in the settled way which would enable him to lead his life in a manner that might arrive at it.

How, though, can Athanasius (or the whole world) justify a set of convictions? In the remaining paragraphs of the present chapter we will mention three elements of justificatory procedure, no one of which, taken alone, will prove adequate, but which employed together have in fact served humanity well in this regard.

In the first place, there are certain widely accepted considerations which go to establishing the adequacy of any belief. One may inquire, for example, whether his convictions, so far as truth is relevant to them, are in fact *true*. Insofar as they are embraced by one community, one may inquire whether convictions are mutually *coherent*. Or if in particular cases these tests are inapplicable or indecisive, one may still raise more pragmatic questions: does the conviction in question contribute to living a good life—to ask a Greek question with a Greek word, does it make for *eudaimonia?* Is the life thus produced really the most *satisfactory* life possible, from the viewpoint of the owner(s) of the convictions under examination? Or, if these latter tests seem unduly subjective, is the life which embodies these convictions a life of justice or *righteousness?* Are not such considerations as these (for the preceding list is by no means exhaustive) the criteria by which all men, of whatever convictional community, do judge and ought to judge their own convictions and those of others?

Those who accept this claim as it stands seem to have the support of St. Paul: "Finally, brethren, whatsoever things are true, whatsoever things are honest, whatsoever things are just, whatsoever things are pure, whatsoever things are lovely, whatsoever things are of good report; if there be any virtue, and if there be any praise, think on these things."[31] There, but for a substituted or added term or two, is the very list we have produced, offered as a guide to the thinking of the Christian community by its chief apostle! However, the occurrence of such a set of criteria *within* a particular religious community may serve, if we were not already wary, to put us on guard. These terms in use may embody convictional elements. Appeals to them cannot be employed to settle interconvictional disputes because they have been preempted to assert the disputed claims. The "justice" of Jesus may not be the same as the "justice" of Muhammad; the "truth" of Aristotle may not be equivalent to the "truth" of Moses. Even if such terms do in a given language have a common content, that content may not be sufficiently precise to allay convictional misunderstandings and conflicts. The process of examining any one of them, say the term "righteousness," across convictional lines is then a means of reintroducing the very pluralist dilemma we have just delineated. Nevertheless there is a point in mentioning these considerations of truth, *eudaimonia,* and the others. The process of justification will in some way make use of such 'ultimate' appeals; they are, if not themselves the judges, at least indicators of the jurisdictions under which convictional judgments are formed; we may call them the *loci* of justification.

In the second place, we may again note the initial thesis of this chapter: the understanding of convictions can be correlated with the understanding of speech-acts, and the justification of the convictions with the happiness of the speech-acts. At the present stage of the investigation of speech-acts, we should not tire of reminding ourselves that these conditions include the affective setting of speaker and hearers (a point widely recognized already), but also the relationship between utterance and the wide world 'outside' the speaker (a point sometimes slighted by present-day analysts of religious utterance), and even more the primary relationship between the utterance and the linguistic-convictional community by means of which it is (if at all) meaningful.

We have claimed that fully to understand a speaker is to be in position to know whether his speech is justifiable; that the analysis of a speech-act is tantamount to the justification or rejection of that speech-act. We are now in position to see the sense in which, and the degree to which, that claim is self-evident: if we understand Aleph, we are also able to say what are the conditions for the happiness of his speech-act. The difficulty we now confront is that a convictional speaker's speech (including some of its conditions for happiness) may be locked into his conviction set, while in a pluralist world we have no ready means of transcending convictional barriers to transconvictional justification.

Perhaps the honest way to put the matter is that, since across these barriers we cannot know when convictional speech-acts are fully happy, we cannot (to that degree) even fully understand those who speak from beyond such barriers. (To understand the language of mathematics, one must accept the conventions of mathematics; to understand the language of Buddhism one must [in some measure?] accept the commitments of Buddhism.) The bright side of this dilemma is that if somehow we can, across convictional lines, understand Aleph, we *will* be able to say how what Aleph says can happily be said, hence how what he believes can be justified. But we grant that so far we have not shown the way to this transconvictional understanding, nor to overcoming the pluralism which creates the need for such understanding. We have only shown that understanding the language must be central to that task.

This brings us to *the third element* of the justificatory procedure. This element involves the recognition that the language of a community is never a hermetically sealed system, that it is never even static, but is in a constant process of adjustment to external as well as internal pressure. Therefore the same must be said of the

community's formative convictions (for they can only be expressed in the language which is itself in flux). *Convictions make us
what we are, but what we are does itself change.* What we said
above about convictionless men applies to convictionless communities as well. If the change is so rapid that the convictions are lost,
the community is dissolved in the process. On the other hand, a
totally ossified community is a contradiction in terms: in a changing world, an unchanging community acquires a new environment,
natural and human, thus a new set of relations to the world.

Recognition of these truisms leads us to ask whether there are
not now ways in which we change our shared convictions in our
common efforts to survive in a changing world—ways which are at
the same time the clues to testing and even justifying our convictions, or some of them, in a pluralist situation? Perhaps there are
characteristic activities—we have in mind the work of the reformer
and the revolutionary, the act of the rebel, the experience of the
convert, for example—by means of which both single individuals
and entire communities may be challenged to convictional shifts
which succeed in meeting the challenges to justification which
have arisen.

Like the two previous elements (the existence of common loci
of appeal; the nature of language itself) this last-named element is
not adequate alone. Alone it cannot show how either Aleph, or
Athanasius, or the whole world can (in principle) justify a conviction set. But what cannot be done by any one element may be
done by three together, and in the two final chapters we shall
attempt to say how this is possible. First, however, we must deal
with some important objections to our procedure, objections
which argue that plurality is not after all so serious a matter, that
our procedures are therefore needlessly cumbersome, and that
there is a simpler way to a world of justified convictions. Those
objections will occupy us in the next chapter.

5

Man is only a reed, the weakest in nature, but he is a thinking reed.
There is no need for the whole universe to take up arms to crush him: a
vapour, a drop of water is enough to kill him. But even if the universe
were to crush him, man would still be nobler than his slayer, because he
knows that he is dying and the advantage the universe has over him.
The universe knows none of this.

Thus all our dignity consists in thought. It is on thought that we
must depend for our recovery, not on space and time, which we could
never fill. Let us then strive to think well; that is the basic principle of
morality.

Blaise Pascal[1]

You will not find me inaccessible to your criticism. I know how
difficult it is to avoid illusions; perhaps the hopes I have confessed to
are of an illusory nature, too. But I hold fast to one distinction. Apart
from the fact that no penalty is imposed for not sharing them, my
illusions are not, like religious ones, incapable of correction. They have
not the character of a delusion.

Sigmund Freud[2]

A Perspective
on Non-Perspectival Reason

THE CLAIM OF PLURALISM IS NOT MERELY THAT THERE ARE A variety of conflicting views in the world, but the immeasurably stronger claim that there is not among these views any which can be clearly established to be the superior of all the others; at least not in the short run. If there were such a conviction set, then its justification would require only an efficient organization of public relations and the passage of time. This might be expensive, time-consuming, and tedious, but it surely would not present the theoretical problems we have outlined in the previous chapter. Of course, any convinced man or community sufficiently isolated or dogmatic might make such a claim for his conviction set. But the vast majority of conviction sets—Christian, Marxist, Buddhist, materialist—are so hotly disputed that we are unlikely, if we are informed men, to take the claim seriously. There are two such putative sets, however, which seem to have such a wide appeal and impressive history of missionary success that we want now to consider the claim for demonstrability on their behalf. We intend first to consider the claim that mere *reason* can be relied upon to settle the disputes among rival conviction sets and establish itself as a principle above all convictions. Afterwards we will consider a like claim made on behalf of scientific reason, or *science*.

I. Reason and Proof

Although we will finally reject the claim for 'reason' in some of its forms, we begin by confessing how much we are committed to rationality and reasonableness in our work, though we are aware that we may fail to live up to that commitment.[3] Our theses in this essay are stated as clearly as we can state them and are

117

supported, as well as we can support them, with evidence and argument. These are, of course, appeals to the reader's reason as well as the products of the writers' reason, and we know of no other way to support or criticize claims. Beyond this, we hold one form of the principle of fallibility, which is also (in a different sense?) a principle of reason. In its most extreme form, the fallibility principle shades over into a view we have already rejected: that one should minimize his convictions, for fear of false belief. Though this may seem attractive at first, it has the unhappy consequence that we should always suspend our judgment. On the other hand, a softer form of the principle, the mere recognition that we can conceivably make mistakes, is so innocuous that it hardly deserves the name of principle.

There is, however, a form of the fallibility principle which is both significant and acceptable. It holds that even one's most cherished and tenaciously held convictions might be false and are in principle always subject to rejection, reformulation, improvement, or reformation. This principle has helped to guide our present effort and, indeed, to make it possible. Granting our desire to correct our errors and extend our knowledge, it follows that we should not only be open to criticism from others, but should seek it out, especially when we are criticizing others.

Nevertheless, the fallibility principle alone is not sufficient. A life of nothing but convinced self-criticism of loosely held beliefs would have little to recommend it. Even Socrates, for all his confessions of ignorance, roamed the streets of Athens striking at pretentious ignorance like a torpedofish. Clearly, he was moved by something more than the fallibility principle. We cannot do without convictions, fallible though we are. But we cannot avoid error, convinced though we may be. We might summarize this point with a motto in Kantian form: Conviction sets without the fallibility principle are blind; the fallibility principle without other convictions is empty. A minimal sort of rationality is therefore essential to our task (or any other in philosophy or theology). But the sort of rationality which is clearly necessary is clearly not sufficient.

Of course, one can add that "rejecting, reformulating, improving, and reforming" convictions are (or may become) rational enterprises. If they were also convictionally neutral ones, that would surely indicate a transconvictional status for reason which would, in principle, ease the task of reaching agreement among holders of rival convictions. Unfortunately, such tasks are not, and cannot be, convictionally neutral. For the work of criticism, evaluation, judgment, or justification requires a stance just as much as the convictions or confessions which may be under criticism.

Take *judgment* as typical of the classes of acts we have just mentioned. It is obvious that utterances like "case dismissed" or "appeal denied" will not count as judgments unless their utterers have some legal authority, that is, unless they are judges. Anyone may say those words, just as anyone may say "time out." But only the referee can call time out in saying it, and only the judge can make a judgment in saying "case dismissed." In such highly formalized contexts it is clear that a special position or stance is required (one has to *be* a referee, or a judge) and also clear what are the characteristics of that stance (being a properly appointed referee or judge). But in informal contexts of judgment, the requirement that one have a proper posture is equally important, even though it is more difficult to say precisely what being in position now means. Still, if I say that Grofé is a better composer than Bartok and it turns out that I have never heard a composition by either, the suggestion that my judgment is poor will have to be taken as jocular understatement. I am in no position to make a judgment, even a poor one, about music I have never heard. Or, in a different vein, consider the utterance "It is easier to starve than accept a handout," where the utterer is the pampered son of the world's richest man. Can he really be said to have judged a situation so utterly alien to his own experience? Surely, it is only by attributing to him heroic powers of empathy and imagination that we can make sense of such a supposition.

A little reflection will show that evaluating and criticizing, like judging, require at least a minimal familiarity and understanding and even some special qualification in order to be distinquished from guessing, surmising, conjecturing, or posing. Of course much more is required of the utterer of these speech-acts if they are to be felicitous: the ability to cite evidence, to distinguish one case from another, and so forth.

In the same way the judge, the critic, the assessor of a conviction set (including the convinced person himself) must at a minimum understand the convictions in the set. Even to judge their mutual consistency, he must know at least their representative force, and to assess the evidence for and against them requires much more. No less than the judge functioning within a particular legal system, the judge of convictions must get into position to make his judgments. And that this latter "getting into position" can be achieved while having no convictions other than "be reasonable" is an arbitrary (and therefore an *un*reasonable) hypothesis. It seems more reasonable to believe that if a person has enough character or stability or selfhood to enable him to make judgments, particularly judgments on such significant matters as the basic religious or irreligious outlooks by which entire human communities live, his character (by definition) will be marked by some definite convictions, though of course they need not be the convictions currently under assessment. Without the requisite standpoint, without some convictions or other, there could be no such judgments, either for or against the convictions to be assessed.

These general conclusions regarding the rational activities of judgment, criticism, and the like apply as well to that more theologically and philosophically central use of reason, deductive proof. The history of theology and philosophy is dotted (some might say, littered) with proofs of the existence of God and to a lesser extent proofs of the non-existence of God. Obviously, we do not mean all these 'proofs' are successful ("proof" is not a success-word), and in fact we are not primarily concerned with their validity or soundness, as many of our distinguished predecessors have been. We intend neither to criticize old proofs nor to construct new ones. Our aim is to account for the fact that such arguments are so ineffective in persuading those who initially disbelieve their conclusions, and to account for the related fact that even the validity of these arguments tends to be assessed or judged differently, depending on the antecedent theological beliefs of the assessor.

It is surely clear, by this time, what our general position is. The conclusions of such arguments are convictions and the proving of them—rational though it is—is a convictional activity as much as criticizing or judging is. Moreover, the construction of a proof requires a getting into position at least to the extent of establishing or assuming the truth of the premises. Now, to derive from premises which are themselves convictional a convictional conclusion may be of great interest and importance to those who share those convictions, but it can hardly be persuasive to those who reject them. To be persuasive across convictional lines, a proof would have to contain premises which were understood in the same sense and accepted both by those who accepted and those who did not accept the convictional conclusion. In our view theistic and anti-theistic proofs fail to persuade because the premises of such proofs, as well as the method of proof itself, are neither convictionally neutral nor agreed upon by all in this way.

Since proofs are simply a special variety of rational assessment, the points we have made concerning the convictional nature of the general activity of assessment or judgment hold as well for proofs. Nevertheless, because proofs have played such an important role in Western thought, it is of some interest to show in more detail how convictional elements do enter into their construction, and how, having entered in, they affect the persuasiveness of the argument.

The *Summa Theologica* of Thomas Aquinas contains the *locus classicus* among theistic proofs.[4] But the proofs there lie under the double disadvantage of being imbedded in an antique world view (so that they must be translated out of that view in order to become effective) and of standing under severe and probably justifiable logical criticism at the hands of Hume, Kant, and other subsequent philosophers. Fortunately, for our purposes, Austin Farrer, a twentieth-century Oxford philosopher and Anglican theologian, has offered in *Finite and Infinite* a theistic proof which is both in the Thomist tradition and fully informed by the criticisms of that tradition.

Every argument for God's existence, says Farrer, must start from "the world of finites," that is, from the world as experienced. Yet it will not do to say, "The world exists, so God must exist"; that proposition carries no force. The world, then, must be examined, and in it certain "distinctions" must be noted. If these "distinctions" can be seen to be explicable if and only if God exists as their ground, then the existence of God will be required as the explanation of the observed distinctions.[5] Before we attend to these distinctions themselves, Farrer warns us to note that such an argument is unavoidably analogical—that is, the argument proposes only to show that there is an analogy between the relationship of God to the world, on the one hand, and certain familiar finite relationships on the other. To neglect the fact that we are dealing with analogy and to treat "divine causality," for example, as though it were a special case of a generally obtaining principle of causality, is to make a "formal false syllogism" or paralogism— the very error against which Kant has effectively warned us. What shall we do, Farrer asks, to avoid this pitfall? The only course is to present the arguments as analogical from the outset, for they present us with "a splintered image of God," and we can "treat the quasi-syllogism as analogical illustration. . . . a challenge to us to recognize a genuine analogy."[6]

Now the form of theistic arguments, we are told, will be

determined in any given case by the particular "finite distinction" which is to serve as its base. By finite distinction, Farrer means the sort of categorical distinction which can be made between "essence" and "existence," or between "actuality" and "possibility," or between "operation" and "interior effect." If one allows that there are such distinctions to be made in the world, he may then propose that the relation between God and the world is in the appropriate respect analogous to the observed worldly distinction. More, it may be argued that only on the basis of the God-world analogy is the this-worldly distinction at hand intelligible. If this is true, the analogy is not merely possible; it is, for the intelligibility of the world, really a necessary analogy. If, further, it is assumed that "relations of reason," in so far as they are valid, correspond to "real relations,"[7] then the admission of the analogy entails the admission of the existence of its terms, including, in particular, the Infinite Being or Activity, namely, God. An illustration of such an argument is found in the essence/existence distinction. We can distinguish the mere fact that things exist (existence) from any particular ways in which they exist (essence). But the relation between existence and essence is not that of belonging to one another as either constituents or properties belong to that which they constitute or qualify. Neither is there any form "which embraces both as constituents, or from which both follow as properties." Putting the matter differently, we quite easily imagine that things might not be as they are, or that as they are they might not have existed at all. Farrer's conclusion is that "every particular union of [essence and existence] is the work of a being in whom existence finds its own full possibility,"[8] that is, of God.

At once, however, Farrer moves on to criticize this argument. Whatever force it has depends upon smuggling in the assumption that whatever forms the union of essence and existence has or is a "form." But it was just the relation of form (i.e., essence) and existence which the argument was supposed to be explaining. "Thus the scheme of . . . causality in its widest sense, is simply an analogy, which points beyond itself to the inexpressible fact of creation,"[9] and why, Farrer implicitly inquires again and again, should anyone take that "inexpressible fact" to be a fact, why take the analogy to hold?

To understand his answer to that question, we must attend briefly to Farrer's exposition of the nature of "finite substance." By "finite substance" Farrer means roughly "selves" and "things." To say that there is finite substance is to recognize the actual existence of selves and things. However, as the use of the term "finite substance" indicates, Farrer does not take selves and things to have a merely phenomenal or haphazard existence. He argues, instead, that substance possesses very special qualities, a very special structure—a structure which can make the force of the analogies referred to in the preceding paragraph evident. Substances, more closely analyzed, are acts, such as the acts of a human being who wills to do this and not that; these acts, according to Farrer, constitute the human will; and the self and its central constituent, the will, then serve as all-important clues to the way things in the world in general are constituted.[10] For example, if it turns out that acts of the human will may properly be placed on a scale of being, if, that is, desiring is a kind of low-grade willing, whereas execution is a high-grade act of will, [11] one thing that follows is that there are degrees of substance. But if degrees, are we not prepared for a highest degree? And, if the will is 'free,' are we not obliged to give place to freedom or creativity in our understanding of the way reality in general is structured? And thus to an ultimate free creativity to which the human sort is analogous? And so forth.

If we are primarily concerned with the perspicuity of Farrer's terms or the validity of his arguments, our exposition of them would certainly have to include both an analysis of his doctrine of "finite substance" and an examination of his introductory exploration of the logic of theistic argument. We might find ourselves in that case quarreling with the appropriateness of this apparatus of metaphysical inquiry, as well as with the particular logical moves made through the maze of argument. Our goal, however, is a different one—it is to show that the first premises of Farrer's arguments, the "structure of finite substance," is taken by him in a way which cannot but express his convictions, or the convictions of those among his readers who find his argument persuasive.

For Farrer, substance is preeminently human substance, including his own substance. Is the self unitary? Is it free? Is the world it apprehends and acts on non-illusory? These are just the sorts of topics about which it is very difficult not to have convictions if one thinks about them at all. So to think, in Farrer's case, is to think not only about human nature but about the relation of all there is to God.

> For the theist, the reality of that unique object [God] and the validity of the construction by which all things are ordered towards Him are, of course, inseparable. To think theistically is both to recognise the being of God *and to construe things in this order.*[12]

And this is just the point with which we began: to think theistically (or deistically, or atheistically, we would add) is to see things in
a certain way, in Farrer's term, it is to *construe* the world thus and
thus.

> And therefore the theist's first argument [and last, we might
> fairly add] is a statement; he exhibits his account of God active
> in the world and the world existing in God, that others may
> recognize it to be the account of what they themselves appre
> hend—or, if you like, that others may find it to be an instru
> ment through which they apprehend, for perhaps apprehension
> here is not separable from interpretation.[13]

To see the world as a theist sees it is already to see the world a
certain way; to see is to interpret, at least in this case. The
intention of theistic argument, then, says Farrer, is to bring a
latent discernment into the view of the reader. The arguer must
start with the scraps of cryptotheism which the reader (perhaps)
possesses and show that they cannot be held consistently save in a
full-blown theism. Thus argument will force men either to give up
their latent cryptotheism (for example, belief in finite substance,
including belief in a substantial self underlying each human person) or, alternatively, to incorporate it into a consistent theism.

What remains to be said? Well, we need to know that the beliefs
which Farrer says theists and cryptotheists share with one another—such beliefs as the existence of finite substance, the reality
of substantial selves, and the freedom of the will—are beliefs which
are persistent, and which to change would be to change their
holders significantly, for it is such beliefs that we call convictions.
In the preface to the second edition of *Finite and Infinite,* Farrer
describes the circumstances in which his essay was composed:
"Eighteen to sixteen years ago I sat down and wrote this book,
because I was possessed by the Thomist vision, and could not
think it false."[14] Now the "vision" is not the dialectic, not the
argument—for in the dialectic section Farrer consciously assumes a
post-Thomist, indeed a post-Kantian stance. The vision, then,
must be just that view of God and the world, of "Infinite" and
"finite," which occupies the second section of his book and forms
the central premise of his theistic proof. There could be no
clearer categorization of this "vision" as convictional than Farrer's
phrase just quoted: "and could not think it false." Could not, that
is, without becoming a markedly different thinker, a different
believer, a different man.

If we are correct about this, then we have established all that we want to establish about Farrer's argument—that its premises, no less than its conclusions, are convictional. Nor is there anything shameful about arguing from premises which are convictions. Convictional ground *is* ground—the only kind of ground on which men finally stand. When, however, it comes to justifying all my convictions, the whole set which I embrace, it is an achievement of limited value to show that some of my convictions entail another, particularly when I know that some of my neighbors share neither the premise-convictions about how it is with the world nor the entailed-conviction, in this case, that God exists.

Proofs of God's non-existence are not as readily available as some who disbelieve in God imagine. Very often arguments which are said to be against belief in God only call attention to apparent logical inconsistencies in a particular concept of God or in particular theistic proofs; sometimes such arguments claim an inconsistency between a concept of God (for example, that he is all-good and all-powerful) and the observed state of the world (which seems full of ills without number). Clusters of such argument seek to persuade, rather than to demonstrate. Our illustrative purpose might indeed be well served by examining one of these clusters of argument, e.g., the nature of evil and its relation to human happiness as these bear on the nature of God and God's existence. In doing this, we would seek to discover the convictional bases which the argument introduces or presupposes.

However, in his current book, *Primary Philosophy*, Michael Scriven provides us with an anti-theistic proof[15] of the more ambitious sort, and we will consider it. Early in his book, while discussing knowledge, Scriven defines rationality as the selection of "the most efficient available means to achieving a rationally acceptable end," where a rationally acceptable end is one which is not inconsistent with another end which is more valued.[16] Given this definition, it is not difficult to see the grounds for being, or trying to be, rational. As Scriven says, "we want certain things and being more rational is by definition a better way to go about getting them."[17] Scriven infers a corollary, important in the present context: "if what we want is knowledge or truth, we must believe those claims which are best and are well supported by the evidence."[18] It also follows from the definition that being rational cannot be the only aim one has. We can and ought to be rational about selecting and achieving our goals, but as Scriven puts it, rationality "can never be the only aim, any more than 'obey the law' can be the only law."[19]

Although there are undoubtedly convictional elements present in Scriven's general discussion of rationality, they are revealed more clearly when the results of this discussion are applied to arguments about the existence of God. Indeed, Scriven begins his discussion of the existence of God by observing that "no other problem has such important consequences for our lives and our thinking about other issues. . . . "[20] Certainly, Scriven agrees with Farrer and with us that whether to believe that God exists or not is (in our terms) a convictional question. Although Scriven's answer to this question is atheistic and based on argument, it is not an argument of the same sort as Farrer's argument for theism, that is, a set of premises about the nature of individuals or causes and effects or purposes which are intended to demonstrate that there is no God. Rather, Scriven regards atheism as the only rational alternative left once he has shown that all arguments for the existence of God fail. "All arguments" here does not mean merely all deductive or demonstrative arguments. Scriven is considering the consequences of failing to find any "evidence which supports the existence claim to any significant degree, i.e., makes it at all probable. . . ."[21] If we assume that God is the sort of Being whose existence would make a difference and that our search for possible evidence has been thorough, then, says Scriven, we do not need a further demonstration that God does not exist. Atheism is "obligatory."[22]

As an illustration of his point, Scriven notes that belief in Santa Claus is a reasonable one only so long as we cannot explain the phenomena in question (the appearance of gifts in a locked house where everyone is asleep) without assuming the existence of a being with the supernatural powers attributed to Santa Claus. Once we find an explanation which does not require such assumptions, we need no further proof that Santa Claus does not exist. Just the fact that there is no reason to think he does is proof enough. Because the belief in Santa Claus involves the attribution of supernatural powers, it is in a less favorable position than belief in the Loch Ness Monster, or the Abominable Snowman, since neither of the latter are supposed to have supernatural (i.e., wholly unprecedented) powers. If there were no evidence for their existence, belief in them would be irrational, but still a 'lesser sin' than a belief in a being whose powers contravene or go far beyond the powers that we know exist.[23] And in this respect, God is clearly more like Santa Claus than he is like the Abominable Snowman, Scriven thinks.[24] Thus, if we examine all the arguments for the existence of God and find all of them wanting, the only rational position to take is atheism. Even agnosticism is indefensible.

Now we are not concerned to examine Scriven's attacks on the theistic arguments or even to question the soundness of his argument for atheism. We intend, as with Farrer's case, to show only that its premises are convictional and that there are alternative premises (also convictional) which would yield an agnostic or even theistic conclusion. We now turn to that task.

Consider Scriven's claim that lack of evidence for a belief makes disbelief obligatory. Suppose someone should claim that next July in Seattle will be the hottest July in its history. Suppose further that he offers various 'arguments' in favor of this claim, none of which have any force (perhaps dreams he has had, astrological predictions, etc.), and suppose further that we find no meteorological evidence against the claim. What is the rational stance with respect to the claim? Should we simply give a Scotch verdict: not proven? Or should we *deny* that next July will be the hottest? If the criterion is plain consistency, surely either will do. Neither stance involves a self-contradiction, and either could be held in conjunction with consistent principles about how we should do all our thinking. One principle of rationality might be that whenever we are presented with a claim which lacks evidence for or against it, we should withhold judgment. Another might be that under the same circumstances we should assume that the claim is false, that is, disbelieve it. If we adopted the first, we would accept fewer false claims (ones which later turned out to be false), but we would also accept fewer true ones.

Is consistency, however, enough? Which of the stances is the best one for getting what we want? There are two difficulties in trying to answer this question in the weather-prediction case. First, by hypothesis there are no observed phenomena which are explained either by the theory that it is, or by the theory that it is not going to be the hottest July in Seattle's history. Second, in the limited context provided, there is no indication of any desires frustrated or fulfilled by the truth or falsity of the hypothesis. Thus there is neither need to adopt nor advantage in adopting any particular stance with respect to the hypothesis. Surely, in circumstances like those, the stance most consistent with the effective fulfillment of the goals I have—including the desire to understand, to know the truth about meteorological phenomena—is withholding of judgment.

Now the hypothesis that God exists is unlike this one in every important respect. As Scriven points out, the consequences of both belief and disbelief are (in William James's term) momentous, not only because of some possible afterlife, but in terms of our attitudes, decisions, and plans right now. Moreover, the sort of God claimed by Jews, or Christians, or Muslims, or Hindus (and denied by atheists of each tradition) cannot be ignored or avoided. If he exists, the world is different than it is if he does not. Thus (again in James's term) the choice of hypotheses is forced. We cannot simply wait until some possible future date when the evidence will be clearer, for that is simply to adopt atheism on a provisional basis. Finally, as this chapter as well as the one on God in Scriven's book attest, both the affirmation and the denial of God's existence have broad current appeal, or, as James would say, they are live options.

James, of course, did in his day regard the hypothesis that God exists as a live, forced, and momentous "option." Because of that, James held that if the evidence both for and against it were indecisive, one had the right either to believe or to disbelieve it. The theist no more than the atheist is being irrational in this case. He is simply following his interest in circumstances where, in James's view, he has every right to do so since nothing else will decide a question which must be decided.[25]

In taking this position, James was directly responding to an essay by W. K. Clifford which maintained that it was a serious crime against the intellect, a gross irrationality, and always wrong, ever to believe anything with less than sufficient evidence.[26] Scriven appears to be taking a position very much like Clifford's. We are not concerned to defend either James or Clifford. But in light of the enormous importance each assigned to his principle and of their lives lived in accordance with them, it is quite obvious that each principle is convictional and that anyone seriously maintaining one will be a significantly different person from one holding the other.

Can Scriven avoid taking a position in this evidently convictional dispute? On our view, of course, there is nothing suspicious or unfortunate about having a conviction and arguing from it. Indeed, it is inevitable in a self-directing adult. But it is inconvenient if one is attempting to prove to everyone of whatever conviction that some particular conviction should be adopted. Those who have significantly incompatible convictions will regard such an argument as unsound or question-begging, however sound and valid it may appear within its own conviction set.

There is the suggestion, in Scriven's argument, of another possible attempt to avoid a convictional stance. Though this attempt would not be successful, knowing the reason for its failure is helpful in understanding convictions and their function in argument. To make this attempt to avoid a convictional stance, Scriven might argue that while the failure of all theistic arguments leaves us with no evidence in favor of the existence of God, there remains one striking bit of evidence against his existence, even if deductive atheistic proofs are ignored. For God is supernatural, that is, possessed of properties which contradict or go substantially beyond all the scientific laws we have. If we can account for all our experience without appealing to such a being, it would not merely be gratuitous to believe in his existence—it would be irrational. Thus it appears that Scriven can show that atheism is the only justified position by appealing to nothing more than an empirical inventory of the universe and a definition of the supernatural. Surely that is convictionally neutral?

Now the claim that an appeal to empirical evidence is convictionally neutral rests on the assumption that we all have spread before us the same evidence. The only question that would then divide the theist from the non-theist is how to account for that common evidence. The atheist, it might be said, explains it parsimoniously and rationally by 'natural' means, but the theist gratuitously and irrationally insists on appeals to the 'supernatural.'

No doubt there are theists who have neatly divided their everyday 'natural' experiences and their 'supernatural' explanations of these experiences in this way, and to such theists Scriven's atheistic argument may be appropriate and sufficient. But there are also other sorts of believers, represented in the present essay by Ramsey, by Zuurdeeg, by Farrer, by van Buren, who differ from the non-believers not just in the explanation they give of the same facts, but in the facts they find to explain. Their world is a different world than Scriven's not because it contains miraculous signs and wonders (if indeed it does), but because it has pervasive characteristics which seem to require 'explanations' of a very different kind than the explanations provided by science. (Indeed, for some such believers, the success of science itself points beyond itself to the existence of God as much as does any other aspect of the world.)

We refer to the sense some people seem to have, both believers and nonbelievers, that the very *existence* of the world is itself a matter of wonder, a matter for awe. "For this is the truth we must reach to live, that everything *is* and we just in it."[27] It is not just that some believers *note* this phenomenon in themselves and others but the notice which they take of it which makes their world of facts significantly different from Scriven's. Thus we are not sure whether to say that they attend to different facts, or that they see the facts differently, or whether these two come in the end to the same thing. This sort of believer takes the world he finds to be itself 'supernatural' (to retain Scriven's term) and quite naturally seeks a 'supernatural explanation' and not just an unusual or unlikely natural one. He would agree with Scriven about the importance of rationality: consistency, examination of all the evidence, acting on the preponderance of the evidence, etc. He and Scriven would disagree, however, on how the evidence should be characterized and thus on what counts as a good explanation for it. Here, then, there is again a conflict of beliefs. And this belief, like the one about rationality, tends inevitably to be convictional since it determines as far as it goes one's stance toward the whole world.

We do not conclude from this that Scriven's conclusion is necessarily false or that his argument is invalid. We do find that certain of his premises are convictional. Not only his conception of what is rational but also his view of this world (about which, incidentally, the present writers disagree with each other). The theist may be mistaken in his conviction that the world is 'supernatural,' and the non-theist may be mistaken in supposing it to be 'natural.' But just as Farrer will not convince Scriven with arguments whose premises contain claims that the world is contingent or that free and finite selves entail Infinite Being, or that nature is designed, so Scriven will not convince such believers as Farrer with an argument resting on a presumption against the 'supernatural.' We are here faced with a convictional conflict which, while neither irrational nor in principle insuperable, will not be resolved by arguments that merely assume contrary convictions.

If we are right about Scriven and about Farrer; if our more general claim is true, and theistic and atheistic proofs *in general* depend upon premises which are the convictions of those who hold them, then the rational shortcut is at this point foreclosed, and we must return, in our search for the justification of conviction sets as wholes, to more gradual, roundabout, but we believe ultimately more satisfactory methods.

Another way of putting our point, perhaps terminologically more satisfactory, is to say, not that rationality or reason is unsatisfactory for establishing convictional conclusions, but that if reasonableness is to be the necessary and sufficient test of the adequacy of any conviction, we must gain an enlarged sense of what is reasonable, of the term "reasonable." Diogenes Allen has argued that one must distinguish between rationales for a given faith and the ground for faith which lies in the satisfaction by that faith of important human needs which cannot be so well satisfied in any other way.[28] In these terms, what Farrer and Scriven have been offering us in the part of their work we have considered has been rationales—reasons (extrinsic to the satisfaction offered by the beliefs for which they argue) to believe that these beliefs are true. An example of a satisfaction-ground, on the other hand, might be the experience of finding by faith the forgiveness of one's sins (Christianity), or the exhilarating discovery of liberation from an oppressive belief in God (secular atheism). Without exploring at this point whether these two kinds of reasons for embracing a conviction set can be separated, as Allen believes, we can note that his thrust is toward the effective enlargement of the current notion of reasonableness, so as to embrace not only questions of truth but also questions of satisfaction—the question of what makes life truly satisfactory. The considerations we have brought forward in the preceding pages seem to demand such an enlargement if there is to be any reasonable justification of anyone's convictions.

We have so far been dealing with proofs which (in our terms) have attempted to prove a presiding conviction by using doctrinal convictions (Farrer) or doctrinal convictions by using presiding convictions as premises (Scriven). Put in these terms, it is easy to see why such proofs would be convictional and therefore subject to the difficulties we have discussed. But suppose an argument could confront a presiding conviction directly. How would this affect our claim? To answer this question we propose an examination of the so-called ontological argument of St. Anselm.

We begin by noting a passing remark upon Anselm's argument made by a currently unfashionable British philosopher of the mid-twentieth century, R. G. Collingwood:

> What it proves is not that because our idea of God is an idea of *id quo maius cogitari nequit* therefore God exists, but that because our idea of God is an idea of *id quo maius cogitari nequit* we stand committed to belief in God's existence.[29]

At first reading, Collingwood seems to be saying that all that Anselm's argument can do is to prove that we think what we think—a particularly vicious subjectivism. Notice, though, that Collingwood speaks, not of proving that we believe, but of proving that we stand committed to believe: whether we believe it or not is another matter. Now, "stands committed" seems to be another way of referring to those deep convictions by which we live, to convictions which are foundations of the form of life of a human community.

In fact, Collingwood further argued that the quest for absolute presuppositions—those presuppositions which prevail in a culture or civilization at a given time and which are 'absolute' not in the sense of being unchangeable but in the sense of not themselves presupposing anything more fundamental still was the proper business of that division of philosophy called metaphysics. "The analysis which detects absolute presuppositions I call metaphysical analysis."[30] Collingwood further believed that the metaphysics of Western culture, that is, the culture or civilization which replaced the Hellenic culture of antiquity, was ascertainably composed of fundamental *propositions* (which Collingwood, interestingly, sometimes called "convictions"[31]) not different from the "metaphysical doctrines" of Christian faith—the doctrines about the triune nature of God.

> A good deal of information about barbarians and Romans in the later Empire is now accessible even to persons who profess no special interest in the subject; and any reader who will spend a little time upon it can satisfy himself that it was not barbarian attacks that destroyed the Greco-Roman world. Further research will convince him that to this extent the Patristic diagnosis was correct: the 'pagan' world died because of its own failure to keep alive its own fundamental convictions.
>
> The Patristic writers not only saw this, but they assigned to it a cause, and proposed a remedy. The cause was a metaphysical cause. The 'pagan' world was failing to keep alive its own fundamental convictions, they said, because owing to faults in metaphysical analysis it had become confused as to what these convictions were. The remedy was a metaphysical remedy. It consisted, as they formulated it, in abandoning the faulty analysis and accepting a new and more accurate analysis, on the lines which I have indicated in this chapter.
>
> This new analysis they called the 'Catholic Faith'. The Catholic Faith, they said, is this: that we worship (note the metaphysical rubric) one God in trinity, and trinity in unity, neither confounding the ὑποστάσεις and, thus, reducing trinitarianism to unitarianism, nor dividing the οὐσία and thus converting the one

God into a committee of three. The three ὑποστάσεις, that is to say the three terms in virtue of whose distinctness they spoke of a trinity, they called respectively the Father, the Son, and the Holy Ghost. By believing in the Father they meant (always with reference solely to the procedure of natural science) absolutely presupposing that there is a world of nature which is always and indivisibly one world. By believing in the Son they meant absolutely presupposing that this one natural world is nevertheless a multiplicity of natural realms. By believing in the Holy Ghost they meant absolutely presupposing that the world of nature, throughout its entire fabric, is a world not merely of things but of events or movements.

These presuppositions must be made, they said, by any one who wished to be 'saved'; saved, that is to say, from the moral and intellectual bankruptcy, the collapse of science and civilization, which was overtaking the 'pagan' world.[32]

What Collingwood seems to be reflecting upon in these speculative lines is the connection between the leading ideas of a religious community, that is its presiding convictions, and the presiding convictions of the civilization to which the religious community stands in creative relationship. If what he says is correct, then the 'necessary' utterances, beliefs, or presuppositions of a community are those which ground the beliefs of that community in the conviction set and thus in the 'necessary' ideas or presuppositions of the civilization in which it appears.

Perhaps we can to some extent test this view and to that degree understand Collingwood more clearly by noting the modern history of criticism of Anselm's argument. A. C. McGill has pointed out in an essay[33] that in philosophy since the time of Kant this argument has been understood as attempting to move (illegitimately) from a purely mental concept to an existence which lies beyond the mental. From the fact that we can think of a being than whom no greater can be conceived, and from the premise that such a being's actual existence would constitute him a greater being than one who 'existed' as an object of thought alone, the argument tries to infer that the being than whom no greater can be conceived does in fact exist, or necessarily exists. And post-Kantian philosophers have in the main held that that inference is invalid.

Twentieth-century historical criticism, however, has argued that however correct these philosophers may have been in their criticism of the argument thus stated, its statement does an injustice to the argument of Anselm. (McGill, in fact, claims that the Anselmic form of the argument was not known either to Kant or to Thomas Aquinas, each of whom examined, not Anselm's work, but that of certain of his successors.) More particularly, twentieth-century historical critics have argued (1) that the Anselmic argument possessed a greater complexity than the philosophers have recognized, consisting at a minimum of three interconnected steps or stages, of which the argument cited above is but the first stage or step: the second stage is the argument to prove that the something-than-which-no-greater-can-be-conceived cannot be conceived as not existing, and the third stage (from *Proslogion* III, neglected, says McGill, by many philosophers) is to prove that this 'something' is actually the God contemplated in (Christian) theology, Creator of heaven and earth.[34] (2) The critics argue, further, that Anselm's motive in undertaking the argument has been misunderstood: his was not the rationalistic motive of establishing the existence of God by reasons which standing alone could refute disbelief, but was (on one view) the attempt of a believer to explicate for himself and his readers the content of his faith, or (on another view) the attempt of a mystical pilgrim toward God, Anselm himself, to use philosophical reflection as a kind of religious aphrodisiac, a means of arousing the religious vision, thus a means of finding God Himself.[35] This last view is supported by the fact that, as the name suggests, the entire *Proslogion* is offered by Anselm as a prayer, a cry to God. (3) Finally, the historical critics have attacked the philosophers in varying ways on the ground of their understanding of the rationale or logic of Anselm's argument. For example, one theory, widely held in the nineteenth century, is that the argument presupposes medieval or Platonic realism, the doctrine that ideas participate in the things which they represent, so that a real idea must represent reality itself. Thus, the historians argue, philosophic criticism cannot properly come to grips with Anselm unless it moves in the realm of such a doctrine of realism. This objection to the work of modern philosophers, however, seems not to take seriously the problem of truth. Philosophers will properly ask whether the realism which it is claimed Anselm depends upon is itself true.

When, however, McGill has surveyed in detail this and other proposed analyses of the rationale of Anselm's argument and has pointed out the difficulties in each, he finally concludes that "the traditional [i.e., rationalistic] view . . . has fallen out of favor, but no broadly accepted alternative has been found."[36] McGill has provided us with an interpretation of his own which (he feels) overcomes that problem. He believes that the modern attempts to find a rationale are all "actually shaped by a common but unrecognized principle, and perhaps that principle is so alien to Anselm that no fully satisfactory interpretation can be achieved."[37] What is this principle?

In the first place, McGill calls attention to the stress which Anselm places upon the *words* which are used, particularly the words of the key phrase, "that than which nothing greater can be conceived." Thus, Anselm says, "However, when this very same fool *hears what I say,* when he *hears* of 'something than which nothing greater can be conceived,' he certainly understands what he hears."[38] And again, in the "Reply" to Gaunilo, Anselm is content to rest his case upon the meaning of the words, and the very *utterance* of them.

> [Anselm] argues that "something than which nothing greater can be conceived" must exist in reality, because otherwise it would contradict *the meaning of these words*. Since he makes no efforts to authorize and verify his phrase, Gaunilo directs some of his most vigorous attacks against this point. How can anything true ever be known simply on the basis of a word heard? In the face of this criticism, however, Anselm simply reaffirms his position. "In my argument nothing else is needed except uttering (*sonat*) the words, 'that than which a greater cannot be conceived.' "
>
> . . .
>
> The description of "conceiving what is heard" from the preacher is exactly parallel to the account of the atheist which Anselm gives in *Reply* VII. In the one case, the believer would never have faith if the preacher's *words* had not first communicated *their meaning* to him. In the other case, the unbeliever denies what is called "God" because he does not know the *meaning of this word.*[39]

However, modern interpreters (and here McGill means, apparently, both the modern philosophers and the modern historical critics) unanimously reject the principle that words can produce knowledge. Moderns, he says, regard language as an epiphenomenon.

> Men use it to *express* or *externalize* whatever lies within their minds. Words, they believe, do not produce thought—thought produces words and gives them whatever significance they may have. This means that if we want to find the meaning of any statement, we must discover what those who use it *have in mind*. We must penetrate their subjectivity.

> Every interpretation of the argument written during the last
> two centuries has been controlled by this hermeneutic prin-
> ciple.[40]

And McGill goes on to claim, against "this subjectivist theory of
language," that an understanding of the *power* and *meaning* of
language would overthrow the inadequacies of the last two centuries of interpretation and enable us to see how the Anselmic
argument works in its own right.

Now, not all that McGill says here is clear. We do not understand how "thought produces words," or how "words produce
thought," either. McGill seems to express himself concerning the
"power" of words in almost an animistic or a mythical fashion.
Yet what he says seems to be interpretable at many points in
terms which we have developed. If we think of our "words" not in
the sense of vocables or locutions, but as our utterances, our
speech-acts, we too want to speak of their objective power. They
have illocutionary force, or rather we exert such force with our
words, our speech-acts. If we can understand Anselm's talk of
uttering (*sonat*), not in terms of the production of physical
sounds, but in terms of the production of linguistic acts; if, that is,
Anselm's talk about something-than-which-nothing-greater-can-
be-conceived can be accounted for in the terms which we have
employed, then such language indeed has objective status. That
does not mean that we merely shift from the claim that "Thinking
it makes it so" to the claim that "Saying it makes it so." While the
former is a distortion of Anselm's argument, the latter is a distortion not only of his argument but of all we say in this essay.
Rather the elements, the several sentences, of Anselm's argument
are to be treated as speech-acts, and they are therefore subject to
the sort of examination for happiness to which we have subjected
another religious speech-act, Aleph's G. In particular, the conclusion of the Anselmic argument

> T$_a$ This God (the being than whom nothing greater can be
>   conceived) necessarily exists

is subject to such analysis.

If the analysis is carried out, what is revealed? It appears that T$_a$
functions for Anselm and for those who share his conviction set as
what we have called a presiding conviction and that Anselm's
argument is to show that T$_a$ does function as a presupposition in
Anselm's conviction set. That is why Anselm finds that denials of
T$_a$ issue in nonsense. Controversies over the validity of the argu-

ment, then, are not pointless—rather, they are efforts to discover whether T_a truly and consistently presides over this set. Thus, those philosophers or 'rationalists' who claim that Anselm's is a purely rational argument have a point. For it is rational in the only way the human mind can be, with not a wordless but a linguistic rationality.

However, there is also a point in the claim that Anselm's argument is a theological argument, which presupposes the faith of the community, or the convictions which embody that faith. This is not negated by the fact that it sometimes takes account of the 'fool' who in a way does and in a way does not participate in that community of speakers. For in the argument the fool is one whose claim ("There is no God") is intelligible to the community, though it is necessarily false. Certainly, Anselm's is not an 'argument from authority' or 'from revelation' in the sense that Anselm was in any special or self-conscious way constricted or constrained in his rational inquiry. He was constrained by the conceptual or linguistic resources which were available to him in the conviction set which he embraced, but that is a characteristically human (rather than any special authoritarian) limitation. In saying that the argument is theological, then, we mean both to say that it is theological in the definitional sense that it is an exploration of the convictions within a conviction set in their interrelations and in their relation to whatever there is;[41] and theological as well in the narrower sense that in the argument Anselm is inquiring about the kind of God who is presupposed by the significance of the language which his linguistic community speaks.

This understanding of the argument and its conclusion T_a further suggests the role which the argument plays in intellectual and theological life today. It may be that Anselm lived in what Paul Tillich called a "theonomous" age. It seems evident that we do not. The existence of God is in no sense taken for granted in our times. Yet it is noteworthy that debate on the validity and force of the ontological argument is at least as lively in the twentieth century as that between Anselm and Gaunilo in the eleventh.[42] Both Norman Malcolm and Charles Hartshorne have put forward versions of the argument, and J. N. Findlay has written a kind of obverse ontological argument designed to show that on its terms God cannot exist.[43] As interesting as this debate is for its technical logical and semantic contributions and for its biographical disclosures concerning various philosophers, it also has a broader and more profound interest. Those philosophers and theologians engaged in it, like Anselm nine centuries earlier, are attempting to discover the foundations of their convictions, to set out the fundamental connections which give their lives the coherence they have. This is not a merely personal or subjective task. The logic and semantics involved are not Norman Malcolm's or J. N. Findlay's, but those of a language they share with each other and with us. And the convictions, if they are not so unequivocally shared, are the convictions of substantial portions of the world whose historical antecedents are Israel, Greece, and Rome. To the extent that we are in this world, we can hardly fail to be interested in the outcome of a dispute concerning its intellectual and convictional foundations. Even if one is separated from or alien to a world, to define one's stance in opposition to it requires a conception of what one is denying. If on the other hand one today wishes to share Anselm's faith, it is significant that such sharing is of a sort which requires restatement of the Anselmic argument in present-day terms.

In all the forms of the ontological arguments, it is either asserted or presupposed that there is a necessary connection among the ideas of goodness, coherence, perfection, and existence, while these ideas necessarily conflict with evil, incoherence, and non-existence. Looked at in one way, disputes about the validity of the argument are really about one or more of these alleged connections. Those who hold that the argument is valid take these connections to be pretty much as the argument implies. Those who find it invalid, take at least one of them (and usually all) to be contingent or even doubtful, so that the argument crumbles. But what is the basis for this finding of necessary connection or the lack of it? It must be the way in which these connections are related to the rest of our concepts, how they fit into the language of those who offer and criticize these arguments. Perhaps, then, the different assessments of these connections reflect different conceptual schemes. If this is so, each philosopher, both one who like Malcolm finds the argument valid and one who like Findlay finds it invalid, may be making a legitimate claim: what he says being faithful or true to the conceptual scheme or conviction set in which he participates. And the finding of validity or invalidity would then come to the same thing as the claim that T_a (or the like) does or does not preside over this (perhaps very general) set of convictions. If this is what he meant, Collingwood was right.

The argument at this point appears to lead to what in chapter 1 we called hard perspectivism: the view that those with a given conviction set are inevitably permanently foreclosed from assessing the beliefs of those with any other conviction set. In fact, as we intend to show, hard perspectivism is not a consequence of our view. But the convictional plurality we are here addressing, as well as our method, does make it a live option, which can be rejected only after some argument. At least in some way we must take account of the fact that what purports to be a purely philosophical argument (the ontological argument) seems to be appraised so nearly along the lines of the prior theological or anti-theological beliefs of the appraisers.

We have been examining the content of one conviction which appears in some conviction sets, notably in Christian ones, with a view to discovering the role such a presupposition can play in the set and the way in which, if at all, it can be singly validated. The Anselmic argument for the existence of God has as its conclusion such a conviction. The point of the argument is to establish the conviction's presiding and presuppositional status. If the ontological argument is valid it does establish that status, and that is all the success it can have. What the argument cannot do is to establish the validity of the argument independent of the conviction set of its users; therefore if the argument is considered in a non-theistic conviction set, it will appear (and be) invalid. And what if it is considered apart from all conviction sets, apart from all linguistic frameworks? But what could such a question mean? To ask that question is to ask what our form of life would be if we had no form of life.

II. Scientific Reason

If pure reason, in the form of self-evident truth or deductive proof, cannot dissolve convictional barriers or leap over them, there is another candidate for these tasks, scientific reason, which will no doubt seem more promising to many a late-twentieth-century reader. Scientific methods are a subtle and powerful blend of experience (in the form of experiment and observation) and reason (in the form of constructs and theories) and their products, the special sciences, have performed so many wonders, from the early triumphs of astronomy to the latest exploits of microbiology, that we have become very cautious about setting limits to their achievements. This caution is especially evident among non-scientists, notably among religious scholars. Surely, some will suppose, a sufficiently careful, subtle, and industrious application of the methods and results of the sciences could determine which of the various competing conviction sets are truly worthy of belief. If that supposition were true, convictional conflict would not disappear immediately, of course, but we could be reasonably confident that with the spread of scientific knowledge and education in the methods of the sciences it would inevitably decline. What differences remained would be differences between those embracing the one scientifically established conviction set and would presumably yield in time to scientific investigation or to scientific education.

Our position here will be similar to the one we have adopted with respect to pure reason. The achievements of science are undeniable; its methods are indispensable to a whole range of problems; therefore our actions should take account of scientific discoveries and methods wherever they are relevant. Our contention is that science is nevertheless a convictionally governed activity and therefore limited in its capacity to settle differences reflecting differing conviction sets. Support of that contention is our next order of business.

Suppose that one should try to assess all conviction sets from the standpoint of the natural sciences. As the word "standpoint" suggests, such an assessment is itself undertaken from a certain stance having its own presuppositions, e.g., that experiments and observations of certain kinds are reliable devices for establishing sound conclusions. If someone, whether or not he is a professional scientist,[44] governs his conduct and determines the acceptability of his beliefs by these presuppositions, then they play a central role in his life, the same role that the Marxist, Christian, or anarchist presuppositions play for their holders. They cannot themselves be justified by the use of scientific methods, for the methods depend on the presuppositions. The apparently non-convictional claim that the methods of science 'work' is not really non-convictional at all. For what counts as working, and what they work for, are determined at least in part by one's convictions about what is valuable and one's (convictional) criteria for rationality, reliable experience, and the like. The consequence is that scientific utterances and those which logically depend on them are in the same situation as utterances belonging to other activities. To understand a particular scientific statement—for example, "Water is composed of two gases"—we must understand the sense of the theoretical terms as well as the relations the statement has with other parts of scientific theory and with observations. Indeed, what we consider an observation report will be determined in part by our acceptance of standards derived from scientific presuppositions. If, in a particular science, we count telescopic sightings, photographic plates, and radar blips, but not dream reports, drug-induced visions, or astrological charts, one reason is the compatibility of counting the former and the incompatibility of counting the latter with our scientific presuppositions. On the other hand, the fact that statements are understood and even accepted within a science does not provide sufficient ground for assenting to them unless we have other grounds for accepting the convictions (or presuppositions) on which they in turn are based.

The growing success and prestige of science in our epoch to some extent obscured the convictional nature of science, for so far as it shared in the thought of the dominant (scientific) culture, the world was increasingly evangelized to accept as convictions the presuppositions of science. This spread of the presuppositions or tenets of a culture meant that it became increasingly easy to justify other beliefs by an appeal to the accepted ones, which were in this case scientific. We must remember, however, that self-defined success, especially short-run success, is not its own justification and that scientific presuppositions still stand in need of justification if they are to be critically maintained. One sort of challenge to such dominant presuppositions, and one which might not seem too farfetched in our times, would be the widespread breakdown of scientific civilization. In any case, the phenomenon of the spread of science, and not the convictionlessness or convictional neutrality of moderns, is the explanation of the failure of religious views which too evidently ran counter to scientific beliefs. And, just as science, or Protestantism, or 'free enterprise' may challenge previous systems by offering convictional alternatives, they in turn may be challenged on the same basis.

On the other hand, it seems inappropriate for scientific convictions to be judged from the standpoint of other, perhaps rival, non-scientific ones. At least it is not self-evident that the scientific enterprise can be or needs to be justified by alien premises brought in from other realms of human life—say from religion or metaphysics or ethics. Our present concern, however, is with the claim that science is to be the judge of other conviction sets, and our claim is that we may not allow it *a priori* to assume such a role any more than we may grant that right to any other conviction set.

As a test of our argument about the convictional limitations of science, let us ask how one might scientifically assess the convic-

tion that baptism cleanses away sin. Begin with a simplistic account. One might observe a baptism and note its effects: the body
immersed in water, the exchange of words, the emergence of the
candidate dripping wet, and so forth. Such observations, together
with what has already been established about water (chemical
composition, boiling and freezing temperature, etc.) and about
human psychology and biology, will warrant a variety of conclusions about what can and what cannot be cleansed away: soil and
pollen can be, tuberculosis and cancer cannot. And what about sin?
Well, we can't observe the sin; indeed, we cannot understand what
"sin" means (what sin is) until we can understand how it figures in
the speech-acts of the community of users of the term. Consider
the parallel in the case of promising. However clearly we hear the
sound of A's promise to B and the sound of B's acceptance, we
cannot at that level observe the obligation (to perform as A has
promised) being created or assumed. The obligation, like the
cleansing of sin, can be understood only by understanding the way
in which the language of the community of users (promisers or
baptizers) functions. And the situation regarding Aleph's G (chapter 3) is similar. Whether God led the Israelites can be established
only after we understand what those who confess this event mean
in making that confession. Someone will object that sin can after
all be observed. Do not the Christian Scriptures (it is Christian
baptism which is here considered) list certain sins: adultery, for
example? And have not certain Christians (G. K. Chesterton?)
remarked that original sin was the one empirically verifiable
doctrine—just look around you, they say. But we could claim to
"observe the sin" only if we *did* regard that hypothesis as suitable,
only, that is, if we saw how the term figured in the speech-acts of
the community of users of the term and entered sympathetically
into its use in that fashion, which would be going beyond empirical evidence narrowly construed and ourselves adopting (at least in
imaginative understanding) the community conviction.

It would be unwise, therefore, for any community of believers
to draw too much comfort from the claim that their convinced
beliefs are empirically supported. We need to remind ourselves
that there was a community of users of the appellation "witch"
and that thousands of witch identifications (and self-identifica-
tions!) were made in that community. Were there witches? If we
say no, we must grant that the fact that an utterance has a place in
a linguistic community does not by itself show that its use by that
community, even what they would take to be its happy use, stands

justified. This point applies equally to all the various sorts of utterance. The fact that in a particular linguistic community there is a conventional device available for enslaving men or putting them in debt or making them kings does not justify slavery, debt, or monarchy, or the beliefs and convictions which those practices require.

The (public) *identification* of a witch, the *coronation* of a king, the *assignment* of one man to another as a slave, are all speech-acts, more or less complex and more or less mingled with other acts. The speech-acts have conditions for their happy utterance—primary, affective, and representative. These conditions are often dependent on one another. As we saw in the case of Aleph's G, checking on 'the facts' (the representative condition) may involve being in a certain position (part of the primary condition) which in turn involves having certain intentions and feelings (the affective condition). The linguistic propriety of the act implies the possibility of fulfillment of all of these. To identify someone as a witch was to adopt a certain set of attitudes and intentions toward the identified person. But that attitude was appropriate only in virtue of certain alleged facts, including the fact that the person had certain sorts of powers and the fact that these powers were the result of certain kinds of relations with demonic beings. In those communities where witch identifications were treated as linguistically appropriate, the possibility of fulfilling the representative conditions was granted, though of course it was possible to argue that they were not fulfilled in any particular case. Given such 'facts,' one could within limits also argue what the appropriate attitude was. The modern (scientific?) view tends to deny the possibility of the representative conditions ever being fulfilled. Thus we moderns regard the attitudes expressed by the identification of someone as a witch as always inappropriate and even the linguistic form ("Mrs. Jones is a witch") is regarded as hyperbole or as a sign of a defect in the accuser.[45] The typical modern view, then, is not merely that Mrs. Jones is not a witch or that there are no witches (now, in the United States) but that there could not be and thus never have been witches. Thus, "There were witches in Salem" is like "Ceres blessed the crops of the Romans."

Beliefs that there are or were kings or slaves are cases which differ in just the degree to which these differ from witches. While the status of monarchs and of slaves has been undergirded by convictions regarding both 'mythical' and 'natural' attributes in various cultures, the 'mythical' attributes have faded into the background of our modern view, so that it may seem easy for us to acknowledge that whoever was treated as a king *was* a king. We do this without regard to the foundation of that treatment in a belief in the divine investiture of monarchs, while we are reluctant to assert that whoever was treated as a witch was a witch. Yet two facts should be weighed in this reckoning: those who in the twentieth century want to recover the institutions of monarchy or slavery often give as reasons the existence of the 'mythical' attributes as well as the 'natural'; whereas those who have opposed slavery and monarchy have strongly argued for the absence of the alleged supernatural differences between persons. Such reformers have implied that an institution which fostered awe of kings and the impressing of slaves was, in the absence of these differences, not merely unjust, but crazy—a lunatic delusion of its perpetrators. Which is the way witch-hunts seem to us.

It follows that we cannot hope to justify a conviction or social practice to those who do not share the conviction simply by pointing out that some community holds the conviction or engages in the practice. If no more could be done than this, then justification across convictional boundaries would be impossible. On the other hand, the understanding of a conviction 'from the inside' *is* an important, indeed essential, step in criticizing or justifying it. To understand 'from the inside' does not necessarily mean accepting the conviction, but it does mean understanding the significance given to it by those who do accept it—understanding the speech-acts they perform in teaching, defining, defending, and attacking it. Attempting to explain a conviction without this kind of understanding leads either to an explanation of a different conviction or to explaining it away.

Consider Vilfredo Pareto's scientific explanation of Christian baptism.

> Christians have the custom of baptism. If one knew the Christian procedure only one would not know whether and how it could be analyzed. Moreover, we have an explanation of it: We are told that the rite of baptism is celebrated in order to remove original sin. That still is not enough. . . . But we do have other facts of that type. The pagans too had lustral water, and they used it for purposes of purification. . . . In cases where taboos have been violated, certain rites remove the pollution that a person has incurred in one set of circumstances or another. So the circle of similar facts widens, and in the great variety of devices and in the many explanations that are given for their use the thing which remains constant is the feeling, the sentiment,

that the integrity of an individual which has been altered by certain causes, real or imaginary, can be restored by certain rites. . . . The human being has a vague feeling that water somehow cleanses moral as well as material pollutions. However, he does not, as a rule, justify his conduct in that manner. The explanation would be far too simple. So he goes looking for something more complicated, more pretentious, and readily finds what he is looking for.[46]

Pareto is here applying what he calls the "logico-experimental method" to the social and religious practice of baptism. But has he succeeded in giving an account of baptism at all? He has managed to designate a class of similar phenomena which includes Christian baptism, but only by ignoring (indeed, denying) the account of baptism given by its practitioners. On what basis does he do this? Not by showing the Christian account he mentions to be inconsistent, dishonest, disputed by other Christians, hypocritical, vague, or unintelligible (any of which might be true, but the proof of which would require Pareto to examine the account). Rather, he rejects it because the explanation the adherents offer does not meet his own previously established standards of appropriate explanation. Regarded thus 'from the outside,' the immersion of persons in water in ceremonial contexts may all seem similar. But *regarded from the outside*, can any sense at all be given to any of the apparently similar actions? Even in Pareto's account, concepts like "lustral water," "pollution," "individual integrity," perhaps even "cleansing," rest on the account given by those engaging in the practices. Suppose we should remove from those accounts even these references, since they are unobservable according to Pareto's standards. Nothing would then remain beyond references to gross bodily movements and the utterance of now unintelligible words. That would mean removing all interest from the practices as human social phenomena.

On the other hand, if we allow some part of the accounts given by the adherents to the practices to govern our classifications, how are we to choose which part to accept? If the standard is amenability to explanation by our theories, that would not only violate the notion of independent confirmation central to scientific method, it would also make clear that the resultant explanation was based on our convictions about the nature of facts, observations, explanations, etc. But the apparent alternative, examining each account on its merits, requires that 'understanding from the inside' which Pareto eschews.

The root error in Pareto's account, as we see it, is the assumption that the non-speech behavior of people and their speech-acts are related as (say) the seeding of clouds and the occurrence of rain: perhaps connected, perhaps not, but regarded as distinct and independent. In contrast, we regard speech-acts and social practices as connected logically, each giving significance to the other. Our discussion of the conditions for happy utterance makes this explicit. If our view is accepted, it is clear both why Pareto goes wrong and how to correct his error.

We have not chosen Pareto's account of baptism because we regard its method as typical of, or necessary to, the social sciences. We are not trying to prove that the social sciences are impossible, or even inferior to the natural sciences (whatever that might mean). We do regard Pareto's errors as endemic to a particular approach to the social sciences, one which assumes that these sciences are non-convictional and which also assumes that human actions can be regarded as simply bodily movements plus perhaps certain thoughts or attitudes plus perhaps certain words. The two assumptions are closely linked, of course. For if the social sciences were conviction-neutral, their descriptions and explanations of the human actions which they study would be logically independent of the convictions held by the agents being investigated. But actions and convictions could be independent of one another in this way only if the convictions were irrelevant to the description or explanation of the action. In sum, the social scientist's explanations are not in the required sense conviction-neutral, because (1) they are logically linked to his (social-scientist) convictions, while at the same time (2) they may rival or support the community's own explanations, which in turn are logically linked both with the explained practices and with the convictions of the community.

Another way of seeing that this linkage is unavoidable is to note that in order to be recognizable as social phenomena, actions must be connected to some aim of the community in which they occur—even if it is a superstitious or illusory aim. Regarding the community's view of its aim as irrelevant and thereby breaking the logical link between action and aim (say between baptism and the point or purpose of baptism) is intelligible only if (as Pareto does) one furnishes some other aim which one attributes to the community. At this point the alleged neutrality or objectivity of the approach becomes altogether spurious.

The preceding argument of course constitutes no denial of the integrity of the procedures of the natural sciences. Many of our readers, we assume, as well as we ourselves, would adhere to the natural sciences' methods as a matter of conviction. However, a systematic error appears when these methods are simply taken over for the explanation and understanding of convictions. For convictions require to be understood 'from the inside' in a way in which the objects of the natural sciences do not. Moreover, if not only understanding but justification is the goal of inquiry, a vicious circle appears, because one rival conviction set (the scientific one) is allowed the privileged role of judge of the other. Our tentative conclusion is that science's usefulness in understanding convictions is achieved only by disqualifying it as the (impartial) judge of convictions. Certainly many of Pareto's successors in social science theory have been sensitive to this point as he was not.[47]

Can such practices as baptism be justified, or even understood, outside the community of baptizers? So far we have ruled out one answer—that which bases itself on the model of the natural sciences and holds that whatever can be affirmed or denied is necessarily a proper object of investigation by these methods. And we have shown that one contrary view is also inadequate, namely the view that no sense can be attached to the question (raised by outsiders) of what baptism means or whether it is justified because the very existence of a community which holds that baptism removes original sin shows that this is a reasonable or well-established conviction. However, we wish to postpone our constructive argument against this hard perspectivism to the following chapter. We merely note here the importance of remaining aware, in any such dispute, of the fact of plurality.

But there is another discipline, the 'science of religion' (*Religionswissenschaft*, also called comparative religion, history of religions) which we have not yet considered. Since this is the science (rather than physics or sociology) whose special field of investigation is religion, some might hope that from this new discipline, having its own methodology appropriate to its subject matter, there can come the desired scientific and impartial settlement of our questions.

In considering this possibility, we must first note a sharp methodological division within the field itself between a 'confessional' school and a 'phenomenological' school. The former, characterized by Hendrik Kraemer and A. T. van Leeuwen,[48] assumes a theological stance and from this stance attempts to relate religions and religion to the (normative) gospel of Christ. Since it thus deliberately occupies convictional ground, its avowed presuppositions are logical homogenes of convictions to be investigated and cannot justify the latter but, like them, stand in need of justification. That is, if on the basis of convictions A, B, and C, one practices a certain science which yields, upon empirical investigation, results d, e, and f, one cannot then without circularity employ merely d, e, and f to justify or criticize either A, B, C or any other conviction set X, Y, Z, where X, Y, Z is a logical alternative to A, B, C. Thus the confessional school is not in position to provide the purported shortcut to justification, nor does it claim to be.

Does the work of the 'phenomenological' school of Mircea Eliade and those who work as he does[49] offer such a solution to our problem? It would be easy to show by direct quotation from the writings of this group of investigators that they do not see their work in this way either. Joachim Wach, for example, writes in a definitive programmatic essay that *Religionswissenschaft* "does not ask the question 'what must I believe?' but 'what is there that is believed?' "[50] It may be useful, however, to show, by a brief examination of the work of the history of religions school, why, and in what sense, this is necessarily true.

We must first recognize that, compared to theology, *Religionswissenschaft* does indeed attain a significant new level of convictional neutrality or impartiality. The religionist approaches the study of a religion not his own with warm sympathy. By reading its documents, by travel to its land, and (especially) by living intercourse with its contemporary practitioners, he acquires a feel for that religion which enables him to understand and interpret its content. These methods are applied not to one religion but to many. The resultant historical data can then be laid side by side, and a 'comparison' yields, not a preference for one religion rather than another, but rather general insights into the nature of religion. Like patterns appear in religion after religion; these patterns can be interpreted by reference to the individual sympathetic investigation just described, and the yield will be a general understanding of the common content and the differentia; in short, an understanding of (this part of) 'the religious outlook' itself.[51]

For example, the religionist may sympathetically collect and then correlate various myths and doctrines relating to sacred time (the time of religious feasts, of Sundays, the time of the occurrence of religious rituals, the time of prototypical or mythical events, etc.). He notes then the common element in these myths and doctrines—in this case, we may say, the view that hierophanic or sacred interludes are all disclosures which reveal, besides ordinary profane or everyday time, another 'time,' sacred time, which is 'absolute' or 'supernatural' or 'superhistoric.'[52] Thus religio-scientific investigation yields a view of the way things (on one religious view) really are, yields a view of reality, a metaphysical viewpoint.

What we should like to know, however, is whether the viewpoint or insight thus gained is *true.* Is there a sacred time? Is the disclosure veritable? Is there any 'absolute' or 'supernatural' or 'superhistoric' ontological realm? Does the science answer the questions which it so clearly raises? One investigator in the field who has honestly faced this question is a Muslim historian of religions, I.R.A. Al Faruqi. He notes that three steps or stages are required in the work of history of religions: first, the reportage or collection of data; second, the "construction of meaning-wholes," that is, the systematization of the data with respect to a particular religion (note that this differs from the Eliade procedure outlined above).[53] Now, however, says Al Faruqi, the religionist is confronted with a variety of meaning-wholes, each (with minor historical exceptions) claiming to be the truth and the whole truth, each merely juxtaposed alongside others which make rival claims. The religionist cannot be content with stopping here. As academician, his concern is above all with the truth. But to present the "meaning-wholes" of the religions and acquiesce in their pluralism is mere cynicism. What must be done, then, is to take a third step, to *judge* the meaning-wholes. To do this is, however, to move on to a kind of "meta-religion," which does not look on the several religions as expressions of a common essence but moves to that deeper reality which underlies all and is common to all, not at the level of "figurizations and conceptualizations," but at the level of a "deeper-lying substratum."[54] And what is the content of this substratum? Why, it is there disclosed that men are standing in "Being's multi-levelled structure," in such a way that they can rationally know God as Creator and can distinguish themselves from other levels of Being by virtue of their possession of "understanding" and "spirit."[55] In this third stage, it seems plain, Al Faruqi has ceased to be the scientific investigator and has become the metaphysician. But how this particular metaphysical enterprise is to be supported is not perfectly clear to us; what is clear is that in the pursuit of truth about religious truth-claims Al Faruqi finds himself appealing to the same sort of rationality which we have considered (and found to be necessarily based on convictions) in the first part of the present chapter. The arguments for going beyond the first two steps or stages of religious inquiry are surely reasonable ones, but in going beyond them he goes beyond any possibility of convictional neutrality as well. And of course the same would be true if atheism, or radical pluralism, or some other stance had been posited in the third step. The point is, not that this was a treacherous or unseemly step, but that any such step will be a step on convictional ground.

Not all phenomenologists of religion are interested in thus becoming metaphysicians or rational theologians. However, attention to their work reveals that, even so, a related problem confronts the most cautious of scientific investigators. For, as we pointed out in connection with science and rationality in general, any particular exercise of scientific rationality presupposes some convictions, so that these convictions themselves cannot without circularity be derived from the data being investigated. This is pointed out for the history of religions in essays by two contributors to the volume in which the Wach article quoted above appears. First, Charles H. Long, in an exploration of the interpretive methods and assumptions which have been employed in the history of religions, shows how from Tylor and Müller in the nineteenth century to Ricoeur and Eliade in our own time, hermeneutic commitments and historical data have interacted in producing the changed outlook of the field as a whole. While Long is quite cautious in his own assessment of "the manner by which the religious phenomena [which science recovers] may be interpolated into our lives,"[56] he believes that the hermeneutical problem in the investigation of archaic religions leads back to a problem about the "archaism of the subject," that is, about the depths of the personality of the investigator, "the shadows of his ego and history."[57] This certainly seems far removed from the possibility that we can find in the science of religions a short way to the objective, scientific justification of some one set of convictions.

A second contributor to the same collection, Kees W. Bolle, is even more explicit in showing that in his view there is in the science of religions no conviction-free starting point and no possibility of interpreting religious phenomena without occupying a hermeneutical standpoint.[58] This is not to say that all possible standpoints are equally viable. Bolle notes that two stances, that of a *philosophia perennis* which is determined to treat all religious phenomena as essentially identical and that of a crisis or positive theology which addresses only particular situations and brings to them concrete moral or theological judgments, are alike unsuited to the task of history of religions. As Wach had earlier noted, history of religions is one of those human disciplines (along with theology, jurisprudence, classical philology) in which the normative question, "what is the image of man?" necessarily arises and which must therefore develop significant heremeneutical theories in order to do their work.[59] The two stances just mentioned cannot do this. Therefore the next question for the scientist, says Bolle, is naturally to ask if there is some hermeneutic which makes it possible "to study religious phenomena *without* setting oneself up as a judge over these phenomena in some individual way or other."[60] Such a hermeneutic must be able to do justice to the universal character of the phenomena, as well as to their changing form.

The actual candidates, Bolle believes, are chiefly three, though he mentions a fourth (and, as we shall see, in a somewhat different class a fifth). The three are a hermeneutic based on Catholicism, one based on Marxism, and one based on what he calls "spiritualism," or a theory of "human creativity" or "cultural creativity." The fourth is that of "the thorough, skeptical, historical-critical scholar."[61] Bolle does not regard this list as exhaustive and clearly regards roughly the same considerations as applying to all the types. Since he does not indicate that the fourth type is in any important way different from the others and does not say very clearly what he means by this type, and since it seems clear that the first two types are instances of hermeneutics based on well-known conviction sets, let us attend to the third, "cultural creativity," which Bolle identifies as Eliade's own view. Bolle believes that the third type also implies "a philosophical stance,"[62] requiring the recognition of the involvement of one's own tradition in the attempt to understand the religion of another people. In the hermeneutic of creativity, it is recognized that no religious symbol can without loss or remainder be translated into the language of the modern West. What is instead possible (and here we seem to find the converse of Long's "archaism of the subject") is bringing the symbol into the life of the investigator so that it functions creatively in his life. "Creativity" is thus not mere novelty; it is, says Bolle, "rather more artistic than that; it is the establishment of human order out of chaos on the basis of the (re)discovered coherence of a symbolism."[63]

What, then, of the question of truth? asks Bolle. Once we have acknowledged that hermeneutical involvements are inescapable and yet in some measure arbitrary functions of individual temperament (all of us cannot be required, says Bolle, to adopt one hermeneutical stance) and once we have recognized that in the history of religions the hermeneutical involvement adopted does not imply a foolproof system but, at best, indicates the direction of scientific inquiry, can we say any more about truth and falsity? It is noteworthy that Bolle asks this question at the beginning of the section of his paper subtitled "Theology?" Are there theological certainties which one can either justly bring to, or rightly infer from, the work of history of religions? We note that (the special nuance introduced by the term "theology" aside) this is a restatement of the central question of the present chapter.

Bolle's answer to this question is a complex one. First, as already said, some hermeneutical starting points show themselves more suitable than others; the viable hermeneutic will be one which permits corporate (as opposed to mere individual) judgments in the field, and it will apply the same criteria to one's own tradition as to alien ones.[64] Bolle wrestles with the proposal that 'Christian faith' is a significantly different (fifth) hermeneutical standpoint. Does the claim that faith is not a phenomenon (Van der Leeuw), and the claim that, therefore, starting from faith is something different than starting from any religious tradition, entitle faith to a special role as a hermeneutical principle? Bolle here issues a firm warning: Christian faith can and does make unique doctrinal claims; e.g., God is revealed in Jesus Christ. It is therefore a faith which has a content and which is dangerously liable to the kind of provincialism that will defeat the work of history of religions. Especially is there the danger of seeing "the others" (pagans, heathens) in contrast with the "we" (who have true religion, revealed religion). When this occurs, 'faith' has become a hindrance not a help. "No hermeneutic can be introduced along the line of such categories since they do not even come up to the level of ordinary human understanding."[65]

Finally, however, Bolle (who writes as a Christian) introduces two practical suggestions. Let us consider them in turn.

My [first] suggestion is that the lack of true respect for "the other" is immediately related to the Christian's lack of humility in himself before God. I mean this both in a very concrete, practical way and with respect to the formation of hermeneutical theories.[66]

What Bolle seems to mean by this is that the historian of religion who would make 'Christian faith' his hermeneutic should be reminded by that faith that in the investigation of "the other's" religion, the Christian is required humbly to expect to learn something worthwhile. This is well illustrated in the history of religions, says Bolle, by the work of Father Wilhelm Schmidt and his followers. However outmoded Schmidt's "high God" methodology may be, it is noteworthy that here was "a whole gr.... of people who were not just faithful Christians, *but who expected to learn something of the utmost theological importance frcm the peoples they studied.*"[67] The fact that the Schmidt research was productive suggests the value of this expectation.

Bolle's second practical suggestion is less clearly stated:

> What the general historian may be forced to admit by experience with his subject matter—that he must serve man by contributing to the orientation of his own world—should be self-evident for the historian of religions who has any inkling of theology.[68]

We take this to mean that the historian of religions whose hermeneutic is 'Christian faith' is to be guided by his study of religions into the constructive criticism of this faith—"his own world." This is taught the Christian, says Bolle, by instances in the New Testament in which 'insiders' learned something crucial from 'outsiders'—Jesus from the Syro-Phoenician woman; Peter from the centurion Cornelius. To those who would arrogantly exclude the religious voice of lesser and ancient peoples, Bolle would reply ("not so much as a historian of religions but as a conservative theologian"):

> Did not Jesus Christ descend to hell principally because he was interested in ancient *homo religiosus* as well as in modern ecumenicists? It may be doubtful theology to speculate on the details of His service down there; but that He did not go down as the risen, triumphant Lord—but just a little earlier—adds one more encouragement for the study of the general History of Religions with a sound and subservient hermeneutic.[69]

Thus the question about truth and theology leads one investigator into so subtle and far-ranging a reflection upon the relationship between truth, hermeneutics, faith, and theology.

It is not part of our program to follow Bolle in examining the special possibilities of Christian faith as a supposition or hermeneutic principle or conviction set. However, one aspect of what he says will be useful to us for our own purposes. In order to see this, let us review the scope of *Religionswissenschaft* as it is now presented. Concerning the question of a scientific method of settling convictional disagreements, we find a spectrum of possibilities. At one end of the spectrum the discipline appears most clearly objective, 'scientific,' and factual. At this pole, the science has no cause to yearn for ontological or convictional truth, for it is fully occupied in discovering facts about the religious life of mankind. The procedures in which this end of the spectrum specializes are quite valuable in their own right. Similarly, if there were a science called 'phanology,' consisting in the study of the plan and function of temples ancient and modern, it would be no reproach to that discipline if it failed to decide on our behalf whether those temples *ought* to have been built, or whether the worship they contain deserved to survive. So it is with the science of religion at its objective pole. By its nature, like 'phanology,' it must omit the question of the value, the relevance, the truth of the rites under examination.

At the other end of the spectrum, however, the questions we are interested in do arise, either as relevant philosophical questions in the mind of the scientist (Al Faruqi), or as necessary hermeneutical questions which affect the success of the investigation (Long), or as finally theological questions which nevertheless both affect and are affected by the investigation itself (Bolle). When this pole is prominent, the science of religion is indeed seen as relevant for the inquiry about justifying conviction sets, only now the interaction between the observed religious practices and the guiding convictions of the observer is clearly so complex that it makes no sense to speak of this process as a scientific or rational *shortcut* to the justification of convictions.

Consider again the proposals Bolle makes for intercourse between the conviction set of the inquirer and the object of his inquiry—the religions in all their multiform variety. Only this time let us ignore the specific Christian form of Bolle's proposals. There is the inquirer, then, who has his own convictions. Some of these are necessary if there is to be any rational activity of inquiry at all,[70] while others will become evident from the particular hermeneutical method which this inquirer adopts as his own. On the other hand, there is the religious material under investigation, itself convictional to the extent that it expresses the pervasive life style of some people, somewhere, at some time. Bolle is suggesting that neither set of convictions can be overlooked or overridden without dishonesty or ineptness. The object set is there, and it provides the investigator with a challenge to come to it with a subject set (or the hermeneutic which the subject set makes possible) sufficiently broad and insightful to cause the object to be seen. Meanwhile, the subject set is there, too, and Bolle believes that one of its member convictions should be the sort of humility which will permit the investigator to see truly and which will permit him, as well, to correct or enlarge or rediscover the subject set by the light shed from the object. Such interaction between subject and object, or in general between two sets of convictions, is precisely one of the themes we must explore philosophically in the coming chapter.

Our immediate conclusion is that neither *Religionswissenschaft* nor any other science fulfills the ideal standards we have tentatively explored in the present chapter. We do believe that there is, or can be, a plural 'science of convictions' which functions as the investigator or adjudicator of all conviction sets, and we will develop this thesis in the final chapter. However, we must admit at once that this 'science' cannot be conviction-free, cannot occupy neutral ground with respect to all convictions, and therefore cannot escape the human condition in answering the human questions concerning what we may believe and do and be. Meanwhile, we have found no single, swift solution to the problem of convictional justification. But why should we expect to find one? Convictions, being those beliefs which govern all our lives, must be judged in the court of all our experience—and that of our ancestors and progeny as well. Nevertheless, our discussion of these problems has yielded results which will help us to delineate the task of justification. To this delineation we now turn.

6

If good or bad acts of will do alter the world, it can only be the limits
of the world that they alter, not the facts, not what can be expressed
by means of language.

In short their effect must be that it becomes an altogether different
world. It must, so to speak, wax and wane as a whole.

The world of the happy man is a different one from that of the
unhappy man.

Ludwig Wittgenstein[1]

It is my impression that many philosophers do not like Wittgenstein's
comparing what he calls his 'methods' to therapies; but for me part of
what he means by this comparison is brought out in thinking of the
progress of psychoanalytic therapy. The more one learns, so to speak,
the hang of oneself, and mounts one's problems, the less one is able to
say what one has learned; not because you have forgotten what it was,
but because nothing you said would seem like an answer or a solution:
there is no longer any question or problem which your words would
match. You have reached conviction, but not about a proposition; and
consistency, but not in a theory. You are different, what you recognize
as problems are different, your world is different.

Stanley Cavell[2]

The Process
of Justification

WE HAVE NOW BROUGHT INTO SHARPER RELIEF THE DISCORDANT
state of affairs presented in chapter 1, our existence in a plural
world whose inhabitants disagree about many things that matter
most. It is not merely that we do not agree: we cannot even
clearly disagree. The preceding chapter explored the claim that by
pure science or pure reason, plurality, so far as it is a problem, can
be straightway overcome. We saw that these claimants do not take
convictional disputes with sufficient seriousness—a fault of all the
shunt proposals for justifying or rejecting convictions. The examination of these shortcut solutions has not been time wasted, nor
merely the disposing of objections to our own thesis; we need such
enterprises as science and reason in the justificatory task, and even
the drive to eliminate convictions may be fruitful in some circumstances.

We now turn our attention to a challenge from those who take
pluralism not too lightly, but too seriously. These see plurality not
merely as a cause for concern, but as a reason for surrender. They
embrace pluralism either with skeptical satisfaction or with sloth-
ful despair: "We are all in convictional prisons; we cannot escape
them if we would." Such hard perspectivists would hold that "I
am my convictions" (that tantalizing motto) means that we are no
more able to adjudicate our convictions across convictional lines
than we are able to jump out of our own skins. To refute this
position will be a hard task if, as they claim, it is immune to
external argument in this way.

But there is a general argument against hard perspectivists: their
view if taken seriously is paradoxical to the point of self-
contradiction. For they hold, first, that one can only view reality
from his own perspective, and, second, that they know perfectly
well that interconvictional justification or criticism of convictions

157

is not possible from *any* perspective. If as they claim they are so enclosed in their own perspective, how can they know what is impossible to all others? If on the other hand they retreat to the claim that at least transconvictional criticisms cannot penetrate *their* perspective, we can respect their testimony about their own view of the matter without assuming that this view is correct. But if they acknowledge that they may be wrong about the convictional prisons in which others are confined, may they not also be mistaken about possible ways of escape from and access to their own outlook? If all this is conceded, hard perspectivism seems a shaky theory indeed. Yet if we are to reject it, we need assurance that transconvictional criticism and justification can indeed occur. We must now show the possibility of this occurrence, or (to speak more accurately) the possibility of this process.

I. The Language of the Process

Both non-perspectivists and hard perspectivists tend to judge the possibility of justifying religious convictions, or disputed convictions of other sorts, without recognizing the historical contingency of the state of affairs they are judging. The present state of religion in the Western world is a historical novelty. For a very long time the Western intellectual and spiritual heritage, Hellenic, Hebraic, and Christian, was not seriously challenged by any outside tradition. There were, of course, Jews as an implicit challenge to Christians, and Christians as an explicit challenge (or threat) to Jews, but that controversy, like the party struggles within the Christian religion itself, could be understood as a family quarrel within a single convictional community. (The more terrible the outcome of those quarrels, the more apt the analogy, for it is ever our kinsman whom we murder.) The Muslim threat to the West was ended by the end of the Middle Ages. From then until the nineteenth century encounters of voyagers and traders, explorers and missionaries with those outside the Western tradition were regarded more as oddities and marvels than as problems for justification across convictional lines.[3] To the degree that convictional differences within the Western family *did* appear profound, they tended to be settled by means of spatial separation—*cuius regio eius religio,* "as goes the sovereignty, so goes the worship," sufficed to define Protestant-Catholic relations, and the ghetto sufficed for the Jew—rather than by one's justifying his belief in terms the other could comprehend, and so the question of inter-convictional adjudication did not forcefully arise.

Thus the pluralist consciousness which is characteristic of con-temporary culture is a relatively recent arrival in our intellectual tradition. If we have found ways to handle the problems it presents, this may be a function of the novelty of the situation. We hold that our solution of these problems is sure to be a time-consuming task, more likely to be measured in centuries than in shorter seasons of time. It will take time to show that secular atheism (or Anabaptist Christianity, or Maoist Marxism, or Vedan-tic Hinduism) is or is not an adequate conviction set, or the adequate conviction set. Present confusion in these matters, then, is not necessarily hopeless or pointless; time may well yield satis-factory changes in our state of convictional disorder. But the passage of time, though it may be necessary, is rarely sufficient for the resolving of serious problems, any more than it is for produc-ing maturity in a newborn infant.

Indeed, our theory of speech-acts and their relation to convic-tions suggests that this analogy is worth more attention. Consider the situation of an infant learning its 'native' tongue. The earliest cooings, gurgles, and blurts of sound give way, ever so gradually, to primitive speech-acts: "da da," or "go by-by," or (perhaps least mistakable) "me!" So crude are these at the outset that listeners are not sure whether the linguistic level, as opposed to mere imitative cries, has been attained: in any case the child's progress depends in part upon very generous appreciation of every success. Part of the learning of a language is saying it the wrong way; that is, issuing speech-acts which are in a variety of ways and degrees unhappy. Yet there is promise in precisely these unhappy utter-ances: once past the threshold, they are indeed functional speech-acts, and the loving family makes even the most ludicrous beginner's talk the occasion for congratulation and shared joy as well as for merriment. Nor is this congratulation in any way ironic; the technically unhappy utterances are stages on the way to happy ones.

Are such circumstances in any way like the circumstances of men of diverse convictional communities living through a time of learning how they may in their pluralist age happily talk together, or justifiably embrace some set of convictions? The illustration is, of course, inept; it presupposes the established linguistic world of adults as a norm which measures the present unhappiness in the

speech of the infant learners. But if we can imagine a race of babes
on its own, groping to know what to say, disagreeing with one
another in many ways, and struggling toward a language in which
to express their disagreements, the analogy acquires considerable
strength. In that way, this infant race represents our own.

As a second suggestive analogy consider a time of political
upheaval in which a traditional monarchy is seized by a fit of
republican fervor. Royalty is deposed, denied its divine right to
rule, denied all monarchical rights. There *are* no kings among us, it
is said. But the discarded 'king' lives on in his country. Was he
once a king? To say that he was is to admit a term which is denied
all status on the new egalitarian theory. On the other hand, to
avoid saying that he once was king makes it difficult to explain
what the revolution has achieved. The time of linguistic uncertainty has come. Neither "we once had kings" nor "we never had
kings" seems quite adequate to the situation. But with the passing
of the years, remembered (and even surviving) kings, no longer a
threat to republicanism, are again mentionable. "Look, there's old
King Julio; I remember when he was the king." Has "king"
acquired a new meaning, then? It seems more accurate to say not
that the *word* has changed but that everything has changed,
including those words once so unspeakable. If anyone believes that
this story of kings is a parable, we shall not quarrel with him, only
adding that similar stories could be told of institutional change
inseparable from linguistic, using "property," or "slaves," or perhaps "witches" in the place of "kings."[4]

Similar crises appear in other fields. Thomas Kuhn records one
in connection with the discovery of oxygen.[5] Who discovered it?
Of the two principal candidates for this honor, one, Joseph Priest-
ly, collected gas released by heated red oxide of mercury and
identified it in 1774 as nitrous oxide and in 1775 as "common air
with less than its usual quantity of phlogiston." The other, An-
toine Lavoisier, started later, but held by 1775 that the gas thus
obtained was a distinct species, one of the two chief constituents
of air, a conclusion Priestley never accepted. So far Lavoisier may
appear the winner, since Priestley never knew what he had found.
Yet Lavoisier's claim, too, must be questioned, for throughout his
days he held that oxygen was "an atomic 'Principle of acidity,' "
while oxygen gas, he thought, resulted only from the union of that
'principle' with caloric, the 'matter' of heat. Was oxygen then not
yet 'discovered' in 1777? Perhaps not, but, says Kuhn,

the principle of acidity was not banished from chemistry until after 1810, and caloric lingered until the 1860's. Oxygen had become a standard chemical substance before either of those dates.[6]

What the history of science requires, Kuhn argues, is a changed understanding of what scientific discovery in such cases amounts to—a new view of the role of anomalies, of scientific paradigms, and of the respective roles of 'theory' and of 'fact' in science, for "until the scientist has learned to see nature in a different way (i.e., acquired a new theory)—the new fact is not quite a scientific fact at all."[7] For us the story of the problematic 'discovery' of oxygen affords another illustration of the barriers to understanding raised by changing conceptions (and, Kuhn would add, changing scientific commitments), barriers at once conceptual and linguistic.

No one of these illustrations, the speech of infants, the linguistic crisis of a social upheaval, or the language changes involved in scientific revolutions, is a full analogue of the crisis of the justification of convictions confronted in contemporary convictional pluralism, but each suggests that the temporary unhappiness of language, or temporary unjustifiability of convictions, may be a necessary and thus desirable state on the way to long-run justifiability and happy utterance. On this view, we humans are a classroom of children learning to express happily our deepest prehensions—our generation (in Lessing's metaphor) a single school-day in the education of the human race.

Such a way of viewing the matter is not inimical to religion, or at least not inimical to all religious traditions. We spoke above of long periods when the shared convictions of our civilization faced no external challenge. It is helpful to remember that during these very periods the chief Western mystics flourished. Some philosophers like to point out that classical mysticism regards all talk about the mystical, including its own, as unsuitable. Often this fact receives ironic treatment—for the mystics nevertheless write such long discourses! But if there is irony here, it lies, according to the mystics, at a somewhat deeper level, not in the fact that they do speak, but in the very situation whereof they speak. For speak they must. Their talk, they feel, is at once inappropriate and unavoidable; in our terms unhappy but not meaningless, not mere babble.

Such a strand is even more deeply imbedded in the biblical

tradition. Thus the Apostle Paul characteristically speaks of (what we would call) religious knowledge as somehow flawed, obscured, partial. "For now we see through a glass, darkly; but then face to face: now I know in part; but then shall I know even as also I am known."[8] And he employs the illustration we have given a few paragraphs above: "When I was a child, I spake as a child, I understood as a child, I thought as a child. . . ."[9] In the realm of convictional utterance, Paul believed, he was still 'childish,' still inept; he awaited an eschatological time when this ineptitude would be removed.[10] Similar instances can be found in the speech of Jesus according to the gospels, and in the prophetic books of the Old Testament. Indeed our earlier remarks about a stable period when convictional speakers knew perfectly well 'what it was in order to say when' in matters of faith may have been misleading. The history of religions, or at least the history of prophetic religion, is the history of turmoil. The normative periods in such turbulent communities are not eras of stable continuity, but revolutionary times when talk of the gods is challenged (often in the name of the gods or of God) by the prophets.

On this view, it might appear that no authentic utterance can ever be acceptable to more than a prophetic minority to whom their own speech, however compelled they may be to utter it, will seem perplexingly at variance with recognized norms. Confessing that one's convictions are absurd, 'impossible,' or foolish is not, on the view of such saints, mere hyperbole. But while the apostolic message may seem foolish, it is "God's foolishness," and therefore wiser than conventional human wisdom.[11] While the apostle now speaks "as a child," he envisions a day when his talk will be mature; when he will know as he is known by God. Thus even the inspired minority appeals to 'wisdom' or 'knowledge' or 'mature speech' *in the long run*.[12] Since this is so, we may do well to move on from our examination of the imbedding of speech in communities to see how these considerations of justification may be affected by the appeal to what are usually called 'ultimate criteria.'

II. The Loci of the Process

Justification, as we have used the term, is not a once-and-for-all yes-or-no achievement but an ongoing task of any who have convictions. That task includes attempts to meet current objections and to present evidence to show that the conditions for happiness of one's convictional speech *can* be satisfied. We have already observed that claims for the adequacy of conviction sets have very often involved broad appeals to considerations like truth, consistency, *eudaimonia,* satisfaction, and righteousness. These considerations cannot be regarded as neutral, for they themselves are convictional in practice; nor are they universally accepted bases of justification, for they are the perennial battle-grounds of convictional warfare. Only their generality and vagueness makes it possible for them to be used so widely as appeals.

To argue here for a particular significance for these considerations or a particular use of them in debate would be an exercise in what we shall (in the final chapter) call theoretics—the assumption of a particular convictional stance and the offering of an *apologia* for it—rather than our present philosophical task of asking how such justifications can in general go. In any event, the appeals we have listed are not mutually exclusive nor is our list exhaustive. For example, it omits the compelling concept of *beauty,* though there are those who might allow it to do duty for all the rest, while others might insist on *peace, love, justice, holiness,* or still others. Moreover, anyone can refrain from appealing to any one of these considerations without being inconsistent or absurd. So we cannot argue that any one of them must be accepted as a criterion for a happy conviction set. But if there is no logically necessary member of the list, and no single list which will satisfy all comers, we think it better to regard the possible terms of all such lists, not as criteria but as possible *loci* of justification. To the traveler negotiating the traffic of justification these will appear as main intersections, junction points of reflection, criticism, debate, and correction. No one justifies his convictions without crossing some of these intersections; many find that they have to negotiate all that we have mentioned and others as well. That this is so is a contingent fact about our world—but it is about the only world, the only form of life, with which we have to do. What we will do here is to consider one important locus of justification, namely *truth,* in order to show how it plays the role we ascribe to the loci. We will then leave to the reader the task of applying our remarks to other loci.

Disagreement about the desirability of truth is extraordinary. Those who, like Braithwaite, hold that religious principles are themselves neither true nor false nevertheless regard it important that their own overall account of religion should be true. Conversely those who reject scientific investigation generally do so not because they question the goal of truth, but because they doubt the efficacy of science in attaining it, or because they see the work of science as conflicting with some other goal which they hold to be equally, or even more, important, or because they hold that another method than the scientific attains truth which disproves the 'truth' (as they say) of science. The widespread commitment to 'truth' implied in these examples has suggested to some that truth is an empty concept. Even in its high generality, however, a term like truth is not devoid of meaning: adoption of it as a goal, as Aristotle saw,[13] does limit the range of choices one may consistently make, though it does not sufficiently narrow that range. We will understand, for example, the man who in his search for truth puts more weight on 'correspondence' between statement and fact or on 'coherence' among statements, and we can be prepared for one who is more interested in 'performative' or in 'pragmatic' features of truth. Yet the failure of such specialized theories to carry the field suggests that the locus truth is broader than any one of them can show.[14]

It is not a part of our plan to engage in a systematic analysis of "truth" and "true." But it may be illuminating to call attention to the way in which one religious theorist, Wilfred Cantwell Smith, has employed the concept and to point out some of the assets and liabilities of his account. Smith notes some disparate uses of "true" in religion. Some speak of a particular religion's being true: "Christianity is true"; "Islam is true." But the difficulty here, he holds, is that it is not at all clear (except in very specialized contexts) what is meant. One possibility is that "Islam is true" means that present-day Islam conforms to prototypical Islam, Islam as revealed by God to Muhammad. Here "true" means "genuine" or "authentic." But to claim that the prototype is true in the sense just indicated would be trivial. Is there any other sense? Smith doubts that there is. Religions, he holds, are not just statements or sentences—they are living historic realities and as such no more to be judged true or false than Mt. Everest is to be judged true or false—it is just *there*.

> Like Mt. Everest, you may like them, or you may not; you may decide to climb them, or you may not; you may feel that you can trust them to bear your weight or not, or the weight of those who, unlike you, have pitched their tents on their slopes.

Yet whatever your attitude to them, they are more like Mt. Everest than they are like a proposition in science. The latter may be true or false, but historical facts and social institutions are existent actualities.[15]

So on this view we cannot speak of a "true" religion (save in the sense "authentic" or "genuine"). Yet Smith claims that we can speak of "true religious life," or "the truth of *my* Christianity (Islam, Buddhism)," and correspondingly of the "truth" of this or that man's Christianity (etc.), and that we can speak of this man's Christianity being "truer than" the Christianity of that man. By such use, he means to distinguish between the man whose religion is mere outward form or show, and the man whose religion is inner life.

We have no quarrel with this use, but we note that there remains a difference, which Smith's account cannot make clear, between sincere attachment to a false belief and hypocritical profession of a true belief. The convictional protestations of a fraud or hypocrite need to be marked as faulty, but they need to be so marked without confusing the issue of the truth or falsity of that about which he is hypocritical. In the assessment of Aleph's speech-act, *one* kind of unhappiness (representative) was liable to arise through the failure of Israel to have crossed the Reed Sea, or God to be God; *another* through Aleph's failure to take up the appropriate stance of one who was issuing such a confession, and to witness thereto, or to fail in the intentions and behavior which are the affective implicates of his speech-act. It was in the latter that questions such as sincerity and hypocrisy were examined, while it was in connection with the former that questions of truth arose.

But it may now be objected that we have argued in a circle. When the justification of individual convictions was at issue, we remarked that in many and crucial cases convictions would stand or fall with the set in which they inhered, the total outlook to which they gave spine. Now we are discussing in summary certain considerations which enter into the justification of whole sets, yet we refer to the earlier discussion of the representative aspect of *particular* speech-acts. Is the reader then in the position of a man handed a card, on the front and back of which is printed merely "See other side"? Not quite. For the interconnected justification of many related convictions, though more arduous, may not be so barren as would the assessment of any one of them while disregarding the others. The assessor of the truth of conviction sets may be like the interpreter of an unclear photograph, composed of many blurred spots and indefinite blotches. Attention to the spots alone (the several singular convictions) may never yield results. Yet the interpretation of the whole photograph cannot be achieved save by bringing each blurred part of it as sharply as possible into focus.

Take this question about the 'truth of' a theistic religion such as Christianity, or of a meta-historical theory of history such as Marxism, or of a typical Western convictional outlook such as free enterprise economy. In such systems, there will be beliefs having representative dimensions relatively easy to examine for truth value, and other representations much harder to bring under such assessment, as our earlier examples have shown. To be sure religions are not mere sets of beliefs—recognition of just this led us to the notion of convictions, beliefs which are crucial clues to life and character. Thus we showed a connection between belief and life even while providing for a discriminable central set of beliefs which could be assessed and found worthy or unworthy. In doing this, moreover, we were prepared to give up the idea that *truth alone* could discriminate worthy from unworthy convictions. So the considerations besides true or false which Smith urges may enter into the assessment of the religion of a given tribe:

> beautiful or ugly, edifying or wicked, rational or grotesque, poetic or prosaic, helpful or obstructive, cohesive or disruptive; . . . the opiate of people, or the form of social progress; the channel through which they know God insofar as they do know Him, or a totally human contrivance. . . .[16]

are all ones which we would regard as potential canons of the adequacy of the conviction set which the tribal religion embodies and reflects, the canons being applied either directly to the convictions themselves, or to the life with which they can be linked by the rules of meaning we have investigated. It seems reasonable that the process of justification should take hold where it can as it can, seeking to know the truth of those convictions capable of direct assessment, the coherence with these of others, and seeking to apply to all the convictions the further relevant considerations—*eudaimonia*, righteousness, and the like.

While the sort of inquiry represented in these pages by Scriven and Farrer produced, we showed, no knock-down, conviction-free results, yet the considerations to which they respectively appealed are certainly relevant to belief in the existence and nature of God, and similar considerations would be relevant to the truth of other religious (or metaphysical) conviction sets. But "true" and "false" are not the only possible assessments. Very often someone will say of a conviction that it is "truer" than another, or that it is the "truest" available, without wanting to claim that it is "true" *simpliciter*. At the same time, "true" and "false," as Austin and others have reminded us, are members of a class of terms which includes also "accurate" and "careless," "rough" and "exact," "fair" and "hasty," and a host of others.

Keeping the preceding cautions in mind, however, we can reiterate our insistence that truth may indeed appear among the loci when religion is at issue. We have recognized that such beliefs as the Christian belief in the existence of God are much more than mere beliefs—are obliged to be convictions if they are to be felicitous. At the same time, we said that characterizations of religious doctrine as "stories plus agapeistic intentions" or as "blik expressions" were an inadequate account of much ordinary religious talk. The conviction that the world is created (and thus that there truly is a Creator and a world) and the conviction that its Creator is Lord of all and active Redeemer of all are just what provide in traditional Christianity the grounds for the claim that the agapeistic way of life is (alone) satisfactory, that the sacrifices it demands cannot be in all senses vain or empty, that whatever the limits and failure of human effort, there is assurance that the poor, the merciful, the seekers of righteousness of whom Jesus spoke are indeed blessed. Likewise Mahayana Buddhism cannot in fidelity to its tradition be merely the inculcation of the Bodhisattva ideal; there must also be the real Manushi Buddhas, whose attainment of the ideal is not a mere tale, but the truth which must be told. These are obvious illustrations, but other, more agnostic styles of conviction also have their representative element, even if these are convictions about what is *not* the case— e.g., no hell in Universalism, no soul in Theravada Buddhism. Although our discussion has throughout insisted on the necessity of recognizing the other elements in convictional language, we have also been at pains to emphasize the widespread importance of this representative element. Without it, religious belief of the sorts we have studied here comes close to justifying the charge made by one of its concerned critics: it becomes only a "retreat to commitment."[17] We have argued above that there is no easy appeal 'to the facts' in questions of convictional difference: our apprehension of facts, the very kinds of facts there are, will be determined in part by the convictions we hold. Yet this does not free us from the task of referring to the discoverable facts, or adjusting our convictions themselves to the way things really are. To seek to do so is to take truth seriously. And if truth or falsity is irrelevant to the most important commitments we make, it will be difficult indeed to insist on the importance of truth in less momentous questions.

We can consider now more briefly the place of consistency among the loci. In a sense, it could be regarded as part of the locus truth. For an inconsistent conviction set is certain to have a false conviction. Consistency, on the other hand, can hardly stand alone. For hardly anyone will consciously embrace false or empty convictions on the mere ground that, being false or empty, they are (therefore) consistent. On the other hand, if someone is genuinely unconcerned with logical consistency, either in the use of his words or in the avoidance of contradictions, then all attempts at justification addressed to him are futile. But this concession in no way constitutes a victory for the irrationalist over his opponents or even a standoff between the two. The irrationalist can't *have* victories, not ones consistently so described; he never knows, is never in position to tell us, when defeat may be victory or victory defeat, for he has renounced such consistencies as knowing that. So they can't be victories from his point of view—he hasn't a point of view—and that hardly constitutes a defeat for the rest of us.

If on the other hand someone takes the position that while logical consistency is necessary he is perfectly content with practical inconsistencies in his life, we are on more intelligible and familiar ground. It is, however, no more comfortable ground for the skeptic. For to be unconcerned about consistency of this kind is tantamount to rejecting the idea of having any convictions other than whatever minimum is necessary to logical consistency itself. And this takes us back to an earlier argument (chapter 4), where we conceded that a person could set out to minimize his convictions, but argued that men who thus seek to make rudderless boats of their lives (1) do after all have *that* (apparently needless) conviction, and (2) turn out to be men who, not knowing what they want, are unable to plan their lives so as to get it, and thus seem especially likely not to live well, not to be happy men. In any case, they are in no position to justify their way of life, since they are men who forfeit every form of those appeals (such as to consistency and happiness) which are the very marrow of justification.

On the other hand it is not a logical necessity that men must have more than a minimal set of convictions. It is just that in general they do, and even more generally they are unhappy when they do not. This conclusion may be disappointing for those who hoped for some logical necessity on which to rest, *ne plus ultra*. It is important, however, to see that this hope is ephemeral. It is the contingent fact that human beings agree as much as they do that makes it possible for them to disagree and argue intelligibly. Men are not content with overt inconsistency; they prefer satisfaction to frustration; they are uncomfortable being ignorant or doubtful about the future. If there were not agreement on such matters, there would be no considerations to offer to incline others in one direction or another, and a shared life (in which justification and attempts to persuade and convert play an important role) would be impossible. There might not have been areas of such agreement; this shared life itself might not have existed; both these are logical possibilities. Given the existing agreements, appeals to these and to consistency are practical necessities in the task of justification, but they are not sufficient appeals; they do not enable us to discard other loci such as righteousness or justice. Influenced by different circumstances, different men may take their stand upon different loci.

To call the appeal to any particular locus no more than a "practical necessity," and to acknowledge that our common fund of agreement is only contingent, may seem to concede too much to unreason. If the loci are not logically required criteria, is there any hope of an acceptable justification? But this complaint forgets or ignores certain features of the complex task we call justification. Remember, first, that utter neglect of such a locus as truth has been seen to be extremely rare, to say the least. Remember, further, that any particular disagreement, even about which loci are to be considered, implies some sort of agreement as well. We should recognize, too, that not every difference in action (including speech-action) rests on a disagreement. Here we invoke in another way the temporal considerations with which we began our discussion of justification. Two persons living in different circumstances may act very differently, even though they have common convictions. A convinced Marxist living in an advanced industrial society will have very different tasks than one living in a rural, semifeudal society. Similar considerations evidently apply to

Jewish or to Christian conviction sets. Thus diverse actions may express shared convictions, and count for the justification-in-practice of the same convictions.

But if circumstances differ, so do men. No two men are exactly the same, and no man at a given time is exactly as he was or will be at other times. It is surely not effete skepticism, relativism, or irrationalism, but common sense both to recognize individual differences within our common humanity and to admit our own changes over the period of our lives. We may be equally devoted to health at seventeen and at forty-seven, but that does not mean that we eat, sleep, and exercise in the same ways at both ages. If, as we are arguing, justification in its broadest sense is a life-long process, we must recognize that fact when we are called upon for justification in its narrower sense of confronting current challenges and meeting them, and must qualify our claims for justifiability accordingly.

We change, and our circumstances change. In the next section we will consider some of the things which, facing certain challenges, men *do* to justify their convictions. There we will see that any device for justifying a conviction set must include some method for making it and its life style intelligible. Often this will require a reorientation, a redefinition of terms, even a change of stance on the part of the one to whom the justification is offered.

In a pluralist world, a conviction set for which changes cannot be induced will fail and deserve to fail as a long-range candidate for commitment. It is essential, however, to having convictions that one does not give them up lightly or in the face of short-run adversity. Indeed, of the most important convictions held by a man or a community we may say (definitionally?) that they are maintained even in face of death. A just man, a faithful man, an honest man must be prepared to be just, faithful, or honest even at the sacrifice of personal advantage, or lose claim to his title. It does not count against a certain style of life merely to say that the convictions it embraces are held dearer than that life. A readiness to sacrifice one's life may even be necessary to the justifiability of such convictions. It will, however, count as a criticism of a sacrifice that it is unworthy, or that the demand for sacrifice is unjustly distributed, or that the good achieved is not that satisfaction at which the sacrifice was aimed.

Within a community an appeal to one or more of the loci may answer a challenge regarding the justifiability of a single conviction: it may even effect a convictional change in those ripe for change. Within Aleph's community, for example, appeal to the facts (the truth) about the sea which *Yam Suph* designates effected a shift in G from Red Sea to Sea of Reeds. A more momentous theological revision in that community might lead to a changed view of the truth about God, and hence to a changed sense of "God" in some not yet expressed G. Where challenges to justification cross the lines of sharply differentiated convictional communities (Marxism *versus* classic liberalism, for example), appeals to truth or justice do not lack importance, but the canons of adjudication may be obscured by convictional disagreements over these loci themselves. In these cases, something more than a simple appeal to 'ultimate criteria' is therefore required. In such pluralist situations we can clearly see the function of the social matrices of justification, which we must now examine.

III. The Social Matrix of the Process

To see the role which the matrix may play, we remind ourselves that convictions are persistent beliefs, beliefs for many if not all seasons. A belief which cannot serve as a guide to other beliefs or actions through changes in time and circumstances simply will not have the persistence to recommend itself as a conviction. One of the recurrent problems faced by religious convictional communities is that many members of the community have identified the action appropriate to a conviction at a particular time and place with the whole meaning of that conviction for all times and places. Of course, if that identification is accurate, if the conviction's application *is* thus restricted, then as times change it will sooner or later cease to incline anyone to commit himself to it. Those who continue to profess (or confess) the conviction will become hypocritical, which is not only unhappy but inherently unstable. Those who cannot or will not become hypocrites will reject the conviction so construed, and will be regarded as modernists or heretics, especially by the hypocritical.

An illustration may be drawn from early Christianity, and another from early Marxism. Both these communities were at the outset apocalyptic. Their earliest adherents thought that dramatic changes, soon to take place, would overthrow the Kingdom of Satan (or selfish capitalism) and usher in the golden age, the Kingdom of Christ (or the classless society). Both were disappointed by the actual course of history. The disappointment was a threat to community existence. Rigorists held unyieldingly to their outmoded view. But both movements showed their vigor by their refusal to be destroyed as convictional communities by the localized disappointment. Surely, they said to themselves, there is *something* right in these beliefs of ours. What is it?

If the convictional community is fortunate, at this juncture a reformer will show by example and by argument how one can live an acceptable life (and perhaps die an acceptable death) guided by the (reformed) convictions of the community. Thereby he enables the community once again to enjoy a justifiable set of convictions. We will examine *reform* as our first example of a matrix of justificatory activity, then a contrasting social phenomenon which we label "interconvictional encounter," and finally, more briefly, some other matrix types which may lead to the challenge and to the justification of convictions.

When we speak of the reform of convictions, we imply a convictional distance between the reformers and their own community, although neither need be aware of this gap at the outset. Such reformers cannot be mere good housekeepers, asserting the community's fundamental convictions and urging conformity to these. For, if convictional reform is needed, it is precisely the relevance of those fundamental convictions which is in question. On the other hand, an appeal to a conviction inconsistent with or radically different from those already recognized is not reform at all but rejection (though obviously we are not dealing with an all-or-nothing question here). A common way of speaking about a conviction set that stands in need of reform is to say that it has 'lost its meaning,' just as one says that a conviction set 'has no meaning' to those who reject or ignore it.[18] Reformers are thus confronted with the task of showing that the conviction set is *or can become* meaningful.

How is this to be done? One method employed by reformers as well as others is what modern philosophers have called the persuasive definition.[19] Briefly described, persuasive definitions propose a (more or less covert) shift in the descriptive force of a term or phrase while maintaining its affective force unchanged. If being a Jew is not, or is no longer, to be understood as entailing circumcision and the acceptance of dietary regulations, but is instead having faith like Abraham's faith in God, then those favorably disposed toward Jewishness can maintain that disposition without being bound to circumcision and diet, though they will be bound to faith. If a 'real Christian' ("real" is a characteristic adjective of persuasive definitions) is not so much one who goes regularly to church and believes in the divinity of Christ, as one who sides with oppressed peoples and who believes in sharing their fate, then the attachment which Christians formerly felt for the old pattern is now to be given to the new.

How radical may such shifts be before the would-be reformer becomes instead a stranger and outsider? We must address this question, but first it will be helpful to examine still other techniques reformers may employ. Clearly a part of the problem confronted by any reformer is that of being correctly understood. If the justification of beliefs is inseparable from their understanding, being understood is not an optional aspect of successful reform, even though the reformer's convictional distance from his community is a crucial barrier to such understanding. In these cases, reformers may turn to paradox or parable.

Any examination of the teachings of Socrates and Jesus reveals an extraordinary use of paradox and (especially in the case of the latter) parable. These devices have been the subject of much discussion by both philosophers and literary critics.[20] While we cannot provide a full investigation of their significance, parable and paradox share several features which are of special interest to us at this point. Most obvious is their ability to bewilder, puzzle, and silence their hearers. How could it possibly be that he who saves his life shall lose it? or that it is better (more profitable!) to suffer rather than to do injustice? He who has ears, let him hear. But the listeners cannot believe their ears. Can those who are cursed and reviled be *blessed?* Can all those leaders of Athens be *ignorant?* How could a *Samaritan* be my neighbor?

Yet the discomfort produced by these stories and puzzles, even when it issues in silence, is not a stultifying or barren discomfort. Those who understand even a little of what Socrates and Jesus are saying are driven to find resolutions to the paradoxes and points to the stories. And—here is the crucial point for us—almost any resolution or point will mean some shift in the meaning of key terms like "ignorant," "blessed," "neighbor," and "justice." Conventional uses are no help, since they led to the puzzlement. Furthermore, often many resolutions are possible, and which one the listener adopts will depend on his openness, his imagination, his sensitivity to nuance, the hardness of his heart, the state of his soul ('heart' and 'soul,' if you like).

Thus the community may find its reformer demanding of it a reformation in the form of a self-discovery, a revision of convictions which is a recovery of authentic community, a re-formation which is also a justification. Is it a justification of the old set? Clearly there is a sense in which it is not, but if in some sense it is, this is because justification is finally the justification of persons in community, and by no means of beliefs apart from persons (or of persons apart from one another). If we grant, however, the newness as well as the historicity of the reformed conviction set, this does not count against our long-range purpose. For we are not seeking in the present book to show how any particular set may be justified, much less every set, but how some set may be. If such justification via reformation entails change, so be it.

The similarity between reformation and the next matrix we shall examine, the *interconvictional encounter,* will be evident. While reform seems to be strictly an insider-to-insider affair and encounter seems to involve groups external to one another, that distinction is too sharp to fit the facts. To the extent that those inside the convictional community are like those outside, apart from their convictional differences, a successful reformation will provide the basis for a successful missionary appeal as well. In making the conviction set the object of (or vehicle for) a renewed or revitalized commitment by those who were nominally convinced, the reformer also makes it a possible object of (or vehicle for) commitment by those who have previously been uncommitted or committed to a different conviction set. If, for example, both Jews and non-Jews fear death, then, to the extent that a Jesus can show that this fear can be overcome with a Jewish conviction set, he offers an inducement to the non-Jew to consider and perhaps accept that conviction set. Again, to the extent that both convinced scientists and non-scientists share a desire to control their environment, a Bacon will be able to attract converts to science at the same time he invigorates the interest of scientists. Thus, these modes of justificatory action are not so much exclusive categories as they are types, distinct timbres which social history orchestrates in a variety of ways.

As we have seen, convictions conflict not only within and between communities, but within the same person. Severe cases of such conflict can be found in prisons and mental hospitals, but most of us have experienced less serious conflicts of this sort at one time or another. Choices of career, of love and marriage, of political or religious allegiance are often painful, not merely because I cannot get my own way, but because I cannot *discover* my own way, cannot discover which of my conflicting convictions is to be surrendered in the interest of the other. It is such dilemmas which make Polonius' maxim "This above all, to thine own self be true"[21] an empty one, save when offered to perfect saints (who will not take it) or perfect knaves (who already believe it). Sometimes the dilemma ends in the wholehearted adoption of one and the giving up of the other conviction (conversions often take this form). Or we vacillate between the choices for a time, trying in some way to reconcile them. More rarely we try to isolate the conflicting sets in our thinking and acting and thereby ignore the conflict. (In the nineteenth century, many intellectuals of religious bent tried this form of solution of the science-religion controversy.) In the long run, however, conflicts between convictions cannot be disguised or ignored: God and Mammon decline a joint appointment, and even the most skillful hypocrite is rarely consistent.

What cases, then, do we characterize as interconvictional encounters? Ones in which representatives of distinct convictional communities meet one another in such a way that one or both parties are thereby convictionally changed. Such encounters range from the relatively benign meetings of the classroom and campus, through the clash and interplay of the social, ethnic, and religious groups in a wider society, to the deadly interaction of cultures epitomized by the meeting of East and West in twentieth-century Indochina. Not least, they include the friction, the fire, and (sometimes) the fruitful engagement in the meeting of diverse religious communities.

An interesting model of such encounters is provided by the Christian ecumenical movement, a movement marked by the successive appearance of 'correct' mutual disdain, of icebreaking courtesies, of a baffling inability to characterize disagreements in mutually acceptable ways, of the emergence of suppressed areas of agreement, and of the discovery of unknown realms of disagreement.[22] Following this model, it appears that a prime element in fruitful encounter must be the location of actual belief differences. As we know, this is a prime element in the work of justification as well. To understand an utterance, or a belief, is to know how it can (conceivably) go wrong; to hold it justifiable is to hold that it does not in fact go wrong in those ways. To this degree, at least, the work of meaningful encounter and the work of justification go hand in hand.

This may be seen more clearly by examining, with William Christian, the transformations we may effect in utterances in order to bring them into direct disagreement with one another.[23] Suppose a Christian issues the confession, A "Jesus is the Messiah." Now it makes sense to say that a Jew may not directly disagree with that utterance, even though he issues as *his* conviction "Jesus is not the Messiah." Not directly disagree, because the speakers do not mean the same thing by "Messiah." For the Jew, "Messiah" means a non-divine being who will restore ancient Israel, making a new nation of her, and bringing about a golden final age of history. For the Christian, "Messiah" means the promised Savior, who will save men from their sins. Since the two speakers mean different things, they have not yet directly disagreed, though of course they have not agreed, either. Doctrinal systems may seem hopelessly cut off from one another by such considerations, but there is a way in which the Jew and the Christian can talk on the same doctrinal topic. This involves the reformulation of the Christian's confession into B "Jesus is the one whom God promised to send to redeem Israel." On this, Jew and Christian can significantly disagree. To be sure, problems may remain. Do the Christian and the Jew have different concepts of Israel? Of God? (Perhaps even of "promise" and of "redeem"?) Still, the concepts may overlap enough to permit disagreement. If not, further reformulation may be needed whereby common elements in the two differing concepts are joined in a new predicate. This should become clear enough in the next illustration.

Suppose, says Professor Christian, there had arisen a dialog between the Apostle Paul and the Stoic philosopher, Seneca. If Seneca were confronted with utterance B above, he might respond that B is neither right nor wrong—it simply makes no sense. For God does not send people or promise things; God does not act in history. Yet it may be that Seneca's concept of God and Paul's concept of God overlap. Both might think, for example, that God rules the world. If (and only if) that is the case, Paul and Seneca might disagree on the following utterance, C "The being who rules the world acts in history." Thus we have moved from an apparent disagreement between Paul and Seneca to a real one. And via C, they may discover that they indirectly disagree about B and A as well.

If we are prepared to revise again we may widen still further the circle of those who are indirectly engaged over the original utterance, A. Suppose Paul encounters a Neoplatonist, say Plotinus. Plotinus may be as perplexed by C as Seneca was by B. For he may say, "The source of all being (to which I suppose you are referring) does not rule the world in any way at all, much less by acting in history . . . . what you are saying does not seem to make good sense."[24] If the game is to be played, then, C must be revised into D "The source of all being rules the world," and about this the Neoplatonist on one side, and Jew, Christian, and Stoic on the other, can disagree. At first sight it may appear churlish for religious speakers to seek, or for philosophers to seek for them, ways to *dis*agree. Yet as we indicate here, and as Christian goes on to show in a valuable concluding chapter of a second book, the logic of disagreement is an indispensable clue to the logic of agreement.[25]

It appears, then, that the participant in encounter can clarify his own convictions for the other by such transpositions, and this is surely a part of the practical logic of encounter. Justification would proceed as each member of the dialog sought to discover and to show how his originial convictions were related to his other convictions, and to whatever he knew to be the case about the world.

However, there is more to be said about this procedure. Suppose it is desirable to transform A into B, C, or D; it is then likely that the champion of A will spend more energy upon the justification of B, C, or D (depending upon who his opposite number is) than upon the justification of A. These may call for different sorts of backing, may interest their champion in different ways, call his attention to different facts, than did A. B brings him, say, to a study of the Hebrew Scriptures, C to an inquiry into the quality of human history, D to metaphysical explorations. To be sure, he might have come to all these inquiries in solitary intraconfessional doctrinal exploration of A, but in practice his procedures will be different. Not only does he engage in a wider range of inquiries; he does so against a different backdrop—that of his counterpart in the dialog.

Missionaries of the 'higher' religions such as Buddhism, Islam, and Christianity sometimes expect that an encounter between religions will result in mass conversions from one to the other. While individual conversions do occur, world history has not borne out the wider expectation. The main instances of mass conversion seem to be the conversion of 'primitive' peoples to one of the advanced religions. The missionary who seeks converts from advanced religions has had to be content with more modest achievements. On the other hand, some philosophers believe that the encounter of the world's religions will produce a single, syncretistic world faith.[26] While our investigation neither favors nor opposes such an outcome, it suggests that overt syncretism is not the inevitable result of dialog. Convictions being what they are, men do not yield them readily, nor with integrity. But the attempt to justify our convictions in the dialog does produce a reformulation and re-clustering of convictions not unlike the renewal involved in the work of the reformer. It is natural that such renewal be aimed at making the reformulated convictions more attractive to both partners in the dialog.

We have been investigating the logical character or structure of actual justification procedures; in order to do this we have examined some characteristic matrices of this process. From our examples it appears that the acquiring of a conviction set and the justification of the set are often simultaneous and always interrelated—not to be understood apart from one another. To speak of choosing one's conviction set is not necessarily wrong, but it may be misleading unless we recognize that "choosing one's convictions" is a shorthand way of talking about many choices made over a period of time, reinforcing one another, accumulating, developing in more and more definite directions until we find ourselves with a conviction set which we acknowledge as our own, as being the way of life, the outlook, which we have chosen.

The apparent counter-example to the preceding generalization is *conversion* or *enlightenment,* for in these matrices one finds oneself dramatically introduced into a new realm, as if a new creature. It would seem appropriate, then, to inquire how strongly such an apparent exception counts against the general rule just formulated, and how different the problem of justification of new convictions may be for the converted or enlightened one. "Conversion" can refer in a derivative way to any new formal attachment to a party, sect, or community. The primary sense, however, is broadly synonymous with the religious terms enlightenment, regeneration, new birth—phenomena which appear in many cultures and communities. In this sense, conversion may or may not involve a change in church membership or party allegiance; if it does, the importance of the external change is its signifying the internal—the new way in which the enlightened one views himself, his world, his god. What does surely characterize conversions is the radical reorientation, occuring dramatically in a few hours, days, or months, of all that is most important to the convert.

All—or is it all that is changed? It seems so. Consider, however, the paradigmatic cases of the conversion of Paul on the road to Damascus, and the enlightenment of Gotama under the bo tree.[27] Surely these are as radical cases of conversion as occur in the literature of religion: Saul the Rabbi, persecutor of Christians, becomes Paul the chief Christian preacher, theologian, apostle, martyr; Gotama the young Hindu prince and seeker becomes the Buddha, the Enlightened One, founder and teacher of the Way of the Lotus. Could there be more profound and sudden reversals? Yet in both cases, we must acknowledge, there were certain continuities as well. Saul/Paul had the same God before and after his conversion, however his conception of this God may have been modified. He revered the same Scriptures, kept the same feasts, worshipped (until ejected) in the same synagogues. One way of understanding the contribution of Paul to Christianity is to say that he brought the background of a broader, more Hellenic, more universalist Judaism to bear upon the narrowly Judean Jewishness of primitive Christianity. However sharp the contrast between Paul's pre- and post-conversion convictions is made to appear, there is still a great tract of continuity. The conversion itself cannot be grasped save within a *certain* context, and that context is Paul's earlier convictional orientation. Thus, when he set out, after his conversion, to explicate and justify the new convictions (as in *Romans*), his method was to relate these convictions to Hebrew Scripture, to the history and hopes of the Jewish people, to the outlook of the Hellenic world in which he had grown up (since he was not a Palestinian Jew), and to Paul's own pre-conversion struggle with 'law,' sin, and the meaning of death.

With allowance for changed circumstances, the same points can be made about Gotama. After the Enlightenment, his first disciples were the intimate friends of the years of his preceding quest. His teaching, the Four Noble Truths, consisted in the formulation of the question which the quest had implied, as well as in the answer to the quest provided in his enlightenment, was governed by the religious texture of the Hinduism from which it sprang. For example, the Buddha's steadfast refusal to give an (acceptable) answer to Hindu texture of the Hinduism from which it sprang. For example, the Buddha's steadfast refusal to give an (acceptable) answer to Hindu questions about God and the soul can be understood as first of all an attempt to correct the distorted otherworldliness of Hindu religion (distorted, of course, from the convictional viewpoint of the Buddha) without rejecting the doctrines of karma and re-birth which he saw as central to that outlook.

Summarizing, we may say that dramatic conversions do indeed contain new convictional elements, but that (1) these are imbedded in a changing body of convictional material; (2) the previous convictional history of the convert contains the seeds of the new material that flowers in the conversion process; (3) in many cases, the conversion is a symbolic concentration representing changes which either precede or succeed it, as well as the changes of the luminous moment itself. And it is in this longer process of change that the convictional revisions occur which justify, as well as being justified by, the concentrated changes of a 'second birth.'

What conversion is to the individual convictional pilgrimage, *revolution* is to the journey of a whole community. We call attention to only one side of revolution, disregarding both its violence and its role as arbiter in the struggle for social power. Our interest is in revolution as the revision of man's understanding of himself and his place in the world. Seen in this way, revolutionary vision may be described as judging the present world by the canons of the world that is to be; against present and (by his lights) reactionary values, the revolutionary pleads the values of the future about to be born. Thus, unlike the reformer, the revolutionary cannot appeal to the authentic tradition of the community against current deterioration of that tradition; the justification he offers is to be found not in the past but in the unattained revolutionary goal. This futurity is at once the lure and the liability of his program viewed in its justifying power, for what he is attesting to is by definition not presently available. This goes far to explain the difficulty and perhaps also the attractiveness of convictional revolution.

> The *revolutionary* wants to change the world; he wants to project into the future, to an order of values which he invents. ... The *rebel* has a need to maintain intact the abuses from which he suffers in order to be able to rebel against them.[28]

That Sartrian aphorism suggests our next matrix of change, that of *rebellion*. It also suggests that the rebel is sometimes unfavorably compared with the revolutionary. Even petulant rebellion may be understood in convictional terms: the cartoon of a white-bearded old man in Confederate uniform, holding the Stars and Bars and snarling, "Forget, hell!" represents a legion who are convinced that the present is insufferably wrong. Such a conviction, however, is not necessarily unworthy. It may be supported, as it is in Sartre's aphorism and in the cartoonist's parody, by the self-deception of an idealized and thus irrecoverable past; on the other hand, it may be a stance which is more clear-eyed and realistic than that of the revolutionary. The latter rebel appeals neither to the past nor to the future, but says of the present order simply, this is wrong.

How justifiable convictional rebellion may be depends, then, as much upon the unsatisfactory state of the community's current convictions as upon any alternative which the rebel may have to offer. In the worst of all possible convictional worlds, the rebel's singular conviction is justified by that world itself. However, not every rebellion occurs in such a world, and perhaps Sartre and Camus are right to typify the rebel in unflattering terms.[29] For the rebel may be one whose significance is found almost wholly in terms of that against which he rebels, while the complete failure of that establishment would be the end of his own convictional existence. Professional anti-Catholics, anti-communists, anti-Semites lead a convictionally precarious existence, which may help explain the ardor of their protestations and the venom of some of their actions.

Finally, we mention one matrix which has perhaps played a larger role in philosophical works on religion than in real life justificatory activity. This is the *quest* for the best or best possible set of convictions. The quester goes tentatively from outlook to outlook, from stance to stance, testing each and finally adopting none, until the fully satisfactory, or most satisfactory, is discovered. This may seem to be the course of some personal histories—Gotama to his enlightenment; Justin Martyr to his Christian conversion—but we doubt that it is a fully accurate characterization. For if the quester maintained a continuous selfhood he cannot have been free of a continuing (though perhaps ill-realized) set of convictions all through the quest. And the idea of tentative exploration of alternative life commitments would seem to preclude the seriousness that would make justification of certain of those alternatives possible. There are today a few religious eclectics who roam over the world of religious knowledge and experience trying on theologies, religions, outlooks, myths, rituals as a shopper tries on hats. Some have approvingly dubbed such gourmet eclecticism 'pluralism,' but it seems to us that this misunderstands the roamers. Religious (or irreligious) convictions, in the present sense, are not a decoration to be added at will to human character—they *are* human character brought to expression. The culture-taster or the religious role-player may be doing something of personal or of sociological interest, but he cannot be trying on convictions and discarding them—we *are* our convictions.

On the other hand, there may be more serious quests, and two of these are worth mentioning, though they are in some tension with one another. Though the quester cannot (purposefully) make a conviction-free pilgrimage, he may on his quest enrich his prior set in such a way as to make it justifiable, or more justifiable. So one sort of quest may be a deliberate and open search for inter-convictional encounters, and these may even produce the sorts of enlightenment or conversion referred to above, in which belief and life seem to tumble together into a happy new pattern.[30]

The second serious sort of quest is of even more general interest. The quester may be at bottom a questioner or *skeptic,* whose present convictions include the determination to challenge every possible conviction, retaining only the refined set which survives such examination. We have spoken of the move to elimin-ate all convictions, and of the absurdity to which that leads, and have urged instead the general usefulness of a principle of fallibili-ty in any conviction set.[31] In this way we have given special endorsement to the place of skepticism in the justificatory task.

Mention of the principle of fallibility, and of others' viewpoints, reminds us of our earlier controversy with the hard perspectivists, and leads us to conclude this section on the social matrices of justification with a fresh reflection on the question, in whose eyes must a justification be effective in order to be acceptable. The only possible answer is that a justification must be effective in the eyes of the community, or the individual, holding the conviction. If it is *not* justified in their eyes, in what sense is it a justification at all? (If I cannot see that my conviction is worth holding, it matters little that someone else thinks it is; if Muslims cannot see that they are right convictionally, it matters little that some non-Muslims think they are.)

"In their eyes alone, then?" Yes, but that requires qualification. The hard perspectivist envisions a world composed of men who, looking each from his own perspective (singular or communal), can neither move nor be moved from that perspective to any other—and who is to say who is right? On this view, there is no truth in general; only "truth to me" or "to him." The hard perspectivist reads "in their eyes alone" to mean that no one can transcend his own perspective by any means. But the radical pluralist, as we may now call ourselves, takes these words in a different way. He does not deny the logical necessity that *I* shall confirm my beliefs, but he holds that men may be conscious of their convictionally plural existence in such a way that that consciousness contains the possibility of transcending the singular perspective of its owners. To the pluralist "in their eyes alone" means "in the eyes of those who may see that theirs are not the only eyes."

That is, though we define the limits of justification as the justification within (in the eyes of) the community of the convinced, that is not so rigid a limit as it would be were there not ruptures of the convictional barriers. If, for example, I am convinced that there is one God (or none, or two) the justification of that conviction is my business, mine and that of my convinced fellows. But the process of justification cannot be altogether the same for me if I so much as know that there are those who disagree (if, for example, I know that "The fool hath said in his heart, 'there is no God' ").[32] And it will be quite different if I come to see those who differ with me, not merely as 'fools' or 'barbarians,' but also as men with flesh like my flesh, brain like my brain, soul like my soul. To that extent, though the justificatory task is still my own, it may draw upon sympathies, correspondences, insights which are not merely private or partisan. And therein lies our hope of transcending the convictional cellblocks to which we might otherwise be confined.

To continue the illustration, if I believe in God (am convinced of God) in a pluralistic world, a world in which I know there are men of good will who do not so believe, then my faith, if justified at all, must be a faith which takes account of that very pluralism which in part denies my faith. It must be faith justifiable (I must be justified by my faith?) *in a world which includes unfaith.* Conversely, if I disbelieve, believe in no God, am convinced no God exists, in a world in which I know there are men who do so believe, then my conviction, if justified at all, must be one which takes account of that fact—it must be atheism *in a world which includes faith.* The pluralism which we envisage, then, does not obviate justification nor require narrowness of outlook, but it does require that the pluralism itself shall be internalized, so that it becomes a factor which my convictions take into account.

IV. Retrospect: Aleph's Task

The role of this chapter has been to expand the idea of justification of convictions with which we began.[33] Just because convictions are ongoing beliefs, their justification in a changing world must be an ongoing task, rather than a once-for-all achievement. If having a (relatively) fixed character is one aspect of having convictions, then even the talk of 'choosing' or 'picking' a conviction (or conviction set) may be misleading. Such talk conjures up a picture

of one standing on some neutral point with the various alternative
convictions spread before him as he demands of each its creden-
tials. But we choose our characters, if we can speak of doing so at
all, in a much different way. We begin life with a certain minimal
set of biological and psychological characteristics. By the time we
can be said to make any choices (as opposed to reacting in certain
ways) these characteristics in interplay with our environment have
already produced in us dispositions with some degree of persistence. (Although recognition of this fact may induce deterministic
Weltschmerz in some, we believe that this reaction is demonstrably
wrongheaded.) These dispositions are reinforced, modified, or
weakened each time we observe, deliberate, hope, choose, and
reflect on the consequences of our choices. Thus while it is true in
a way that our dispositions determine our choices, it is also true in
a way that our choices create our dispositions, not all at once but
over a period of time. And of course if we do not deliberate and
reflect on the consequences of our choices they will remain more
like reactions, and we shall turn ourselves into the desperately
unhappy men portrayed by Plato and others.

What we have said of our relatively practical dispositions applies
to our relatively theoretical ones as well. As we learn to talk and
think, we have initial inclinations to make various statements,
guesses, conjectures, judgments, and the like about how the world
is, and these inclinations are reinforced, modified or weakened as
we consider them and reflect on the evidence. So our inclinations
determine our beliefs, but only at the same time that our beliefs
are determining our inclinations. What follows is that having
convictions is as 'natural' as having human life itself—a naturalness
which consists neither in sheer fortuity nor in sheer grit, but which
is the natural product of being or becoming human, the world
being what it is. In the broadest sense, one tries to justify one's
conviction set (or one's life) by living it. Yet life includes talk, and
persuasion, and reflection, and certainly change, and thus it can
include the special dynamics of justification we have been describing in these pages.

Seen in this perspective, the justificatory techniques which we
rejected in chapters 4 and 5 also have their role to play in the task.
While we rejected there the skeptic's simple-hearted faith in the
elimination of all convictions, we have seen that the principle of
fallibility may play a useful role in the selective thinning of a set.
While we have denied to 'science' the role of supreme judge of all
convictions and to 'reason' the claim that it occupies conviction-

free ground in offering proofs of God or the like, we have not foreclosed the possibility that some science or sciences may play a more modest role in convictional explorations, or that a modest reasonableness can inform even interconvictional justificatory activity. (One way to characterize the present essay is as an attempt to redefine "reasonable"; to discover how a not disinterested reason may yet justify its convinced interest.)

It may be helpful, before enlarging these themes in the remaining pages, to mark our conclusions so far by considering their application to Aleph's convictions as represented in chapters 3 and 4. Our task is not to attempt the justification of his hypothetical set but to show what might be involved in such a justification. Aleph, it will be remembered, uttered his confession as a member of a conservative, traditional religious community. When for convenience we furnished him with a related set of religious convictions of just five members (one of which was expressed by G), we left open the question of Aleph's relation to the wider set shared by his community. Is God triune? Is His nature summed up in self-giving love? Are all men sinners by nature? We did not define Aleph's position on these matters, or his relation to his community's position. Yet it may be that his confessional/convictional attachment to a historic community (cf. G and J) shows our list of his religious convictions to be artificially limited. Perhaps Aleph can be understood, and his set justified, only by an understanding of all the shared convictions of his community. This is not to say that, in order to be justified, Aleph must go along with each and all of the defining (or orthodox) convictions of his community. If his community's set is at some points infelicitous, his own felicity may require dissent at those points. It is to say that the understanding of his speech and his belief involves understanding of the community or communities of speakers and believers in terms of which his own life is formed.

Though understanding is necessary to justification or rejection, it is sufficient for either only where judgments of truth or falsity, consistency or inconsistency, righteousness or unrighteousness are so immediate as to go unnoticed. In a convictionally plural world, these judgments are often conscious, and sometimes seem imponderable. Did Israel cross the Reed Sea? Does God act in history? Does He exist? In such cases, Aleph inevitably enters the arena represented by our (partial) list of loci, risking the convictional disputes which such loci may stake out. Historical inquiries (the Reed Sea; the Jesus of history) and rational arguments (the theis-

tic proofs; the bases of ethics), while quite relevant to his task
here, cannot by themselves settle his convictional questions on
grounds independent of the convictions themselves. In any case, if
Aleph's set is justifiable, its justification will require implicit or
direct appeal to one or more of these common loci, for example to
the claim that life lived in his way is a truly *happy* life. Failing to
make (or make good) such claims, he will have failed to justify his
set.

If the preceding activities prove inadequate for justification,
Aleph may be aided by a third element. We remember that
justification is a demand to meet a finite number of actual objections (not hypothetical, not innumerable). Sometimes these objections are suggested by outsiders, but the important thing is that
they arise for Aleph himself. Such crises are at once challenges to
justification, and occasions of justification. To show how Aleph
will justify his set if he does justify it is thus dependent upon a
contingency—what challenge, what matrix will form for him an
occasion of justification? Will Aleph become, or will he meet, a
reformer, a revolutionary, a rebel? Will the form of his justificatory activity be a profound interconvictional encounter, or an
internal pilgrimage or quest? As these matrices differ, so do the
form and content of the justification to which they may give
birth. And so will the time which they may require.

If such a summary of one hypothetical justification appeals to
some as displaying the 'crooked lines' of actual life, others will be
distressed at its chanciness and disorder. Can we men do no better
than this? Is there no highway to order in the convictional wilderness, no return to reasonableness, no science of convictions? The
present writers share to some degree both the delight in jagged
veracity and the desire for greater order in this work. While we
cannot in the present pages give full vent to the latter desire
(having indulged the former) we will now say something more
about a science of convictions and its relation to philosophy.

7

Here as elsewhere in philosophy, analytic techniques help to answer the penultimate questions, while the ultimate ones, being incapable of answer, *must be come to terms with in some other way.*

Joel Feinberg[1]

In its defense of truth against sophistry, philosophy has employed the same literary genres as theology in its defense of the faith: against intellectual competition, Dogmatics; against Dogmatics, the Confession; in both, the Dialogue.

Stanley Cavell[2]

Give me somewhere to stand and I will move the earth.

Archimedes

Theology as
a Science of Convictions

IT HAS OFTEN BEEN THE ROLE OF PHILOSOPHY TO BREAK THE
ground for the construction of a new science. Many previous
philosophic proposals have seemed to suggest the possibility of a
convictionally neutral science of convictions. Let us look at two
such proposals, one classic and the other contemporary, as prelude
to our own suggestion. William James, toward the end of his
Varieties of Religious Experience, suggested that the old dogmatic
theology was about to be replaced by a new, philosophically pure
"Science of Religions," to which the *Varieties* itself was making "a
crumb-like contribution."[3] James must have had the development
of experimental psychology, with which he had so much to do, in
mind as a model. The "science of religions" would be impartial
and would "presuppose immediate experiences" as its subject
matter. The fruit of this science, James hoped, would be a common body of conclusions about religion. To this common body
each scientific inquirer would add, according to his predilections
and faith, his own (more dubitable) superstructure of "over-
beliefs." James thought, for example, that the new science might
be able to conclude from the facts of experience that each man is
continuous with a wider self, a "more," through which saving
experiences come, while James's own corresponding over-belief
was that the "more" was on its higher side to be denoted "God."[4]

James's early-twentieth-century view seems far too uncritical,
far too sanguine about the possibilities of a science independent
from what we have called conviction sets. Against his scheme, so
briefly presented, there seem to arise all the objections to a
sovereign role for science in convictional matters which we raised
in chapter 5. Indeed James was conscious of the difficulties: while
the science might be "impartial" to any one of the several religions
(as theology was not), it would have its "internal difficulties";

189

notably, it would be biased against the claim that "the essence of religion is true," a bias James sought to overcome partly by argument, partly by assigning an ultimate role to the over-beliefs.[5]

Two elements in James's program, however, seem commendable still. (1) If there are indeed religious data which can be brought into view by a scientific suspension of some of our convictions, then this is one set of facts which any conviction set in the modern world worthy of adherence must reckon with. It may not be enough for present purposes, but it cannot be ignored, either. One thinks of the present-day discipline of history of religions in this connection. (2) It is noteworthy that James makes no hard and fast distinction between the methodology which yields the over-beliefs and that which yields the common core of conclusions in his science of religions. Both spring from empirical investigation and from reflection and are subject to correction from either of these sources; nevertheless, they may contribute to the sum of our knowledge. (It would be a mistake, James holds, to say that all men should have identical religious views, pending any final resolution of our differences in one harmonious system.)[6] Perhaps, then, the science of convictions which *we* envisage might make room, not only for common empirical data, but also for those aspects of convictional belief in which men are (and so far ought to be) separated. There may be a *scientific exploration of convictions* even in a convictionally pluralist world.

Consider, second, the argument made by a contemporary analytical philosopher, Kai Nielsen, for "the primacy of *philosophical theology*" in settling the questions both of religion and theology.[7] Philosophical theology, on Nielsen's view, analyzes fundamental religious concepts and claims. Once he has completed his analysis, the analyst can judge the religious convictions that rest on these claims. The judging standard which Nielsen seems to favor is the concept of coherence. For example, opponents of Christian claims may with reason argue that the concept of God central to Christianity is incoherent. Christian theologians may well reply that belief in Christian revelation excludes the recognition of any point of view external to revelation which can understand and assess the truth of the latter. Offering these as appropriate moves in "philosophical theology," Nielsen then leaps into the demonstration himself, arguing in response to the last move that the concept of revelation is itself incoherent.[8] And so forth.

We can heartily agree with Nielsen that certain elements intrinsic to religious belief and discourse are subject to philosophic examination—indeed such examination is the stuff of the present essay. Even those teachers of doctrine who, like Karl Barth, consciously eschew philosophic discussion continually take up positions on matters which philosophers discuss in their own way. If we disregard those cases in which (it could be argued) philosophers are actually engaging in tasks theological not philosophical, still there are other cases where theologians tread on historic philosophical preserves. For example, theologies sooner or later make direct or indirect appeal to one or more of the loci, such as truth and consistency, for which philosophy has always held itself responsible. Nielsen reminds us of this fact.

It is not clear, however, in what sense we should speak of a "primacy" of philosophy in such cases. The loci, for example, are arenas of combat, not realms in which philosophy as such can somehow settle theology's business, or anyone's business. We have pointed out in chapter 5 the inability of 'rational theology' *or* philosophy to settle fundamental convictional disputes on non-convictional grounds. Nielsen seems to us another of those philosophers whose arguments against religious convictions are based on contrary convictions.[9] It is significant that he finds religious men's talk of God, or of God's self-disclosure, not so much mistaken or unproved as "incoherent" and "utterly opaque": "Language seems to have gone on a holiday."[10] Is this a non-convictional assessment?

But what if we relax the impractical requirement that the 'philosphical theology' which investigates convictions shall itself be convictionally neutral with regard to the investigated convictions? May we not then borrow from Nielsen (and of course from a tradition as old as pre-Christian Greece) the term "theology" to designate the 'science of convictions' in which we are interested? From Nielsen and others we would borrow not only the term but also the license to employ in theology whatever philosophic methods offer promise in the inquiry and from William James the hint that the investigation of convictions can proceed simultaneously down many corridors (the several sorts of over-belief). Then we would have a discipline, called *theology,* that is consciously convictional, plural in form, responsive in many ways to many sorts of empirical data, and open to the rational modes of adjudication suggested in the previous chapter. More than any rival candidate we know of this discipline would deserve the name 'science of convictions.' Perhaps this claim too must be qualified (we have not forgotten the fate of the medieval 'Queen of the Sciences'), but before we qualify it, we must say more exactly what it is.

By theology or theoretics (terms to be distinguished in what follows) *we mean the discovery, examination, and transformation of the conviction set of a given community, carried on with a view to discovering and modifying the relation of the member convictions to one another, to other (non-convictional) beliefs held by the community, and to whatever else there is.*[11] We intend this to be a descriptive definition, singling out the characteristic activity of those who call themselves, or are called, theologians. It can embrace both theologies whose source is 'revelation' and those which draw upon 'reason' or 'experience'; it indicates the work of theologians in communities where ethos or style or still other commitments are determinative. Our definition could thus be criticized if it failed to refer to all (or almost all) instances of what we do in fact call "theology," or if it failed to distinguish theology from non-theological activities, such as history or philosophy proper. It cannot, of course, be a full explication of the several varieties of theology and thus will not seem an ideal definition to those whose goal is the furtherance of a certain sort of theology.

The theologian's is an intellectual enterprise; he is concerned with confession, with doctrine, with beliefs, and we are now in position to see that this theoretical concern is indeed warranted. Whereas earlier much was made of belief, more recent students of religion have tended to deplore the concentration upon doctrine alone, arguing that what a community does is just as important as what it believes or says. But we have shown that such a bifurcation is not itself easily made, that speech, action, and belief are necessarily intertwined. How is it that doctrines matter? They matter not because of some alleged primacy of theory over practice, or of belief over action, but because, *if the doctrines are convictions,* to change them is substantially to change their holders. Not all beliefs matter, but (by definition) all convictional beliefs do. When convictions exist at all, they are central for their holders, and if the theologian would deal with what is central to his community, he must deal with its convictions.

Etymology-minded theologians like to tell us that theology is the 'science of God,' though sometimes we are not sure whether they intend the genitive to be construed subjectively or objectively. In any case, it is traditional to say that theology is about God, or about God and the world. On the other hand, another sort of theologian writes that theology is "critical concern with alternative images of human identity, human community, and the relation of man to his world."[12] In fact, theology as we observe it is not usefully characterized by its subject matter: its topical range is as wide as the range of convictions of the subject community itself—or as narrow. Thus the definition we have offered does not restrict theology to 'God' or to 'religion' or 'religious' topics however conceived. Indeed, historically "theology" is an older and more honored term in communities of faith than is "religion." But if anyone thinks it strange or unseemly that we should refer to the exploration of the conviction sets of secular or 'non-religious' or atheistic communities by the name "theology," we have at hand an acceptable synonym in "theoretics." Indeed "theoretics" (or "theoretic") is already in the language in this sense—as in "Communist (or New Left, or Black Nationalist) theoretics," or "Marxist theoretician." We intend normally to use "theoretics" to refer to every investigation and transformation of the shared conviction sets of convictional communities, while using "theology" to refer to the theoretics of religious convictional communities. Theology is religious theoretics; theoretics is convictional exploration, whether religious or not.[13]

How small or large may be the community to which the theologian attends? We know that convictions are the tenaciously held formative beliefs of a community or of an individual person, and our first extended examination of convictions concerned those of a hypothetical individual, Aleph. Why, then, do we speak of the *community* as the object of theological interest, especially since it would seem a strain upon language to speak of the individual as the limiting case of community? Consider further that although Aleph was depicted as a representative member of his community, we all know of solitary Kierkegaards whose very individual conviction sets are of great interest theologically. May not the theologian treat "the theology of S.K."? In answer, we might note that in the view of many significant theologians (for example, Schleiermacher) theological work is necessarily engaged with the faith of a church (or, as they might say, "the church"), not with any private faith alone. However, our own judgment is founded on linguistic, not theological, grounds: convictions are convictions, beliefs are beliefs only in a frame of language; the convictional/linguistic community thus has logical priority in placing, understanding, and assessing convictions. Even the Kierkegaards are to be understood, and their theological contribution appreciated, only in terms of the community of belief (or disbelief) to which they react. Thus the theologian is necessarily concerned with a community or with some subset thereof. The convictions of an individual can be understood (and examined theologically) only as such a subset.

What of the other alternative? Can the 'community' which

theology explores be the human race as a whole? Well, it is not
without meaning to speak of a theology or theoretic of mankind;
i.e., the discovery and creative transformation of the shared conviction set of the human race. In a convictionally divided world,
however, effective theologizing will not likely take place on so
grand a scale. To attempt it is either to be content with very
modest results, or it is to ignore the problems of pluralism which
have engaged us in the present work.

Before we can say how theology or theoretics may serve as a
'science of convictions,' we need to explain more fully the relation
of theology to the convictional communities which are its normal
sphere of investigation. Is theology as we have defined it actually a
historical inquiry? It is evident that it calls for, includes, historical
investigation. Whether the convictional community be the Westminster Assembly, the Roman Catholic Church, or a commune in
the Arizona desert, the discovery of its convictions is a historical
task. Even if the immediate object is the theology of Kierkegaard
or any other individual, say the theologian himself, the ascertain-
ing of his actual convictions is a biographical or autobiographical
task and thus again historical.

As historian, the theologian faces the critical problem of determining the actual tenacious formative beliefs of his community, as
opposed to its putative ones. Some items in the confessional
documents (if these exist) may be dead letters, while living convictions may not have found their way into any formulary. Most
difficult for the theologian are those beliefs which are indeed
present within the community, perhaps hailed as convictions (the
term, of course, may well be "dogmas," "axioms," "self-evident
truths," "our heritage of faith,") by some, but which are in fact
only marginally convictional.

It might appear that the theologian's burden is lightened in
communities where a fixed dogmatic tradition 'defines' the convictions that matter for his work. Thus it might be supposed that the
Roman Catholic theologian could confine his attention to the
dogmatic definitions found in Denzinger, or the Protestant bibli-
cist to the propositions of Scripture. But that only shifts attention
from one historical problem to another: from the location or
identification of historic formative doctrines to the investigation
of their historical meaning or force. In all communities loyal to
the past the theologian is compelled to ask what the historical
doctrines meant, but he is also compelled to ask what they mean
now—what it means to say in this community here now that the
church is infallible, or that Allah is God. Thus the hermeneutic

task is an inescapable part of the theologian's historical work, playing a critical role especially in communities of fixed tradition.

The burden of history is perhaps lightened for the radically revisionary theoretician, but it is not lifted. The mere intention to *be* radical requires for fulfillment a sense of the convictional place of the community thus radically addressed; our earlier remarks about reformers, rebels, and revolutionaries should make it clear that these roles, no less than that of the traditionalist, imply the existing convictional community with its history. Of course the mere propagandist of change need not be a historian, but then he need not be a theoretician either. In our definition of the theoretician's task, such terms as "discovery," "examination," and "transformation," while chosen to avoid dictating too narrowly the mode of the theoretician's work, do require an orderly investigation to discover what is the case in some convictional community, even if this is only the means to a radical overturn.

In the widest sense, our claim is that theology or theoretics is a discipline whose form is some human language, the language of some community however broadly or narrowly defined. The very imbedding of language in history requires that any serious investigation which involves language involves history as well: this is a conclusion which springs from all the preceding chapters of our work. In this minimal sense, all theology is descriptive because historical. In the usual case, there are even more stringent demands upon the theologian to attend to history. Indeed our problem now is to show how the theologian or theoretician is anything other than a historian of ideas.

It is worth noting that one important twentieth-century school of theologians, the Lund (Sweden) tradition, held that theirs was a purely historical task; that theology is merely a descriptive science. This school assigned to philosophy in Kantian style the task of guaranteeing *a priori* the possibility of religion as a mode of human experience; theology was left with the task of exploring the historical forms of this experience; thus Buddhist theology would discover and explore the organic whole which is Buddhism; Christian theology the organic whole which is Christianity, all on strictly historical lines.[14] Their motive in this division of labor between philosophy and theology seems to have been twofold: on the one hand, theology was relieved of an intolerable burden of apologetic prolegomena to its doctrinal inquiries; on the other, the importance of the theologian's fidelity to given history was underscored.

Clearly there are parallels between this understanding of theolo-

gy and our own. We part with the Lundensians in our belief that
theology not only is but ought to be prescriptive as well as
descriptive; normative as well as historical. Evidence that it is so
can be found on any shelf of theological works; not only radical
revisionists but reactionary conservatives are constantly telling
their readers what to believe. Even the excellent theological works
of the Lundensians themselves display this feature.[15] This is not
because the Lundensians forget their principles and lapse into
adjuration, but, we think, because of the nature of the convictional material theologically addressed. It is part of the meaning of a
conviction that its holder wants others to share it in appropriate
ways. Lundensians can hardly provide a sympathetic account of
"organic wholes" such as Christianity without providing thereby a
more or less effective argument for the adoption of those very
wholes. (A further step, which we will not pursue here, might be
to argue that because the very identification of convictions as
convictions involves judgment, insight, and interpretation, 'normative' considerations cannot be effectively filtered out.)

When we shift attention from this historico-descriptive task of
theology to its innovative and creative task, no great gap inter-
venes. If the theologian, while investigating the convictions of his
community, finds them incoherent or in tension with one another
or otherwise unhappy, he cannot leave the matter there. He must
transform them and continue from there. His vision of the community to be formed grows directly out of his understanding of
the present community. For matters to be otherwise implies a lack
of seriousness in the theologian at his work. (He cannot be a mere
dreamer and be in the workaday sense a theologian.) Theology is
no conviction-free discipline, and (except in extraordinary cases)
the theologian's convictions are intimately related to the shared
convictions of the community he addresses.

It is just this convictional seriousness which drives the theologian to investigate convictions, their meaning, and their happiness.
It is just this seriousness about what *is* which leads him to ask
what *ought to be,* what can be. He is the man whose work requires
that he keep one eye (so to speak) on the already and the other on
the not yet, and that he do this with eyes wide open, and yet not
be cross-eyed. If the convictional transformation or innovation he
proposes seems sometimes radical, it may be just this serious look
at what is the case, this seriousness about the community's convictions, which requires so radical a proposal for convictional revision.

Once we acknowledge that theology is in two senses a convictional inquiry, since it both attends to and is guided by some convictions, many interesting questions arise. What relations may obtain between the set which guides the theologian and the set which he examines? Must the theologian belong, convictionally, to the subject community? What role may imagination play in theological work? By what means are the actual, as against the supposed, convictions of a community discovered? (In particular, will sociologists' questionnaires do the trick?) By what criteria can some indispensable subset, a community's 'essential' convictions, be distinguished from its other real but 'contingent' convictions?[16] What are the possibilities for objective or at least intersubjective recognition of success in theoretics?

The wide curve of the theologian/theoretician's net, when cast out over the objects of his concern, need not surprise us. Long ago we noted how language and thus convictions are related to the speaker in his situation and so to the cords of language tying him to his fellow men and to the factual world in which his speech occurs. Wherever convictions bear upon the real world, or upon what the believer mistakes to be the real world, there the theoretician's writ of inquiry runs, too. Whatever the conviction he investigates, it is this conviction whose meaning he must determine, whose interconnections he must trace, whose termini in the community, and in the language, and in the wide world he must explore. In a word, the real world (whatever that may mean) is the theologian's dish. It need hardly be added that the demands placed upon him by a given community's convictions may be herculean and that the ratio of entrants to successful finishers is obviously high.

We began our discussion of theology by proposing it as a candidate for the 'science' which might in orderly fashion carry forward the work of justifying (some) convictions. We have tried to describe theoretics (theology and its non-religious counterparts) as that variegated enterprise in part already exists. If our description has been an accurate one, then it is a philosophical question whether the enterprise can fulfill the conditions of a 'science of convictions.' Perhaps the question can be best asked in a negative form: is there anything which would disqualify theoretics *a priori* from fulfilling this role? We think that there is not. Theoretics is convictional, but that does not disqualify it, for it is consciously so, and theoretics is as diverse as are the interesting candidates for examination and justification. The very business of theoretics is the sort of discovery, examination for happiness, and transformation of convictions which, as we have seen earlier, tends toward the justification of some set or sets. And theoreticians or theologians may be or become aware of the pluralist world in which their community's convictions stand alongside others, so that they can manage the special problems created by plural perspectives.

Will theology/theoretics in fact come to serve as a 'science of convictions'? It seems to us that the future of theoretics depends upon whether it incorporates the sorts of considerations we have brought together here. If that happens, the 'science of convictions' will still not be a discipline whose workers all subscribe to some one set of convictions, nor will it be composed of those who eschew all conscious convictions or those who attempt to embody in themselves all convictions (a grotesque or meaningless undertaking). Theology will be undertaken by many workmen in many camps, each, while alert to others, doing his best to bring into focus the set of convictions available in his camp, precipitating and testing it, transforming it as best as he can, until it fails or stands justified. If anyone thinks this is too denominational or partisan a view of the theoretical task, let him remember (1) that the 'camp' may be as broadly defined as he likes, but (2) there is no reason to suppose that such breadth, any more than the standpoint of the narrowest schismatic or deviationist, affords that neutral platform which was not available to Archimedes.

Justification is by definition justification in the eyes of the community who embrace the conviction in question. This logical truth leads to hard perspectivism in practice only if those whose task is the examination of convictions, and preeminently those who examine them in the practice of theology, ignore all voices but their own. Theology need not listen to every ranter, but it cannot be deaf to its own inner voice, repeating in its own way those outer voices. There are ruptures in the convictional walls that divide us from one another, and if theology in a pluralist age works in painful but productive awareness of these ruptures, it will thereby become the science of convictions.

It is surely plain by now that we hold that philosophy is subject to the same convictional restraints and has the same kinds of opportunities as other disciplines dealing with convictional matters. There is considerable resistance within the philosophical community to this view of philosophy. Before we turn to the implications of our theory for the practice of philosophy, it is worth investigating the grounds for this resistance.

Philosophers have claimed independence of convictional barriers on two main grounds: One is that true philosophical thinking transcends mere cultural or historical barriers and is, in that sense, "pure." The other is that philosophical thinking does not rise to the importance of convictions, being merely an underlaborer, a brush-clearer for science or theology or some other discipline. To the first we have already responded. Philosophy is a human activity, and if it confronts fundamental human problems our previous arguments show that it cannot do so without being convictional. Purity or transcendence can be purchased only at the cost of emptiness. As for the second ground, it is not altogether false. Certainly much that is called philosophy (in professional journals, for example) while it may be of technical interest, has little to do with convictions. No doubt philosophers could resolve to limit themselves to such concerns. But the probable result would be that others less devoted to standards of clarity, precision, and rationality would seize the field of convictional inquiry. We would do well to remember that some of those who have announced the most modest aims for philosophy have also spoken most readily of convictional matters: Locke, who aspired only to be an underlaborer, wrote the *Second Treatise on Government,* and Wittgenstein, who characterized philosophy as (a very special kind of) nonsense, could nevertheless make remarks like the one used as an epigraph for chapter 6.

But there is another, more practical ground for resisting convictional restraint and we have considerable sympathy with it. No philosopher, conscious of the life and death of Socrates, Spinoza, or Russell, and cherishing his independence, will readily consent to making himself a partisan of a particular class or culture. Unlike theology, philosophy seems to have no institutional identification to begin with; therefore it is tempting to elevate this appearance into a necessary truth and to assert the freedom of philosophy from all intellectual restraints—including convictional ones.

To yield to this temptation, however, is to misunderstand convictions and the restraints they impose. As we pointed out in the case of theology (and this point is equally valid for politics, economics, history, etc.) convictions need not be conservative or orthodox or tailored to the dogmas of any given group. A philosopher can be as radical or heterodox as he likes. But to be intelligibly radical or to have a point of view recognizable as heterodox requires that he take a position with respect to what is understood as orthodox or conservative. This is likely to be convictional in two ways: first, since it is the taking of a position, it involves the adoption of standards of rationality, coherence, morality, and so forth—and such standards are almost necessarily convictional. Second, in taking one position over another, he is opposing views which are likely to be convictional, and in doing so, proposing logical homogenes to them. Socrates, Spinoza, and Russell were radical and independent not because they lacked convictions or identified with no community, but because the smaller community out of which they grew (and which grew around them) was devoted to standards of rationality and rigor which the hostile larger society could hardly understand.

As these examples show, the restraints produced by the holding of convictions are not barriers to independence or intellectual freedom in any intelligible sense. Test oaths, censorship, and other legal threats are barriers to philosophical development. Convictions, on the contrary, are the result of philosophical development as well as a standard for further development.

In our discussions of Scriven, Farrer, James, and Nielsen, we have suggested some of the limitations our theory implies for philosophy. But it would be more accurate to speak of limitations on the claims made for certain philosophical techniques. We have produced no basis for calling into question either the interest in or the validity of philosophical proofs or disproofs of the existence of God, free will, or any other convictional matters. We *have* argued that such proofs, insofar as they employ convictional premises or appeal to convictional standards of rationality or coherence or significance, are incapable of settling those convictional conflicts which have been the focus of this book. Proofs may nevertheless be (as we think) indispensable for establishing and exhibiting the internal coherence and significance of a conviction set and for indicating common ground with other conviction sets. They may certainly lead to an appreciation of the complexities and profundities within a conviction set. And the aesthetic appeal of such proofs—like many proofs in mathematics—is obvious to any who have taken the trouble to follow them rigorously. We regard these as enormously important and interesting properties of convictional arguments, not to be ignored or deprecated. To be disappointed because they cannot settle convictional disputes is to weep because the jet engine is not a perpetual motion machine.

But this is not to say that philosophy is useless in convictional disputes. That would not be true even if philosophical techniques were exhausted by the proofs and disputes we have been discussing. The exhibition of conceptual connections in a precise and perspicuous way is an aid—perhaps an indispensable aid—to the self-understanding that precedes a fruitful dialogue on matters as fundamental as convictions.

But philosophical techniques are not, in fact, exhausted by deductive argument and the application of established or *a priori* standards of significance, rationality, coherence and the like. Another technique (on which we have depended heavily) is the patient searching out and exhibition of the distinctions revealed to us by common speech, including, of course, the speech of adherents of rival convictions. It was this technique which Austin believed offered the "fun of discovery, the pleasures of cooperation and the satisfaction of reaching agreement"[17] (and we can testify to the accuracy of his belief). As our own efforts show, this is neither a mechanical process, nor one guaranteed of success. Indeed, to understand fully the speech-acts of a community requires no less (but no more) than understanding its corresponding beliefs and convictions. Speech-acts, however, have an immediate availability which convictions (traditionally conceived) lacked. If our thesis concerning the relation of convictions and speech-acts is correct, that traditional conception is in error, and the significance of speech-act analysis is broadened all the more.

The speech-act analyst may be denied the pleasures of cooperation and agreement precisely because of the linguistic convictional barriers which in fact exist. If so, there remain the variety of devices for redefinition which have as long a philosophical history as deductive argument: whether the philosopher proceeds by paradox and Socratic *elenchus, de more geometrico,* dialectically, or through depth grammar, he will not lack for models. Indeed, there is considerable ground for claiming an enhanced role for philosophy if we are correct about the nature of convictional pluralism. For philosophers since Thales have perennially dealt with convictional matters, and they have been made unusually sensitive to the dangers and opportunities in convictional conflict. What may be obscured by narrow concentration on *one* kind of philosophical approach may be revealed by patient and imaginative use of the variety of alternatives philosophy has provided through its long history.

What contribution is to be made by the philosophy of religion? Much philosophy of religion is clearly what we call theoretics—the assertion and reasoned defense of a point of view. The same is true of philosophy more generally. When a Scriven or a Farrer sets out to prove that God does or does not exist, we think he is engaged upon a theologian's task. Since not all convictional exploration concerns religion, we prefer to say that the work thus undertaken is theoretics. It is no criticism of philosophers to say that they are sometimes theoreticians as well. But in other cases, the philosopher merely comes to the aid of the theoretician in the untangling of his puzzles or the checking of his work. In these cases, the philosopher clearly cannot replace the theoretician, though his advice may be indispensable. How easily the theoretician's job may shade over into the philosopher's and philosophy into theology again, is a matter for philosophical attention itself.

The present work, with its interest in just such distinctions, represents another strand in philosophy than that described in the preceding paragraph. Our work may be called philosophy of religion, not because it sets out to decide religious (or convictional) questions, but because it seeks to show what kinds of speech-acts religious speakers perform, what sort of belief a conviction is, how the former may be found happy, or how the latter may be justified. Philosophy of religion, in this understanding of the term, investigates the concepts and practices of religion and explores the limits of theology, but is not itself theology or theoretics and cannot replace these. Theoretics is (or may become) the 'science of convictions'; philosophy of religion done as we have done it is not that science but rather (to borrow an old metaphor) its servant or handmaid.

We have not set out to do theoretics in this essay, and we have conscientiously avoided arguments on behalf of this or that conviction set. We have also made a point of our own widely differing religious convictions. Nevertheless, we acknowledge that we share convictions which have guided our work and even made it possible. Some are so common that we undoubtedly share them with any reader: the veridical nature of some of our experience, the genetic continuity of our selves, and more. Others, though not equally common, have contributed in a specific way to our ability to work together in spite of disagreements: we are convinced that dialogue and cooperation are preferable to dispute and hostility, and, at a more general and philosophically interesting level, we subscribe to the fallibility principle, the conviction that any of our convictions might be false and that all are open to criticism, modification, and even rejection.

This is a fairly small list of fairly particular convictions, not perhaps of great interest in a world racked by conflicts between authoritarian and democrat, Arab and Jew, radical and reactionary. There are other convictions guiding our work, however, which do seem to share the character of those convictions over which men argue and fight and die. Perhaps our own rather similar life-histories have given us similar views on religious issues that are not made explicit in our work. Our arguments and disagreements and their (sometime) resolution suggest that we share common views about rationality and coherence and about the relation of our theories to our experience. Discussions with friends and colleagues persuade us that not everyone shares these views. Those who do not may expect to find our work not (merely) mistaken, inadequate, or inaccurate but unintelligible, incoherent, or incredible. Not every criticism reflects such a convictional difference, of course; and not everyone who differs with us on some conviction will necessarily disagree with all we have said.

No doubt there are still other convictions which have helped to make this work what it is. To the extent that the argument of this essay is cogent, these convictions, whatever they may be, are supported and can be recommended to others. But happy or not, our convictions, like everyone else's, must stand their turn in the dock, for they too require subjection to the ongoing process of justification, with whatever adjustment that process may in turn demand of the authors of this book.

Notes

Understanding Religion

1. "The Modes of Thought and the Logic of God" in John Hick, ed., *The Existence of God* (New York: Macmillan, 1964), pp. 297–298.

2. Karl Marx, "Theses on Feuerbach," in Friedrich Engels, *Ludwig Feuerbach and the Outcome of Classical German Philosophy* (New York: International Publishers, 1941).

3. On the newly discovered pluralism of American religion, for example, see the opening historiographic chapter of Sydney E. Ahlstrom, *A Religious History of the American People* (New Haven and London: Yale University Press, 1972). Ahlstrom says any new general history "should above all do justice to the fundamentally pluralistic situation. . ." (p. 12).

4. Jonathan Edwards, *Concerning the End for Which God Created the World,* in Ola Elizabeth Winslow, ed., *Jonathan Edwards' Basic Writings* (New York: New American Library, 1966), p. 238.

5. For the terms "hard" and "soft" perspectivism we are indebted to Van A. Harvey. See his *The Historian and the Believer* (New York: Macmillan, 1966), pp. 205–230.

6. In ordinary language, what one 'believes' may be distinct from what one 'knows'; thus to call convictions a kind of belief might seem to suggest that we cannot know what we are convinced of, but this is not what we mean to say.

7. Cf. John L. Austin, *How to Do Things with Words*, ed. J. O. Urmson and G. J. Warnock (Oxford: Clarendon Press, 1962, and Cambridge, Mass.: Harvard University Press, 1962), chap. 12.

8. This is a form of what John R. Searle calls the Principle of Expressibility. See *Speech Acts* (London: Cambridge University Press, 1969), pp. 19–22. On 'happy' utterance generally, see our chap. 3.

9. Freudians would remind us here that not all 'beliefs' are within the conscious possession of their 'believers.' We think our method allows for dealing with these also. If one has unconscious beliefs, then if discovered they can be expressed by way of speech-acts, and we can proceed from there with a speech-act analysis. To the extent that one's interest in such beliefs is only

in their causal relation to behavior, however, such an analysis will be uninteresting.

10. Henry Fielding, *The History of Tom Jones, a Foundling* (London: Collins, 1955 [1st ed. 1749]), p. 107.

11. On the history of the terms "religion" and "religious" see Wilfred Cantwell Smith, *The Meaning and End of Religion* (New York: Macmillan, 1963), chap. 2, "'Religion' in the West," with extensive notes found on pp. 203–245.

12. Ibid., p. 45.

13. Frederick Ferré, in *Basic Modern Philosophy of Religion* (New York: Scribner's, 1967): "Religion, then, we define as the conscious desiring of whatever (if anything) is considered to be both inclusive in its bearing on one's life and primary in its importance. Or . . . *Religion is one's way of valuing most comprehensively and intensively*" (p. 69). See also, same author, "The Definition of Religion," *Journal of the American Academy of Religion,* March, 1970.

14. We note here, in passing, that it is one virtue of our analysis of convictions that it can explain the variety of meanings of "religion" and the conflict it engenders. See our chaps. 3 and 4.

NOTES TO CHAPTER 2

Rival Interpreters of Religious Language

1. Braithwaite, *An Empiricist's View of the Nature of Religious Belief,* The Eddington Memorial Lecture for 1955 (Cambridge: Cambridge University Press, 1955), reprinted in Ian T. Ramsey, ed., *Christian Ethics and Contemporary Philosophy* (New York: Macmillan, 1966), p. 62. Our subsequent citations of Braithwaite's lecture will be from the Ramsey reprint.

2. Zuurdeeg, *Man before Chaos* (Nashville: Abingdon, 1968), p. 108.

3. Ramsey, *Religious Language: An Empirical Placing of Theological Phrases* (London: SCM Press, 1957), p. 47.

4. See Gottlob Frege, *Translations from the Philosophical Writings of Gottlob Frege,* ed. Peter Geach and Max Black (Oxford: Basil Blackwell & Mott, 1952), and *The Foundations of Arithmetic,* trans. J.L. Austin, 2nd rev. ed. (Oxford: Basil Blackwell & Mott, 1953). For Bertrand Russell's logical contributions, see especially Bertrand Russell and A.N. Whitehead, *Principia Mathematica* (Cambridge: Cambridge University Press, 2nd ed., 1927); Bertrand Russell, *Logic and Knowledge,* ed. R.C. Marsh (London: Allen & Unwin, 1956). On Russell's analytical work, see especially *The Problems of Philosophy* (London: Oxford University Press, 1912, often reprinted); *The Analysis of Matter* (New York: Allen & Unwin, 1927); and *An Inquiry into Meaning and Truth* (London: Allen & Unwin, 1940). For G.E. Moore, see *Philosophical Studies* (London: Kegan Paul, 1922); and *Some Main Problems of Philosophy* (New York: Macmillan, 1953).

5. First English edition, London: Kegan Paul, 1922.

6. For a brief account of the Vienna Circle's understanding of the *Tractatus,* see John Passmore, *A Hundred Years of Philosophy* (London: Duck-

worth, 1957), chap. 16. Wittgenstein, however, intended the *Tractatus* to be taken in a much more paradoxical way than the positivists recognized. For him the literally "senseless" questions of philosophy and religion were of unlimited importance, as the concluding sentences of the *Tractatus* show. And subsequently, Wittgenstein revised his philosophical beliefs, while presenting them in a deliberately casual and allusive style; see the posthumous *Philosophical Investigations*, trans. G.E.M. Anscombe (London: Macmillan, 1953). On Wittgenstein and his interpreters, see Norman Malcolm's article in Paul Edwards, ed., *Encyclopedia of Philosophy* (New York: Macmillan and Free Press, 1967); and D.F. Pears, "The Philosophy of Wittgenstein," *The New York Review of Books*, January 16, 1969 (the latter especially for Wittgenstein's views on religious language) and the literature cited in these. See also *Ludwig Wittgenstein, Lectures and Conversations on Aesthetics, Psychology, and Religious Belief*, ed. Cyril Barrett (Berkeley and Los Angeles: University of California Press, 1967).

7. To the extent that religions were logically untouched by these developments in Western thought, the next few paragraphs do not directly apply to them.

8. Cf. Acts 26:19.

9. A handy summary of the verification criterion's fortunes in philosophy as they bear upon the questions of religious belief is to be found in Diogenes Allen, *The Reasonableness of Faith: A Philosophical Essay on the Grounds for Religious Beliefs* (Washington and Cleveland: Corpus Books, 1968). See chap. 2, "The Real Challenge of Logical Positivism."

10. This section and the next one on Zuurdeeg depend partly on material we published in an article, "Saturday's Child: A New Approach to the Philosophy of Religion," *Theology Today*, October, 1970.

11. A.S. Eddington, *The Philosophy of Physical Science* (1939), p. 189, cited in Braithwaite, p. 53.

12. Ibid., p. 58.

13. Ibid., p. 60.

14. Ibid., pp. 61f. "Assertions" and "assert" are Braithwaite's own terms. Since however later philosophers (and we) use these in a more restricted way, we shall retain quotations marks (" ") whenever we use the terms in Braithwaite's sense, in reporting him.

15. Ibid., p. 66.

16. Ibid., p. 69.

17. Ibid., pp. 66–71.

18. A contribution to "Theology and Falsification," *University*, 1950–51, reprinted in A. Flew and A. MacIntyre, eds., *New Essays in Philosophical Theology* (London: SCM Press, 1955), and "Religion and Morals," in Basil Mitchell, ed. *Faith and Logic, Oxford Essays in Philosophical Theology* (Boston: Beacon, 1957).

19. Psalm 75:4 (PBV).

20. "Religion and Morals," pp. 189–192. Our account is also indebted to an unpublished paper by R. Linwood Urban, Jr., which he very kindly let us read.

21. Braithwaite, p. 63.

22. We recognize that "God is wrathful" is not in Christian theology on all fours with "God is love." The love of God is viewed as primary in historic

Christianity; wrath is understood as loving wrath. Yet even to give that account seems to presuppose reference to an at least imaginary or delusive God, references which on this alternative reading of Braithwaite are altogether excluded, so that the objection cannot even be *made* in these terms.

23. See Wallace Matson, "Bliks, Prayers, and Witches," *Pacific Philosophy Forum,* December, 1966.

24. Willem F. Zuurdeeg, *An Analytical Philosophy of Religion* (Nashville: Abingdon, 1958).

25. Ibid., p. 26.

26. Ibid.

27. Ibid., pp. 27–40.

28. Cited by Zuurdeeg, ibid., p. 35.

29. Ibid., p. 49.

30. Ibid., pp. 47ff. In the era of the Bomb, physicists have been confronted vividly with the difficulties sketched in these sentences. Compare, for example, the sometime judgment of Robert Oppenheimer that the U.S. H-bomb program must be continued because it was "technically so sweet that you could not argue about that." See Philip M. Stern, *The Oppenheimer Case: Security on Trial* (New York: Harper & Row, 1969), pp. 177f.

31. Zuurdeeg, *An Analytical Philosophy of Religion,* pp. 54–56; and cf. his chap. 5.

32. Ibid., p. 58.

33. Ibid., p. 56.

34. We remark that "use" seems to us quite different in the terminology of Marxists, Freudians, etc., than in philosophical analysts.

35. Zuurdeeg, *An Analytical Philosophy of Religion,* pp. 59ff.

36. "Man speaks . . . to establish his existence. . . . The language in which man establishes his existence is always convictional language." Ibid., pp. 89f. See also Zuurdeeg's posthumous book, *Man before Chaos* (Nashville: Abingdon, 1968).

37. Zuurdeeg, *An Analytical Philosophy of Religion, p. 58.*

38. Ibid., pp. 32–35.

39. Ibid., pp. 27–40.

40. See for example Rudolf Bultmann, "What Does It Mean to Speak of God?" *Faith and Understanding,* ed. R. W. Funk, trans. L. P. Smith, Vol. 1 (New York and Evanston: Harper & Row, 1969 [6th German ed. 1966]).

41. Zuurdeeg, *An Analytical Philosophy of Religion,* pp. 54–56. The illustration, however, is our own.

42. Ibid., chap. 5.

43. We published most of this section in an article, "Ian Ramsey's Model of Religious Language: A Qualified Appreciation," *Journal of the American Academy of Religion* 41, no. 3 (September, 1973).

44. Besides the works listed in the following notes, we have consulted the following: *Freedom and Immortality* (London: SCM Press, 1960); "Contemporary Empiricism, Its Development and Theological Implications," *The Christian Scholar* 43 (Fall, 1960); "Empiricism and Religion: A Critique of Ryle's *Concept of Mind,*" *The Christian Scholar* 39 (June, 1956); *Miracles: An Exercise in Logical Mapwork,* Oxford Inaugural Lecture (Oxford: Clarendon Press, 1952); "A Logical Explanation of Some Theological Phrases" in *The Chicago Theological Seminary Register* LIII (May, 1963); "Polanyi and

J.L. Austin" in *Intellect and Hope,* ed. T.A. Langford and W.H. Poteat (Durham: Duke University Press, 1968); Ramsey's introductions to *Prospect for Metaphysics* (London: Allen & Unwin, 1961), to *Christian Ethics and Contemporary Philosophy* (New York: Macmillan, 1966), and, in the last-mentioned, his "Reply to Braithwaite" and "Towards a Rehabilitation of Natural Law." More recently have appeared a posthumous book, *Models for Divine Activity* (London: SCM Press, 1973), and a Ramsey collection which includes several of the articles just mentioned: Jerry H. Gill, ed., *Christian Empiricism* (London: Sheldon Press, and Grand Rapids: Eerdmans, 1974).

45. Ian T. Ramsey, *Religious Language* (London: SCM Press, 1957), chap. 1.

46. Ibid., pp. 25, 38; Ramsey, "Paradox in Religion," *Proceedings of the Aristotelian Society,* supplementary vol. 33, 1959, reprinted in Dallas High, ed., *New Essays in Religious Language* (New York: Oxford University Press, 1969), p. 160.

47. Donald Evans, "Ian Ramsey on Talk about God," *Religious Studies* 7 (1971), 126–127.

48. Ramsey, *Religious Language,* pp. 23–24. For a handy catalog of Ramseyan disclosure-situations, see Donald Evans, "Ian Ramsey on Talk about God." p. 126.

49. Ramsey, *Religious Language,* p. 69.

50. Ibid., pp. 19ff.

51. Ramsey, "On the Possibility and Purpose of a Metaphysical Theology," in Ian T. Ramsey, ed., *Prospect for Metaphysics* (London: Allen & Unwin, 1961), p. 168.

52. Ramsey, "Moral Judgments and God's Commands," in Ian T. Ramsey, ed., *Christian Ethics and Contemporary Philosophy* (New York: Macmillan, 1966), pp. 152–171.

53. Ramsey, *Religious Language,* p. 42.

54. Though moral disclosures, according to Ramsey, *may* take a religious form, not all do, nor are all religious disclosures moral disclosures. The relation between the two is an important and delicate problem for Ramsey's philosophy. See his "Moral Judgments and God's Commands."

55. Ibid., pp. 167–168.

56. See editor's note, Ian T. Ramsey, ed., *Words about God: The Philosophy of Religion* (London: SCM Press, 1971), p. 237.

57. See our chap. 1, p. 12.

58. Has not, save by amassing analyses of various religious texts, from Bible, Church Fathers, other religious traditions, etc. If successful, however, these illustrations at best make the thesis a plausible one. On the other hand, we have argued that "religion" represents a family of meanings and that definitions of the 'essence of religion,' missing this fact, are bound to fail.

59. Ramsey, *Models and Mystery, The Whidden Lectures for 1963* (London: Oxford University Press, 1964), p. 1; Ramsey, *Religion and Science: Conflict and Synthesis, Some Philosophical Reflections* (London: S.P.C.K., 1964), chap. 1.

60. Max Black, *Models and Metaphors: Studies in Language and Philosophy* (Ithaca: Cornell University Press, 1962), cited in *Models and Mystery,* p. 2.

61. *Models and Mystery,* p. 7.

62. Ramsey, *Religious Language*, chap. 2.

63. Ramsey, "Paradox in Religion," pp. 144–146.

64. Cf. for example Ramsey's remarks about "perfection" in *Religious Language*, p. 58.

65. Ludwig Wittgenstein, *Philosophical Investigations*, see e.g. no. 28, pp. 13f.

66. Lewis Carroll, "What the Tortoise Said to Achilles," *Mind*, n.s. IV, no. 14 (April, 1895), pp. 278–280, reprinted in I. M. Copi and J. A. Gould, *Readings on Logic* (New York: Macmillan, 1964).

67. Ramsey, *Religious Language*, p. 18.

68. When philosophers of language speak of a connection's being part of the meaning of a word, the sort of paradigm they often have in mind is found in the word "murder." If someone says that murder is wrong, we may be reminded but we cannot (if we know English) be *informed* thereby. For that murder is wrong is what we *mean* by "murder"; to call a killing murder is to judge it wrong. (Nor does it count against this that murder may sometimes be justifiable—so may 'doing wrong' sometimes be justifiable.) Similarly, (everyday) kindness has built into its meaning that it deserves (everyday) gratitude. (As before, the exceptions are only apparent ones.)

69. Ramsey, "Paradox in Religion," pp. 155ff.

70. *Religious Language*, p. 45.

71. E.g., by Ninian Smart, "The Intellectual Crisis of British Christianity," *Theology* 68 (January, 1965), 33–35.

72. See e.g., Ramsey's letter of reply to Ninian Smart in *Theology* 68 (February, 1965), 109–111.

73. Ramsey, "Religion and Science, a Philosopher's Approach," *Church Quarterly Review* 162 (1961), reprinted in Dallas High, ed., *New Essays in Religious Language*, p. 40; Ramsey, *Models and Mystery*, p. 17.

74. Ramsey, "Religion and Science, a Philosopher's Approach," p. 52.

75. Ramsey, "Talking about God," in F. W. Dillistone, ed., *Myth and Symbol* (London: S.P.C.K., 1966), as reprinted in Ian T. Ramsey, ed., *Words about God*, p. 214.

76. Ibid., pp. 214–215.

77. *Models and Mystery*, p. 17. See also Ramsey, "Talking of God: Models, Ancient and Modern" in Gill, ed., *Christian Empiricism*.

78. Ramsey, "Talking about God," in *Words about God*, p. 215; "Models and Mystery, Reply," *Theoria to Theory* 1, no. 3 (April 1967), 267.

79. "Talking about God" in *Words about God*, p. 216. See also Ramsey, *On Being Sure in Religion* (London: Athlone, 1963), passim.

80. See D.Z. Phillips, *The Concept of Prayer* (London: Routledge & Kegan Paul, 1965); *Faith and Philosophical Enquiry* (New York: Schocken, 1971); *Death and Immortality* (London: Macmillan and St. Martin's, 1971). See also D.Z. Phillips, ed., *Religion and Understanding* (New York: Macmillan, 1967); H.O. Mounce and D.Z. Phillips, *Moral Practices* (London: Routledge & Kegan Paul, 1971); and Ilham Dilman and D.Z. Phillips, *Sense and Delusion* (London: Routledge & Kegan Paul, 1971). A very different case is the interesting (and too much neglected) work in Wittgensteinian perspective of Dallas M. High. See High's *Language, Persons, and Belief* (New York: Oxford University Press, 1967).

81. *Faith and Philosophical Enquiry*, pp. 96f.

82. Ibid., pp. 143f. Phillips's notion of religion is termed a "picture-preference" by Herbert Burhenn, "Religious Beliefs as Pictures," *Journal of the American Academy of Religion* 42, no. 2 (June, 1974); we are also guided here by Peter Slater's unpublished paper, "From World to God and Back Again."

83. A good account of the tension by one sympathetic to much of Phillips' work is Donald S. Klinefelter, "D.Z. Phillips as Philosopher of Religion," *Journal of the American Academy of Religion* 42, no. 2 (June, 1974).

84. A good account of these is found in Robert W. Funk, *Language, Hermeneutic and Word of God* (New York: Harper & Row, 1966). See further the bibliography there, and also James M. Robinson and John B. Cobb, Jr., eds., *New Frontiers in Theology*, vol. 2: *The New Hermeneutic* (New York: Harper & Row, 1964), and Gerhard Ebeling, *Introduction to a Theological Theory of Language*, trans. R.A. Wilson (Philadelphia: Fortress, 1973 [German ed. 1971]).

85. For example Funk refers to "what J.L. Austin has called performative discourse [sic]," but misses completely (1) Austin's rejection of the performative, and (2) Austin's insistence that 'performatives' depend on what the facts are, as do other utterances. Nevertheless, Funk says that anyway Austin is only identifying what students of primitive cultures have known about for some time, namely the primitive bond between the linguistic and the mythico-religious consciousness. (This explanation will astound most readers of Austin.) Funk then adds that "the effort to relate language event to the category of performative language is as much in the interest of saying how language event may not be understood as it is in saying how it may be understood" (Funk, *Language, Hermeneutic, and Word of God*, pp. 26–28). And with that dark saying, he abandons the comparison for good.

NOTES TO CHAPTER 3

A Speech-Act Theory of Religious Language

1. *Philosophical Papers*, ed. J. O. Urmson and G. J. Warnock (Oxford: Clarendon Press, 1961), p. 33.

2. Stanley Cavell, *Must We Mean What We Say?* (New York: Scribner's, 1969), p. 19.

3. Evans' work is published as *The Logic of Self-Involvement: A Philosophical Study of Everyday Language with Special Reference to the Christian Use of Language about God as Creator* (London: SCM Press, 1963). The second part presents a 'performative' doctrine of creation theological in intent.

4. Austin's principal work (cut short by his early death) is available in three volumes: *Sense and Sensibilia*, reconstructed by G.J. Warnock (Oxford: Clarendon Press, 1962); *How to Do Things with Words*, the William James Lectures for 1955, ed. J.O. Urmson (Oxford: Clarendon Press, 1962); and *Philosophical Papers*, ed. J.O. Urmson and G.J. Warnock (Oxford: Clarendon Press, 1961, 2nd ed., 1970). Also see "Critical Notice of J.L. Lukasiewicz'

Aristotle's Syllogistic: From the Standpoint of Modern Formal Logic," Mind 61 (1952).

The chief advance upon Austin's theory of speech-acts is the work of John R. Searle. See his "What Is a Speech Act?" in *Philosophy in America,* ed. Max Black (Ithaca: Cornell University Press, 1965), and his *Speech Acts: An Essay in the Philosophy of Language* (London: Cambridge University Press, 1969). See also Mats Furberg, *Saying and Meaning, a Main Theme in J.L. Austin's Philosophy* (Oxford: Basil Blackwell, 1971), and the essays in K.T. Fann, ed., *Symposium on J.L. Austin* (London: Routledge & Kegan Paul, and New York: Humanities Press, 1969).

5. See "Performative Utterances" in *Philosophical Papers,* and *How to Do Things with Words,* pp. 45–91.

6. *How to Do Things with Words,* pp. 45–91; "Performative Utterances" in *Philosophical Papers.* After noting that relation to the facts is a significant test of the happiness of the 'performative' and 'constative' utterances alike, Austin remarks with his characteristic irony: "This is in itself no doubt a very trivial part of our investigations," *How to Do Things with Words,* p. 45.

7. Some philosophers have argued that Austin was mistaken, that there are sure-fire tests for a narrowly defined class of performative utterances. But for what follows their cavil, even if sustained, does not matter. For the importance of performatives in Austin's thought (and in ours) was heuristic; it helped to free him from the grip of the "descriptive fallacy" and enabled him to develop the theory of speech-acts, and it is the latter which is our interest here.

8. See for example Gilbert Ryle, *The Concept of Mind* (London: Hutchinson's University Library, 1949); Anthony Kenny, *Action, Emotion and Will* (London: Routledge & Kegan Paul, 1963); Myles Brand, *The Nature of Human Action* (Glenview, Ill.: Scott, Foresman, 1970); Stuart Hampshire, *Thought and Action* (London: Chatto & Windus, 1959); Charles Taylor, *The Explanation of Behavior* (London: Routledge & Kegan Paul, 1964); and the literature cited in these.

9. This is our term; Austin and John R. Searle distinguish differently than we do the ways in which in speaking we act. Austin speaks of phonetic, phatic, and rhetic acts, and of locutions *vs.* illocutions (*How to Do Things with Words,* pp. 91ff.); Searle of utterance acts (uttering words, morphemes, sentences), propositional acts (referring and predicating), and illocutionary acts (stating, promising, etc. ("Austin on Locutionary and Illocutionary Acts," *Philosophical Review,* October, 1968; and *Speech Acts,* pp. 24ff.). Our distinction of phonetic acts (issuing sounds), sentential acts (uttering sentences in a language), and illocutionary acts = speech-acts (stating, promising, etc.) is for present purposes clearer and more manageable, we believe.

10. *How to Do Things with Words,* pp. 98ff.

11. Regrettably, there is no uniformity in the usage of "speech-act." Austin usually (cf. *How to Do Things with Words,* pp. 52, 147; *Philosophical Papers* (1961) p. 238) but apparently not always (cf. *How to Do Things with Words,* p. 146) used "speech-act" (or "speech act") of the illocution in its context—the "total speech situation." Searle instead uses "speech act" as a *generic* term for utterance acts, propositional acts, and illocutionary acts (*Speech Acts,* p. 22). We stick closer to the usual Austin, differ from Searle, and use "speech-act" = df. "illocutionary act" (including, thereby, its implied

sub-acts, the sentential act and phonetic act) because Austin's term "illocutionary act" is such a mouthful.

Paralleling the speech-act could be the 'graphic-act'; each would entail a
sentential act; in the former case the sentential act would be also the acts of
saying words, and of moving one's jaw, issuing sounds, etc.; in the latter case
the sentential act would be also the acts of *writing* words, moving one's pen
(or typewriter) upon the paper, etc. But since little is to be gained for present
purposes by making these distinctions in each case, we shall employ "speech-
act" in a sense which includes written as well as spoken language.

12. This may be seen by noting the number of works on religious language
which refer to the Austinian work but continue blithely to treat "religious
statements" or "religious assertions" as if they were self-evidently satisfactory
linguistic categories.

13. Financial statements are useful examples to keep in mind for bringing
together several of these points: (*a*) While the treasurer or accountant may
prepare such a statement, the office boy cannot (special position required).
(*b*) If the treasurer or the C.P.A. does give us this information in proper form,
it is a *statement*, not an assertion, a guess, or a telling (i.e., responsiblity is
fixed in a particular way upon the issuer of the statement, and the same thing
is true if it is an institution which issues the statement). (*c*) Although the fact
that you owe $250.37, or that the Bank of Angel Island has on deposit
$135,791.35, may appropriately appear in a statement, the fact that you are
a dead-beat, or that the bank is in trouble, may not, even though you are, it
is, and the C.P.A. knows it (limitation of appropriateness).

14. J.L. Austin, *Philosophical Papers* (1961), pp. 236f.

15. A similar speech-act humor characterizes a Ring Lardner line (reporting what he said to his children): "'Shut up,' I explained carefully."

16. This section is based in part on James M. Smith and James Wm.
McClendon, Jr., "Religious Language after J.L. Austin,' *Religious Studies* 8,
March, 1972.

17. Some might contend that the conditions we are about to lay down are
too stringent. After all, isn't a mumbled request or one for an impossible task
still some sort of request? This misses our point, however, in using "happy"
or "unhappy" of speech-acts. We want to call attention to the wide variety of
ways in which acts, including speech-acts, can go wrong or be subject to
criticism or question. Just as non-speech-acts can be clumsy, graceful, careless, or clever as well as morally wrong or legally authorized, so speech-acts
can have many virtues and vices besides existing or not existing as such. It is
to avoid undue concentration on traditional categories of assessment that,
with Austin, we use the very broad terms "happy" and "unhappy" (or
sometimes, for stylistic convenience, "felicitous" or "infelicitous") as assessments of all the faults and virtues of speech-acts.

18. Cf. a similar attempt by John R. Searle, *Speech Acts*, p. 66. Searle
tabulates the conditions for requesting as follows:

Propositional content	Future act A of H.
Preparatory	1. H is able to do A. S believes H is able to do A.
	2. It is not obvious to both S and H that H

> will do A in the normal course of events of
> his own accord.

Sincerity   S wants H to do A.

Essential   Counts as an attempt to get H to do A.

19. Searle does call such a condition "essential."

20. Searle, *Speech Acts*, p. 66, incurs the latter risk by listing the essential condition of requesting as 'Counts as an attempt to get H to do A.' That seems to disregard the distinction between requesting and ordering, for one thing; for another it seems to disregard the (really essential) difference between linguistic and non-linguistic ways of getting 'H to do A,' a difference Searle is in general deeply interested in.

21. Of course, "Hello" and "Thank you" are not in the usual technical sense 'referring expressions,' but the speech-acts which they are used to perform require certain things to be true of the world if they are to be happy.

22. On this point, cf. Searle, *Speech Acts*, pp. 44f.; cf. also the articles by H. Paul Grice: "Meaning," *Philosophical Review*, July, 1957; "Utterer's Meaning and Intentions," *Philosophical Review*, April, 1969; "Utterer's Meaning, Sentence-Meaning, and Word-Meaning," *Foundations of Language*, August, 1968.

23. *How to Do Things with Words*, pp. 115f.

24. *The Confessions of St. Augustine*, trans. E.B. Pusey (New York: Washington Square Press, n.d.), p. 1.

25. See H. Richard Niebuhr, *The Meaning of Revelation* (New York: Macmillan, 1941), chap. 2.

26. However, Isaac Newton himself believed in miracles and was thus not a 'Newtonian' in the present sense. The plainest Newtonian in our sense is La Place, who felt no need to use the "hypothesis of God" to explain the heavens.

27. Clearly, then, these remarks are not offered as settling the question of whether it is proper *to say* that God acts in history or the question of whether he does so; we are at best providing a kind of linguistic footnote to those related questions.

28. Psalm 105:37–40, RSV.

29. Psalm 105:1.

30. W.J. Harrelson, "Blessings and Cursings," in *Interpreter's Dictionary of the Bible*, ed. G.A. Buttrick (New York: Abingdon, 1962), vol. 1; our emphasis.

31. 1 Cor. 11:23f, RSV.

32. A good instance of a classic liturgy which displays these elements clearly is the Liturgy of St. James of the Eastern Church.

33. *Sabbath and Festival Prayer Book* (Rabbinical Assembly of America and the United Synagogue of America, 1946), p. 28.

34. *The Passover Haggadah, with English Translation, Introduction, and Commentary*, based on the commentaries of E.D. Goldschmidt, ed. Nahum H. Glatzer (New York: Schocken Books, 1953).

35. Ibid.

36. If the uptake of confession requires genuine understanding of *what* is confessed, it follows that the solitary believer is one whose speech is (necessarily) unhappy—a linguistic point of great theological interest.

37. Our guide to Buddhagosa is Ninian Smart, *Reasons and Faiths, an Investigation of Religious Discourse, Christian and Non-Christian* (London: Routledge & Kegan Paul, 1958), pp. 95–104.

38. None, that is, which is not presupposed by the conviction expressed by Aleph's G, or its contradictory, but not both.

NOTES TO CHAPTER 4

How Are Convictions Justifiable?

1. Ludwig Wittgenstein, *Philosophical Investigations*, trans. G.E.M. Anscombe (New York: Macmillan, 1953), I, 373, p. 116e; II, xii, p. 230e.

2. Norman O. Brown, *Love's Body* (New York: Random House, 1966), pp.82f.

3. The appropriate changes would be those which allowed for the evident differences between a speech-act and a thought or belief: speech is faulted, often, if it is not heard; it requires a certain degree of uptake for its success; it is a performance or act; it occurs at a given time and can be repeated; these features give rise to differences which could be explored in detail, but, our interests being different, we will not do so here.

4. It might be possible to examine systems of religious belief, and the apologies for such systems, in terms of these three categories.

5. We are not concerned here with legal rights.

6. It may be worth noting that a suspicion, though once justifiable and even justified, meeting every available challenge, may cease to be either. The police chief was justified, given the evidence, in suspecting Roberts, but now that Randall is caught red-handed, the suspicion of Roberts is no longer justified.

7. For example we may not know when to count a growing youth as an adult or an immigrant as acculturated, nor when to count a play or a novel as 'great.' Yet without doubt there are full-grown adults, acculturated immigrants, and great plays, and there are as well callow youths, obvious newcomers, and slight or insignificant novels. In case of need, we define the border: an 'adult' may then be one who has reached his eighteenth birthday; the great novel, one which has endured 100 years and enjoyed a million readers. But these acts of precision are themselves but approximations, rules of thumb.

8. Cf. Willem F. Zuurdeeg, *An Analytical Philosophy of Religion* (Nashville: Abingdon, 1958), pp. 40–44.

9. Luke 10:38–48, RSV.

10. Indeed, several stories in the gospels and in Christian tradition. However, let us assume that these coalesce in Aleph's mind (he may believe that many of them are variants of a single story in the gospel tradition), or that one, e.g., the healing in John 9, assumes prototypical importance for him.

11. A fact which tends to explain the resistance of many believers to critical examination of sacred texts. The critic is tampering with words which express, which are, another man's convictions.

12. Wilfred Cantwell Smith, *Questions of Religious Truth* (New York: Scribner's, 1967), p. 89. Cf. our A, p. 22.

13. 2 Sam. 11 and 12.

14. Thus Braithwaite's claim for the importance of stories is quite justified, though we believe he does not accurately identify the basis for that claim. Cf. our chap. 2.

15. See for example the "Christology" article in any convenient handbook or encyclopedia of Christian theology.

16. *Summa Theologica,* 12ae, Q.109, Art 8. We have quoted from the Library of Christian Classics edition of selections: *Nature and Grace,* trans. A.M. Fairweather (Philadelphia: Westminster, 1965), p. 151.

17. *The Christian Faith,* trans. H. R. Macintosh & J. Stewart (Edinburgh: T. & T. Clark, 1928), § 100, p. 425.

18. Cf. the discussion of the context of the representative force of G in our chap. 3, pp. 68—74.

19. Van A. Harvey, *The Historian and the Believer* (New York: Macmillan, 1966), pp. 265ff.

20. *An Analytical Philosophy of Religion,* pp. 32—35.

21. "Is 'Transcendence' the Word We Want?" *Theological Explorations* (New York: Macmillan, 1968), p. 164.

22. *Tractatus Logico-Philosophicus,* ed. D. F. Pears and B. F. McGuiness (London: Routledge & Kegan Paul, 2nd impression, 1933), p. 44 (our translation).

23. *Theological Explorations,* pp. 169-170.

24. Ibid., p. 171. We remark that the capacity to be puzzled or astonished at what most men take for granted is a characteristic shared by geniuses (and madmen) in many areas: science, poetry, and philosophy as well as religion.

25. Ibid., p. 172.

26. Save by specifying a code, a possibility which presupposes the very conventional structure of language which we are here invoking.

27. Cf. for example *How to Do Things with Words,* p. 27 (divorce among Mohammedans, etc.).

28. Some of these convictions are, of course, at a different level from the ones which are our models in the present chapter. They do not, as far as we know, entail entirely different considerations than do the latter, however.

29. On the relation between convictions, character, and morality, see also James Wm. McClendon, Jr., *Biography as Theology* (Nashville: Abingdon, 1974), chaps. 1 and 7, and the literature cited there.

30. We take these character traits to involve not just urges in one direction or another, but beliefs about the preferability of certain policies or goals; e.g., the ambitious man is one who believes that success of certain kinds is of great importance, while a malicious man believes that the interests of others are readily sacrificed to his own pleasure. If then we consider the case of the malicious man who is (therefore) conscience-stricken, we will say that such a man is not one lacking in these convictions, but rather, if "malice" and "conscience" correctly apply to him, one who has two (painfully contrary) convictions. Thus his is not the case we have in mind in the text.

31. Phil. 4:8, KJV.

NOTES TO CHAPTER 5

A Perspective on Non-Perspectival Reason

1. *Pensées*, trans. A.J. Krailsheimer (Harmondsworth: Penguin Books, 1966), p. 95.

2. *The Future of an Illusion* (Garden City, N.Y.: Doubleday, Anchor, 1957), p. 86.

3. Roger Trigg (in *Reason and Commitment* [Cambridge: Cambridge University Press, 1973], pp. 145–157) argues that it makes no sense to speak as we have here of a "commitment" to reason: reason underlies all language and cannot sustain a commitment or require a justification. It is interesting that Trigg, who is on our classification a non-perspectivist, makes the same sort of claim for reason here that hard perspectivists make for the central contents of their own perspectives. Thus our own main arguments for soft perspectivism apply equally against both views. Trigg's particular mistake seems to us to be a confusion of the notion of "commitment" with that of "voluntary endorsement": but I may endorse a political candidate without being (convictionally) committed to him, and I may be committed (e.g., to reason) without choosing it. Reason may simply be presupposed by my thinking and speaking.

4. *Summa Theologica*, Part I, Q.2, Art.3.

5. Austin Farrer, *Finite and Infinite*, 2nd ed. (Westminster: Dacre Press, 1959), p. 262.

6. Ibid., p. 263.

7. Ibid., p. 266.

8. Ibid., p. 268.

9. Ibid., pp. 268f.

10. Ibid., Part II.

11. Ibid., pp. 168–170.

12. Ibid., p. 9, our emphasis.

13. Ibid., pp. 9f.

14. Ibid., p. ix. After eight more years, Farrer published a restatement of his views on rational theology under the title *Faith and Speculation* (London: Adam and Charles Black, 1967). In this work, he criticized and revised his old argument at some points, especially retracting its "formalism" as opposed to the "voluntarism" he now favored in the conception of God which was the conclusion of his argument. Yet Farrer stood by the general argument. See especially pp. 104–118. Farrer also wrote there, "We take it as axiomatic that the straight path of rational theology must be the prolongation of that basic theism which precedes all philosophising" (p. 122).

15. We remind the reader again that we are not using "proof" as a success-word.

16. Michael Scriven, *Primary Philosophy* (New York: McGraw Hill, 1966), p. 11.

17. Ibid., p. 13.

18. Ibid., p. 14.

19. Ibid., p. 15.

20. Ibid., p. 87.

21. Ibid., p. 102.

22. Ibid., p. 103.

23. Ibid.

24. Regrettably, as far as the aptness of our choice of illustrations of argument is concerned, Scriven's argument leaves something to be desired here, since his discussion of the nature of God does not make it evident either that God is, in Scriven's sense, supernatural, or that the sort of God he has in mind is a sort attended by believers.

25. See the title essay in William James, *The Will to Believe and Other Essays in Popular Philosophy* (New York, 1897). See also, in the same collection, "The Sentiment of Rationality."

26. See W. K. Clifford, "The Ethics of Belief," in his *Lectures and Essays*, ed. F. Pollock, vol. II (London, 1879). See also Ralph Barton Perry, ed., *The Thought and Character of William James, Briefer Version* (New York: Harper & Row, 1964), p. 153; Richard B. Brandt, "Epistemology and Ethics, Parallel Between," in *Encyclopedia of Philosophy*, ed. Paul Edwards (New York: Macmillan and Free Press, 1967); Rudolf Carnap, "Probability as a Guide in Life," *Journal of Philosophy* 44 (1947), 141–148; Roderick Chisholm, *Perceiving: A Philosophical Study* (Ithaca: Cornell University Press, 1958), chap. 1.

27. Dag Hammarskjöld, *Markings*, trans. Leif Sjoberg and W. H. Auden (New York: Alfred A. Knopf, 1965), p. 51.

28. Diogenes Allen, *The Reasonableness of Faith* (Washington and Cleveland, Corpus Books, 1968), pp. xv–xix.

29. R. G. Collingwood, *An Essay on Metaphysics* (Oxford: Clarendon Press, 1940), p. 190. The Latin phrase is the familiar "something than which no greater can be conceived."

30. Ibid., p. 40.

31. Ibid., p. 198.

32. Ibid., pp. 224–226.

33. A. C. McGill, "Recent Discussion of Anselm's Argument," in John H. Hick and Arthur C. McGill, eds., *The Many-Faced Argument* (New York: Macmillan, 1967).

34. Ibid., pp. 39–41.

35. Ibid., pp. 50–69.

36. Ibid., p. 104.

37. Ibid., p. 105.

38. *Proslogion* II, in ibid., p. 4, our emphasis.

39. McGill, pp. 105f., 108.

40. Ibid., p. 109.

41. For this convictional definition of theology, see further our chap. 7.

42. Cf. the bibliography in Hick and McGill.

43. Norman Malcolm, "Anselm's Ontological Arguments," *Philosophical Review* 69, no. 1 (January, 1960), reprinted in Hick and McGill; Charles Hartshorne, *Man's Vision of God* (New York: Harper, 1941) and *The Logic of Perfection* (La Salle, Ill.: The Open Court, 1962); J. N. Findlay, "Can God's Existence Be Disproved?" *Mind*, April, 1948, reprinted in A. Flew and A. MacIntyre, eds., *New Essays in Philosophical Theology* (London: SCM Press, 1955).

44. We hope it is clear that our concern here is not with the foundations of the special sciences: physics, biology, chemistry, et al. Rather it is with the

broader and more widespread beliefs which characterize what has been variously called the scientific attitude, the scientific temper, and the scientific world view. We are not attempting the sort of task exemplified by Carnap's *Philosophical Foundations of Physics* or Popper's *The Logic of Scientific Investigation*. Our enterprise is if anything more like that undertaken by Collingwood in his *Essay on Metaphysics*, by Weber in *Protestantism and the Rise of Capitalism*, or by Ernst Troeltsch throughout his work. An interesting and recent work which concentrates on the foundations of the sciences but reaches conclusions of the broader scope with which we are here concerned is Stephan Körner, *Categorial Frameworks* (Oxford: Basil Blackwell, 1970).

45. Yet it is noteworthy that at this writing (1975) there are 'post-moderns' in the Western world who again take up the earlier view.

46. Vilfredo Pareto, *A Treatise on General Sociology* (New York: Dover Publications, 1963), II, 506f.

47. See e.g., A. R. Louch, *Explanation and Human Action* (Berkeley: University of California Press, 1966); Peter Winch, *The Idea of a Social Science and Its Relation to Philosophy* (London: Routledge & Kegan Paul, 1958) (however Winch seems to us sometimes to fall over into the opposite fault of suggesting that one cannot understand the group unless he is a *member* of the group); Barbara Wootton, *Social Science and Social Pathology* (London: Allen & Unwin, 1959). Disputes involving many of the issues we raise above can be readily found in current literature. See, e.g., Theodor W. Adorno, et al., *The Authoritarian Personality* (New York: Harper, 1950); Richard Christie and Marie Jahoda, *Studies in the Scope and Method of the Authoritarian Personality* (Glencoe, Ill.: The Free Press, 1954). Two areas of sociological inquiry which illustrate the problem of transconvictional investigation are represented by the investigation by Charles Y. Glock and Rodney Stark of the relation of a community's doctrines to its attitudes and behavior (see Charles Y. Glock and Rodney Stark, *Christian Beliefs and Anti-Semitism* [New York: Harper & Row, 1966]) and by the discussion of the use of intelligence testing across cultural lines (see Arthur K. Jensen, "How Much Can We Boost IQ and Scholastic Achievement?" *Harvard Educational Review* 39 [Winter, Summer, 1969], 1–123, 449–483 and the subsequent discussion.)

48. See Hendrik Kraemer, *The Christian Message in a Non-Christian World* (New York: International Missionary Council, 1947); Kraemer, *Religion and the Christian Faith* (Philadelphia: Westminster, 1957); Arend Theodoor van Leeuwen, *Christianity in World History*, trans. H. H. Hoskins (New York: Scribner's, 1964).

49. See especially Mircea Eliade, *Cosmos and History, The Myth of the Eternal Return*, trans. Willard R. Trask (New York: Harper & Bros., 1959); Eliade, *Patterns in Comparative Religion* (Cleveland: Meridian Books, World Publishing Co., 1963); also Mircea Eliade and Joseph M. Kitagawa, eds., *The History of Religions, Essays in Methodology* (Chicago: University of Chicago Press, 1959); and Joseph M. Kitagawa with Mircea Eliade and Charles H. Long, eds., *The History of Religions, Essays on the Problem of Understanding* (Chicago: University of Chicago Press, 1967).

50. Joachim Wach, "The Meaning and Task of the History of Religions," in Kitagawa, Eliade and Long, p. 2.

51. We note again our skepticism about the existence of an 'essence of religion' such as these writers seem to assume. Cf. our chap. 1.

52. Cf. Mircea Eliade, *Patterns in Comparative Religion,* pp. 388–408.

53. I.R.A. Al Faruqi, "History of Religions: Its Nature and Significance for Christian Education and the Muslim-Christian Dialogue," a 1964 lecture at the University of Chicago, with responses by Charles H. Long and H. N. Wieman, published in *Numen* 12, Fasc. 1, 2 (1965), pp. 35–95.

54. Ibid., pp. 53f.

55. Ibid.

56. Charles H. Long, "Archaism and Hermeneutics," in Kitagawa, Eliade and Long, p. 86.

57. Ibid., p. 87.

58. Kees W. Bolle, "History of Religions with a Hermeneutic toward Christian Theology?" in Kitagawa, Eliade and Long, pp. 89–118. See also Bolle, "The History of Religions and Christian Theology," in *Anglican Theological Review,* October, 1971.

59. Bolle, "History of Religions with a Hermeneutic . . .," p. 98.

60. Ibid., p. 100.

61. Ibid., pp. 100–103.

62. Ibid., p. 108.

63. Ibid., p. 102.

64. Ibid., p. 108.

65. Ibid., p. 111.

66. Ibid., p. 113.

67. Ibid.

68. Ibid., p. 114.

69. Ibid., p. 116.

70. See above on the role of judgment in rational inquiry, pp. 119f.

NOTES TO CHAPTER 6

The Process of Justification

1. *Tractatus Logico-Philosophicus* (6.43), trans. by D.F. Pears and B.F. McGuinness (London: Routledge & Kegan Paul; New York: Humanities Press, 1961).

2. "Aesthetic Problems of Modern Philosophy," in Max Black, ed., *Philosophy in America* (Ithaca: Cornell University Press, 1965), p. 86.

3. We would hold that known exceptions to this generalization, e.g., Hugo Grotius' apologetic poem *De Veritate religionis Christianae,* did not set the tone of the Western community's self-understanding regarding the demands of justification. Nevertheless the situation we are describing did in time change; every change has its harbingers; and most attempts to draw a line distinguishing new eras in history will meet claims that the line is not early enough.

4. Cf. chap. 5.

5. Thomas S. Kuhn, *The Structure of Scientific Revolutions,* 2nd ed., enlarged, constituting vol. II, no. 2 of *Encyclopedia of Unified Science,* Otto Neurath, editor-in-chief (Chicago: University of Chicago Press, 1970), pp. 53–56.

6. Ibid., p. 55.

7. Ibid., p. 53.

8. 1 Cor. 13:12, KJV.

9. Ibid., vs. 11.

10. It is noteworthy that in the later 'Pauline' writings, this linguistic reserve is diminished; for example, 2 Tim. 1:12 makes 'Paul' say "*I know* whom I have believed. . . .*" And in the Gnostic writings the adept flourishes. As the apostolic revolution wanes, is the sense of the ineffable replaced by dogmatic confidence?

11. Cf. 1 Cor. 1.

12. If the prophet's or apostle's appeal is to a longer run than history itself, as is suggested in John Hick's appeal to eschatalogical verification, special problems are introduced which we do not explore here. We note that it is possible that appeals to a life to come are not cogent. Our present point, however, is that the appeals are *made.* See John Hick, "Theology and Verification," *Theology Today* 17, no. 1 (April, 1960), reprinted in John Hick, ed., *The Existence of God* (New York: Macmillan, 1964), and see the criticisms of Hick's theory cited there (p. 253).

13. *Nicomachean Ethics,* p. 1095a, lines 14–22.

14. See the articles cross-referenced under "Truth" in Paul Edwards, ed., *The Encyclopedia of Philosophy* (New York: Macmillan and Free Press, 1967).

15. Wilfred Cantwell Smith, "Can Religions Be True or False?" in *Questions of Religious Truth* (New York: Scribner's, 1967), pp. 78f.

16. Ibid., p. 77.

17. W. W. Bartley, III, *The Retreat to Commitment* (New York: Random House, 1962).

18. The latter form of speech, by the way, should be used with caution. The present essay maintains that the meaning of our talk lies not merely in the mind of a single hearer (or speaker), but in the act of utterance embedded in its linguistic and thus conventional context. One who fails to get the meaning of an utterance, then, does not evacuate it of meaning.

19. See Charles Stevenson, *Ethics and Language* (New Haven: Yale University Press, 1944), chap. 9.

20. An interesting brief discussion of parable which also provides a guide to the literature in the field is Sallie M. TeSelle's "Parable, Metaphor, and Theology," *Journal of the American Academy of Religion* 42, no. 4 (December, 1974).

21. *Hamlet,* act 1, sc. 3.

22. See for example Ruth Rouse and Stephen C. Neill, eds., *A History of the Ecumenical Movement,* vol. I, 1517–1948, 2nd ed. (London: S.P.C.K., 1967), and for inter-religious awareness, George Rupp, "Religious Pluralism in the Context of an Emerging World Culture," *Harvard Theological Review,* 66, no. 2 (April, 1973).

23. William Christian, *Meaning and Truth in Religion* (Princeton, N.J.: Princeton University Press, 1964), chap. 2.

24. Ibid., p. 18.

25. *Oppositions of Religious Doctrines: A Study in the Logic of Dialog among Religions* (New York: Herder & Herder, 1972).

26. See for example F.S.C. Northrop, *The Meeting of East and West* (New

York: Macmillan, 1946); and William E. Hocking, *The Coming World Civilization* (New York: Harper & Bros., 1956).

27. For Paul, see Gal. 1:13–17; Acts 8, 9, 22, 26. For Gotama, see Henry C. Warren, *Buddhism in Translations* (Cambridge, Mass.: Harvard University Press, 1922), pp. 38–87, and Kenneth Morgan, ed., *The Path of the Buddha* (New York: Ronald Press, 1956), pp. 5–10.

28. J.-P. Sartre, quoted without further reference in J. C. Hoekendijk, *The Church Inside Out* (Philadelphia: Westminster Press, 1966), p. 46.

29. Cf. the paradoxical description of rebellion in Albert Camus, *The Rebel* (New York: Vintage Books, 1956), Part 1.

30. This is illustrated by the concept of "passing over" in the work of John S. Dunne. See for example his *The Way of All the Earth* (New York: Macmillan, 1972).

31. See chap. 4, pp. 110f.; chap. 5, pp. 118f.

32. Psalm 14:1.

33. Cf. the discussion of the expansion of the notion of reason in chap. 5, pp. 117f.

NOTES TO CHAPTER 7

Theology as a Science of Convictions

1. "Action and Responsibility," in Max Black, ed., *Philosophy in America* (Ithaca: Cornell University Press, 1965), p. 160.

2. "The Availability of Wittgenstein's Later Philosophy," reprinted in George Pitcher, ed., *Wittgenstein, The Philosophical Investigations* (Garden City, N.Y.: Anchor Books, 1966), p. 183.

3. William James, *The Varieties of Religious Experience: A Study in Human Nature*, The Gifford Lectures in Edinburgh for 1901–2 (New York: Modern Library, 1902), pp. 422–424.

4. Ibid., pp. 505–507.

5. Ibid., pp. 479ff., 500f.

6. Ibid., pp. 476ff., 494f.

7. Kai Nielsen, "The Primacy of Philosophical Theology," *Theology Today*, July, 1970. Our emphasis. For Nielsen's position in philosophical theology generally, see his *Contemporary Critiques of Religion* (London: Macmillan, 1971); *Scepticism* (London: Macmillan, 1973), and the succinct account in "On Speaking of God," *Theoria* (28), 1962.

8. Ibid., pp. 162ff.

9. It is relevant to note here, as previously, that one of the present writers is by conviction more sympathetic to Nielsen than to Nielsen's religious adversaries. If we are biased, it is not against Nielsen's basic religious stance.

10. Nielsen, "The Primacy of Philosophical Theology," p. 166.

11. Cf. James Wm. McClendon, Jr., "Theology," in Wm. M. Pinson, Jr., and Clyde E. Fant, Jr., *Contemporary Christian Trends* (Waco, Tex.: Word Books, 1972).

12. Michael Novak, in the Introduction to *American Philosophy and the Future* (New York: Scribner's, 1968), p. 17.

13. Cf. Stephan Körner's characterization of metaphysics as "the exhibition of implicitly accepted categorial frameworks . . . their critical examination and, sometimes, also . . . their modification." *Categorial Frameworks* (Oxford: Basil Blackwell, 1970), p. 59.

14. The Lundensians, especially Anders Nygren, Ragnar Bring, and Gustaf Aulén, as represented by Nels ·Ferré, *Swedish Contributions to Modern Theology* (New York: Harper Torchbook, 1967 [1st ed. 1939]), make a vigorous effort to separate the *a priori* justification of religion-in-general from the historical *identification* of particular religious strands; the former is the task of philosophy; the latter that of theology. "Theology is thus a special form of religious history with a special working hypothesis, according to which it accomplishes its systematic task, namely the discovery and the systematic exposition of each religion in accordance with its organic distinctiveness. '*Nicht die begriffliche Einheit, sondern die organische Ganzheit muss das Ziel der Dartstellung sein,*' " Ferré, pp. 58f.; the German quotation is from Bring, "Die neuere schwedische Theologie," in *Die Kirche in Schweden,* p. 74. The present enterprise parallels Nygren and Bring in several interesting ways; we depart from both their Kantian transcendental underpinnings and their view that the theologian necessarily cannot by any means "prove the value of the disclosures of faith" (Ferré, p. 73)—the present essay aims to show just how such a 'proof' can be undertaken.

15. One can hardly read Anders Nygren's *Agape and Eros,* or Gustaf Aulén's *Christus Victor,* without feeling himself under strong persuasion that *agape* not *eros,* in the first case, and the 'victor' theory of atonement, in the second case, really ought to be determinative for Christian thought.

16. This question engaged John Henry Newman in his work on the development of Christian doctrine—what, he asked, are the "notes of a genuine development?" See *An Essay on the Development of Christian Doctrine,* John Henry Newman (Garden City, N.Y.: Image Books, 1960 [1st ed. 1845]).

17. J. L. Austin, "A Plea for Excuses," *Philosophical Papers,* ed. J. G. Urmson and G. J. Warnock (Oxford: Clarendon Press, 1962), p. 175.

Index